Unloved, Unworthy, Unknown
A JOURNEY TO A NEW LEVEL OF CONSCIOUSNESS

By Allura Halliwell
Founder of *The Consciousness Method*™

DISCLAIMER

The information contained in this book is for educational and informational purposes only. It is not intended as a substitute for professional medical, psychological, legal, or financial advice, diagnosis, or treatment. Always seek the advice of qualified professionals regarding any questions you may have about your specific situation.

The author and publisher make no representations or warranties of any kind with respect to the accuracy, completeness, or suitability of the information contained herein. The author and publisher shall not be liable for any special, consequential, or exemplary damages resulting, in whole or in part, from the reader's use of, or reliance upon, this material.

Individual results may vary. The strategies, techniques and suggestions presented in this book may not be suitable for every individual or situation. Any application of the recommendations set forth in this book is at the reader's sole discretion and risk.

Copyright © 2026 Allura Halliwell

All rights reserved. No part of this publication may be reproduced, distributed, or transmitted in any form or by any means, including photocopying, recording, or other electronic or mechanical methods, without the prior written permission of the publisher, except in the case of brief quotations embodied in reviews and certain other non-commercial uses.

Identifiers: ISBN 978-1-7644374-0-0 (pbk.) | ISBN 978-1-7644374-2-4 (ebook)
Editorial Assistance: Mikala Dind and Nicky Prince
Interior designer: Loren Bousfield (Gemini Creative Studio)
Cover designer: Šimon Očkáš

www.unlovedunworthyunknown.com

Infinite Love and Dedication to:

Wren Hiranni Jean, Sienna Lake & Fox Alexander

The Invitation

The concepts offered in these pages are expansive, profound and designed for ongoing exploration.

They offer you an access point into my unique method of understanding yourself and reality called
The Consciousness Method ™.

The journey is vast and multi dimensional and I want to offer you the support to orientate yourself in this powerful process of realising yourself.

Via this code you will find:

Meditations
Masterclasses
Community
Resources
Mentorship

Yours in Evolution,

Allura

Table of Contents

Preface

Part I

Chapter One	The Power of Awakening	1
Chapter Two	The Return to Source	15
Chapter Three	The Core Wounds as Gateways	27
Chapter Four	The Addiction to Your Wounding	52

Part II

Chapter Five	Unifying Your Fragmented Self	79
Chapter Six	Freeing Your Nervous System	101
Chapter Seven	How Fear Maintains Your Limitation	118
Chapter Eight	Pain is the Path to Freedom	133

Part III

Chapter Nine	Dying to the Limited Self	159
Chapter Ten	Dying to the Limited Self	180
Chapter Eleven	The Energetic Liberation	204

Part IV

Chapter Twelve	Conscious Engagement with Reality	221
Chapter Thirteen	Your Limitless Potential	236
Chapter Fourteen	The Divine Design	252

Glossary 270

PREFACE
Your Destined Awakening

We are living in an extraordinary time in human history. Right now you are being called towards a profound recognition that you are no longer a victim of your reality.

The old paradigms of limitation, separation and wounding that have governed human experience for millennia are dissolving within you.

The perception that you are separate, powerless and at the mercy of external forces is giving way to an understanding so revolutionary it is reshaping everything.

You are a conscious creator and your reality is far more malleable than you ever imagined.

Every experience you have had, every challenge you have faced, every moment of pain and every realisation of truth has been preparing you for this recognition.

In fact your journey to this moment has not been random, it has been orchestrated to bring you to the exact place where you can receive what your soul is now ready to remember.

Every healing modality, spiritual practice and personal development experience you have had contributes to these insights and revelations.

This book is now evidence of your emerging Consciousness.

In the pages that follow, we will explore the mechanisms that have kept humanity trapped in cycles of suffering and separation and the path to expansion and liberation through that contraction.

More importantly, we will discover the pathways that lead beyond these patterns into a reality where you are the conscious architect of your experience.

I have divided it into four parts to remind you to take space and time to integrate and apply what you have read.

This is not another 'self-help journey'. It is a conversation of Consciousness, yours and mine, a recognition between souls who remember the experience we have come here to have.

To activate this remembrance I will share my direct experience and offer a handbook of realisations and processes for you to integrate your own understanding of this Consciousness.

Loved, Worthy and Known is your birthright. It is time to activate and catalyse the remembrance of your true nature.

Part I

CHAPTER ONE
The Power of Awakening

The design you intend for your life is one thing. Your soul's evolution is another. Beneath the Consciousness I offer, is my own profound journey of awakening. I am going to share with you the event that split my timeline, from the predictable to the complete Unknown. The event that expanded my Consciousness and rewrote my trajectory. The event that showed me the design of reality and a path of self realisation and a comprehensive understanding of the human experience. This reflection is here to remind you of the power of your own awakening and that in every moment you can access this evolutionary Consciousness.

Before the dissolution of my former self in November 2018, an ego death so complete it was indistinguishable from physical death, I was pretty much asleep in my life. I lived an ordinary existence as a devoted mother of three children, trapped in a prison of emotional distress, with a stressed out husband and a life brimming with pain. On the surface, I was surviving, going through the motions of daily life but within, I was already dead, disconnected from any genuine aliveness or purpose. I could feel something wasn't quite right and pressure was building in my system but I remained largely unconscious of it all.

I was stuck in repetition, caught in loops of arguing and feeling misunderstood by my partner, experiencing chronic anxiety about my kids, eating and drinking to numb out and avoid my pain, trapped in the chaos and overwhelm of life. My life wasn't bad and my childhood trauma wasn't chronic. But I was deeply separate from my authentic self, consumed with constant uncertainty, pushing to be loved and heard and sucked dry by it all.

I would cry in the shower, have panic attacks in the car and hide away, then push to connect. Cycles of numbness and pain would move through me. Yet I was driven by an understanding of what I 'should' be doing in life: I 'should be' a devoted wife (even when there was intensive stress and overwhelm). I 'should be' a devoted mum (even when I was crippled with separation anxiety and depletion). I 'should be' forging a career, studying, working, showing up. All the 'shoulds' left me empty inside, disconnected and lost.

The exit point came unexpectedly. A friend called, breathless and excited asking me to attend a meditation retreat with her. I wasn't really listening, the phone was half-pressed to my ear as I wrangled a child into the car. I wasn't on any kind of spiritual journey. I was overwhelmed by daily existence, no time or desire for enlightenment or meditation. To be honest, I was just trying to survive from one moment to the next. But something in this invitation captured my attention. My heart said "Yes" and I hadn't heard my heart in a very long time.

What happened at that retreat was nothing short of Divine intervention, though I wouldn't have used those words then. The Consciousness I encountered there didn't arrive with fanfare or dramatic visions. Instead, it slipped in through a crack in my defences, a momentary surrender born of complete exhaustion.

The Return to Source

The retreat was held on the Sunshine Coast in Australia and on one brilliant blue sky morning, I walked down to the beach to meditate with the group. We all filed down the path and onto the sand. As I walked towards the water I could feel a powerful force beginning to move in my body. My heart started thumping heavily. Something was happening that I couldn't quite grasp. Standing facing the ocean, all my attention was suddenly drawn to my body. I felt a tremendous weight growing within, almost like cement, dragging me down to the ground.

I can't do anything, I thought. *There's nothing I can do to stop this.* I decided to trust the energy and consciously let go.

Like a magnet pulling a sliver of metal, I was pulled to the ground. I surrendered and allowed it. Lying in the sand, I felt an energy moving from the soles of my feet, gathering momentum as it moved up my body. As it moved upward, the parts below became more lifeless. I realised it was my Consciousness that was moving, building momentum. When it reached the crown of my head, whoosh...my Consciousness left my body.

While my body lay breathing peacefully on the beach, I was rapidly ascending. As my Consciousness rose higher, I could see my body lying motionless in the soft sand.

As I ascended higher and higher, I began to completely lose awareness of my body. My Consciousness began dissolving into a field of extraordinarily bright light, the most immaculate, purest, cleanest, Divine light imaginable. Its intensity was overwhelming and in that moment, my Consciousness began to expand. I shimmered with the bright light until... I merged with it.

I would later understand this pure light is the brightest source of Divine information and a gateway home. It is the light that lies at the foundation of our being, the spark we carry as we are conceived into human experience and the light we journey through as we return to the Divine.

My Consciousness merged with this celestial light completely, inexorably and definitively. Then suddenly, I was plunged into a darkness, a profound void stretching infinitely in all directions.

In that void, I suddenly became the infinite frequency expression of all timelines: all-knowing, all-energy and simultaneously nothing. As I merged with that void, I lost all connection to the concept of self, of being human, of being anything. All of my Consciousness began to get absorbed into that void. And as I was absorbed, I experienced this incredibly profound sense of being absolutely everything, everywhere, all space, all time, infinite, eternal, with no barriers, no separation. Just pure Consciousness and pure connection.

The Death and Rebirth

This merging was the moment I died, not physically, but to the version of me that had previously existed. The intensity of the experience wiped away my awareness of life as I had known it. I could no longer connect with the version of me that was tethered to a personality, a life, to limited Consciousness. My preferences, programs and even attachment to being human had dissolved.

In this space, I experienced being released into the infinite, eternal Consciousness: the Divine essence of everything. This is the field of infinite Consciousness, what some call the quantum field, the whole of existence in non-material, energetic form. The field of everything. God.

Infinite frequencies exist in this energetic space. I merged with and experienced the truth of the frequency of joy, of enlightenment, of truth. Eventually, I reached the frequency of pure, unconditional love.

The moment I merged with that frequency of love, I dropped out of the void back to the light. *Where am I going?* I thought. But I was being pulled back to this earthly dimension. In that moment, I understood that unconditional love needs a degree of separation from the All to truly experience it. I realised that the foundation of human experience is this frequency of profound unconditional love. It is the core motivation for our inception here: to consciously experience that love.

In that expanded state, I could see a body on a beach that looked vaguely familiar. My Consciousness was being magnetised back into my body. I could feel the re-entry, my body having lain very still, breathing almost imperceptibly for the last hour and a half.

As my Consciousness moved back into my body, I felt an extreme level of constriction, as if I was a giant being stuffed into an ant's body. It felt suffocating to be back in physical form and deeply disorienting. But something else had changed too, my body was now connected to a massive energy source, as if I'd plugged my spine into a thousand-watt generator. Waves of this powerful, precious and life-changing energy kept surging through me.

This force, or Kundalini energy, caused my whole body to tremble and shake for hours on end. Imagine being a snow globe and all the density that had settled in your body needed to be violently shaken and released. Between the disorientation of being back in a body, the surging Kundalini force and the deep longing for expansion into Source tormenting me, I entered a state that from the outside might have appeared like psychosis. However, within me I had truly retreated from the physical world into my own inner domain.

The Chaos of Integration

When I came home from the meditation retreat and walked through my front door, I experienced an overwhelming sense of disorientation. Looking around, I couldn't properly recognise anything. It was like having a vague memory that I should know this house and these things, but I didn't really. I felt like I was underwater, looking at a blurry version of the articles of my life.

I didn't know how I had come to create this life, live in this house, this relationship, none of it felt like mine, yet I didn't know what I could do. I was completely stuck in it. While it was my material reality, my energetic being felt so removed, like landing in a foreign country and being told it had always been your home. The structures and patterns of my former life now seemed like an ill-fitting costume I was expected to wear, despite having outgrown it entirely.

The powerful energy current continued its profound work through my system. I felt shocks of electricity pulsating up my spine and reverberations through every cell of my being. I was physically shaking myself into a new alignment, though, at the time it felt like seizures were overcoming me. I had difficulty driving; when I went for walks, I would end up being pulled to the ground. I refused medical help; there was nothing physically wrong with me. My body had become a Divine conduit for processing these vast energetic forces.

I was plugged into a massive planetary power source, a primal current that runs through the earth itself. This energy is a brutal force. It brings so much to you and takes so much away. It charges your system while simultaneously moving you away from anything that is not in alignment. It has its own intelligence and I had no choice but to succumb to it. It didn't give me another option.

I came to understand it was giving me the codes of the energetic force available here on the planet. It was helping me come to terms with separation and duality while inviting me into more truth and honesty with myself and my experience. Yet, at the time, it felt like being caught in an endless cosmic earthquake.

The energy would physically move me when I got close to my then husband, pushing me away across the room. When I had a misaligned thought, it would push me down and vibrate through me. When I wasn't where it wanted me to be, it would pull me to the ground. It was a harsh but firm teacher, I could feel both the destruction of my old self and the loving support in every moment. It was a profound gift, a profound shift in my entire energetic system.

The Dark Night of Transformation

While this energy was having its way with me, I went into a deep state of being sequestered from life. I could barely relate to anyone. I could barely communicate or function. The pressure to be around others weighed heavily on my soul. I felt held in a prison of Consciousness, looking at my children and family from my darkest recesses with nothing to give them. I was in complete absorption of my process, gripped by something beyond my choice or control.

My immediate family sensed a profound change in me. They were not sure how to approach or connect with me. My mother said she mourned me as if I had died. And she was right, in a way, I had. My human form was reorientating. My Consciousness was elsewhere, exploring other dimensions. This is where my mystical experiences were about to take off, as I navigated the complete dismantling of everything I'd known myself to be.

It wasn't that I suddenly accessed all wisdom or became instantly enlightened. Rather, I became aware of a presence, a field of knowing that had always been there but that my busy, frightened mind had never allowed me to recognise. This Consciousness wasn't separate from me, it was actually more essentially me than the identity I had constructed and defended for decades and beyond. It annihilated the predictable pathways of my energy and design patterns that had been etched across lifetimes.

My out of body experience revealed a truth: we are here to remember our infinite and eternal connection to the expanded field of Source Consciousness.

This truth became the default of my inner design. I knew innately that we are all here to experience this. Living like it is heaven on earth is the evolutionary trajectory we are here to realise. When we know we are internally Source and inseparable, then we orient our energetic signature to connection and presence. We can experience all of life; because we are life. We can know the power of creation; because we are all creators. When I experienced this truth, every cell of my being reset to that freedom and expansion. It was as if the human, limited, wounded version of me had been released and I'd found something vast and real.

At first there was no place I wanted to be but back in Source. The period after the awakening became a time of deep, consistent meditation where I escaped into what became my safe place. For up to six hours a day, I could merge back with Source and dissolve my Consciousness into the connection I now knew was always here. I was able to close my eyes and travel via Source to any timeline and any physical space on the planet. Sometimes by will, but other times I was taken and shown what I needed to see and understand. I witnessed countless versions of me in other iterations. I began to understand how to use the space to create inner completion and to redesign patterns of my experience that had been expressing my energy for millennia. I became timeless and boundless in the most beautiful ways. Meditation I realised was an escape hatch and it took the pain out of living, it kept reminding me of the truth of myself on the most expanded level. It kept showing me miracles.

Yet when I opened my eyes and met reality, the fracture was

almost unbearable. The contrast between my expanded soul essence and my lived human experience was so vast, it felt in many ways like it was insurmountable. My nervous system had gone into overdrive. The extreme sensitivity and anxiety were intense and unending. It felt like being tied up and consistently poked with hot spears, the searing pain of my wounding continually moving through me and reflected all around me. I wanted to remain with my eyes closed and in Nirvana. But there was a place I had to be: here. The journey to merge my inner awareness of Source Consciousness with my outer experience of reality became the only focus.

The Emergence of Truth

I realised I felt radically unsafe. The fear that had been laid in my nervous system was coming to the surface like tsunami waves. I had dropped the program of numbing and suppression that had previously kept this dormant and the power of it was unleashed and intense.

My nervous system was raw and, I realised, very underdeveloped. It couldn't discern a true threat from an imagined one, so it reacted consistently in a state of hypervigilance. This level of contrast continued for a year and I began to witness the primal drives that had unconsciously ruled my life.

As I continued this intense process, my marriage crumbled. I had become a ghost of the woman my husband had married, not only was I unrecognisable to him but my former self had become a distant memory. During this time of profound isolation and fear, I met someone who lived hundreds of kilometers away and we began a torturous long-distance relationship filled with craving, anxiety and longing. My addiction to trying to get someone to love me reared its head like a monster. I could see how powerful this addiction was from my higher mind. When we were in contact, my nervous system was soothed; when I was waiting for his call, I was a complete mess. This was when the deeper questions began emerging:

- ✦ Why am I perpetuating this sense of separation between myself and another?
- ✦ Why is my nervous system so addicted to the drug of this connection?
- ✦ Why am I in a continual flood of emotion?
- ✦ Why is my mind telling me I need this relationship to be okay, that without it, I will die?
- ✦ How will I find peace?

These questions became the pathway to understanding the Unloved Core Wound and ultimately, all the wounds that shape our human experience. But more about this later...

What I came to understand through this process is that awakening often descends into immense levels of chaos. It is as if all the information of the universe opens up at once, creating a radical internal disruption. Nothing is clear, everything is up for review and the disorientation becomes epic.

My past reality had been detonated. My future reality was deep in the Unknown and my present moment was manic. The true relationship I now had with the Divine, with the truth of the universe, was anchored within me but had almost no translation into the human experience around me.

This began three solid years of the deepest reflection and realignment. I had to take the complete confusion and disorientation and merge it with the truth that was being shown to me in my inner world, in my meditations, in my thorough and conscious explorations of reality. It was also at this time the world descended into chaos and shut down externally, as global mandates locked everyone in their homes. I stayed sequestered with my children, walking the beach, finding hidden tracks in the forest, re-orientating my whole being.

Gradually, what arose was my understanding of how to make a quantum leap in Consciousness and arrive home within myself. This process led me to move from incoherency to a new level of coherency, guided me to metabolise the radical shifts in my nervous system and showed me how to reconcile the three-dimensional life that was already established around me with the vast new reality I had glimpsed.

This experience has completely changed my life. It has initiated a vast reclamation of my energy and expansion of my Consciousness, but in real time this looks like moving into greater levels of sovereignty, Wholeness, awareness and connection. A life that I truly love and is loving to me.

This path has revealed how reality is designed and how we, as humans, co-create with it. This knowledge allows us to systematically move towards becoming the true creators of our reality. It is like finally understanding the design of the game of life and giving ourselves permission to make up our own rules.

Living this truth was a process of testing reality, testing myself and challenging the limits of what I believed our existence to be. I first had to recognise where I was unconscious and not free in my personal relationships, within my identity, with my physical body, with my concepts of what it means to exist in this dimension.

So I began to challenge all parts of me. I tuned into the strongest essence of myself and focussed on living with the greatest levels of authenticity and commitment to personal liberation and connection to others. These two things at first felt paradoxical because as I forged my inner freedom, many of my external relationships began to collapse, revealing their wobbly foundations. Yet as I continued to align with myself and my inner compass, I began to cultivate a new level of internal relationship that holographically reflected healthier connections all around me.

I moved out of the relationship with my husband to a deep relationship with myself, out of co-dependency with my children to a deep unconditional love, out of isolation in my friendships to an acceptance of others and most importantly I began to move from self-abandonment to radical acceptance and truth.

I want to be clear, my path was extraordinarily intense and abrupt, like being thrown into the deep end without swimming lessons. Your journey does not need to be this dramatic. What I have done through years of integration is distill the essential understanding and methods that can guide you through this process in a more gentle, deliberate way. You do not need to have a Kundalini awakening or out-of-body experience to access the wisdom I am sharing. The Consciousness work I will guide you through allows you to navigate these waters more gradually, with the support and understanding I never had. Your path to this Consciousness will be uniquely yours.

The wounds that have shaped you, the defences you have built, the gifts you carry, all of these create the particular doorway through which expanded awareness will enter your life. There is no right way, no formula, no prescribed sequence of steps that guarantees awakening but this book is here to help you to make sense of the journey.

Forming a Relationship with Consciousness

What I have discovered in the years since that life-changing day is that there exists a relationship with Consciousness that transforms everything, not by escaping our humanity, but by embracing it more fully. This relationship does not require dramatic mystical experiences or years of ascetic practice. It simply asks for your willingness to turn towards what you have been turning away from and to expand into the vastness of the truth of your human experience.

Underpinning everything is Consciousness and from this relationship everything can change. This was the impetus for the creation of *The Consciousness Method* ™. A comprehensive system that guides you through the human experience and expands you beyond any loops, limitations, lack and loss into a state of creation and connection to all of life. Unlike conventional spiritual approaches that often bypass our wounds, this work insists on travelling back through the very fracture points of our wounding to reclaim the Wholeness of self. This relationship with Consciousness develops through active engagement with the very elements most spiritual paths encourage us to transcend:

Pain: Rather than avoiding pain, we use it as a doorway. Each moment of pain marks a fracture in our Consciousness.

Fear: Instead of calming or overcoming fear, we follow it to its source. Fear is a messenger, pointing to the places where our Consciousness has become disconnected and needs reclamation.

Triggers: Our emotional triggers are not problems to be managed but maps leading us to our core wounding. When something triggers us, it is Consciousness calling us to attend to a fragmented part of ourselves.

Patterns: The repeating patterns in our lives are fractals or repetitive expressions of the same design form. The patterns reflect how our Consciousness attempts to bring our attention to what creates our repetitive experience and alerts us to what we need to redesign to experience greater levels of understanding and awareness.

Active Engagement: Rather than witnessing from a distance, we actively engage with our reactions, emotions and thoughts. We do not observe them, we enter them fully to recover the Consciousness trapped within them. Through this approach, Consciousness becomes a dynamic reality to reclaim piece by piece. It becomes your primary relationship, by fully embracing your humanity and every fragmented aspect of it, life begins to transform from the inside out.

The Truth of Your Journey

I also want to reassure you, if you have been committed to a healing journey and still feel trapped or limited in some way, it is important to understand that many healing methods, spiritual practices and psychological interventions do not always address the deepest dimension of our being and our reality. This missing piece exists in the less tangible realm of our own relationship to Consciousness itself, which holds both the content and context for everything we experience.

What I discovered is that the healing journey as we have known it, often leads us in circles because it operates from a fundamental misunderstanding. When we believe we need to heal something broken within us, we reinforce the very separation we are trying to overcome. Instead, we are creating a radical new level of connection to the field of expanded Consciousness that permeates and surrounds us at all times. This Consciousness is not separate from us, it is our true nature, though our identification with smaller aspects of ourselves prevents us from recognising it.

Sometimes awareness becomes blocked because we do not incorporate and see all parts of ourselves, denying elements of our being that seem threatening, uncomfortable or contrary to our self-image. We cherry-pick a reality that complies with a limited version of ourselves, shutting out aspects of Consciousness that might challenge our carefully constructed identity. In doing so, we create the very fractures we later try so desperately to heal.

For so long, my own 'victim Consciousness', survival patterns and wounding protected me from full-spectrum Consciousness. By victim Consciousness, I mean the deep-seated perception that I was at the mercy of outside forces, other people, circumstances, even my own emotions, rather than a co-creator of my reality. This state of awareness views life through the lens of 'things happening to me' rather than 'responding meaningfully to what is'. These patterns kept me trapped in an illusion where I misinterpreted and reacted to a version of reality locked in my nervous system rather than experiencing the truth of material reality. I lived as if the distorted perceptions of my wounded self were objective truth, unable to distinguish between actual threats and the ghosts of past pain. All of this awareness became a catalyst for me and the questions that underpin this whole journey:

+ How do we truly reconcile the experience of living?
+ How do we move from illusion to truth?
+ How do we connect and experience true safety in our human experience?
+ And how do we genuinely become the creators of our reality?

I truly believe there is a path to live an expanded, meaningful life and the path arises through our direct relationship to Consciousness. This Consciousness serves us entirely, facilitating our evolution through this life and beyond. The inner work is powerful, but there is a greater awareness here for you to know and it is not just within you, it is all around you. It is in what I call the 'interface', the space between your inner world and your external experience. It is understanding how you are truly designing your reality and your life with the application of another level of expanded awareness.

This Consciousness brings a vast understanding of how your humanity is defining the expression of life and, most importantly, what unconscious mechanisms are limiting your capacity to be present for all of it.

In these pages, we will journey together through an understanding of the internal spaces of your pain, your fear, your programming, your nervous system and merge with the Consciousness that shows you how to redesign your relationship with the world around you in a new way. The vehicle for this is understanding the greatest unconscious patterns that all of humanity has to meet: feeling Unloved, Unworthy and Unknown. These wounds create the template of separation for life and the portals for deep reconnection.

I offer a blueprint to follow and a mirror in which you might recognise aspects of your own journey. The Consciousness that speaks through me is the same Consciousness that lives within you. The connection is beyond any limitation of language, space or time.

As we begin this journey together, I invite you to approach these words with your whole being. Let your body's wisdom and your heart's knowing guide what resonates. Hold both trust and discernment. Take what resonates and leave what does not.

Question everything, including what I share. Let your own innate wisdom guide you towards what serves your evolution. For in the end, this book is merely a conversation between Consciousnesses, yours and mine, both expressions of the same infinite Source seeking to remember itself through our unique human experiences. The authority on your journey to Consciousness is not me or any teacher, it is the Consciousness itself, speaking directly through your heart, your body, your lived experience of being human.

We are here to feel the true extent of this unconditionally loving dimension and feel liberated in our lives.

CHAPTER TWO
The Return to Source

After the complete chaos of my journey to Source and back, I became increasingly aware that no one was going to save me and no one truly understood the extent of the experience I went through. The only person with the capacity to save me was me. Yet I felt ill equipped. I could see how trapped I felt in the human experience and leaving this realm was not an option; I had three beautiful children. I needed to find my way back to them, myself and my life.

My soul was calling me louder than before, so I set to work taking apart my experience of reality, piece by piece, I began to challenge the perception I was a helpless participant and started to see myself as an active creator. I was being flooded with mystical experiences and profound insights and could virtually see the design fabric of reality. I simply had to make sense of it. I could feel I was being driven by the ultimate quest for freedom here. To experience life as a liberated being, fully conscious and sovereign, not held prisoner by the mechanisms of reality.

My exploration began at the very core: that intense reverberation of feeling wounded, the inexorable hurt created by perceptions that isolated me from everyone and everything around me. I knew there was nothing wrong with me, yet these ingrained patterns of separation needed to be met with a new level of potent awareness. I began to challenge this space with an unprecedented focus and as I did, the understanding of how the wounding emerges and persists within us was revealed. In this chapter I will reveal this mechanism and the Consciousness that is needed to see your core wounding as one of the most important aspects of your humanity to understand and work with.

The Paradox of Your Wounding

As you travel through life, you may have noticed patterns that seem to repeat, relationships that have similar themes, challenges that resurface in different forms or an inexplicable sense that something essential continually remains just beyond your reach. These looping patterns are signposts pointing to where your Consciousness has temporarily forgotten its Wholeness.

It is in this space there lies a profound paradox: we can only recognise what is missing if we already know it exists. When we find ourselves searching outside for proof of our lovability, worth or recognition, we are actually reflecting an internal knowing of these truths. Some vast, eternal part of us already recognises our inherent nature as loved, worthy and known as a baseline of truth, hence the confusion as to why that is not our dominant experience. I want you to consider: you can only know you are lost if you know there is a way home. This aspect of forgetting your true nature so you can remember again, is an important foundation. You already know it and are it, it is simply the realisation of it.

This awareness changed everything because it ignited a deep cellular remembrance that we must have the templates of the realisation of self within us, embedded deeply below the fractures. It simultaneously created profound sadness and relief. The grief that I had not had access to this state of completion for my lifetime and beyond burst through me, while an all-knowing part of me knew the path home was already here and available, it was simply a matter of walking it. More so I realised this separation is a sacred doorway that illuminates the distinction between your limited, wounded existence and your authentic self as boundless awareness.

The Split from Source

Through this journey, I recognised that each wound carries within it a piece of our fragmented Consciousness waiting to be reclaimed and integrated. In my meditations and past life visions I began to see the deep integral pattern my wounding had imprinted across space and time. The version of me as a slave kept showing itself and I felt the crushing lack of freedom constricting every cell. I could see the wounds do not have boundaries and are deeply embedded in our energetic signature across our incarnations.

I began to understand that the Core Wounds, those profound feelings of unworthiness, abandonment, rejection, confusion or shame, are essentially distortions in how we perceive reality. They represent areas where our connection to Source Consciousness has become clouded, generating an illusion of separation. These wounds carry the energetic signature of our human experience and gather strength as we repeat the patterns through life. It is as if the core fracture creates a series of ongoing fractals that replicate through our existence. Their true power does not stem from the original events that formed them but from how they function as hidden programs, continuously filtering our perception through their warped perspective. Through our unconscious behaviours, these wounds self perpetuate, influencing our relationships, career choices and self-image, ultimately manifesting the exact circumstances that seem to validate their existence.

The true healing of these wounds is bigger than simply analysing the past or changing your behaviour, it is about bringing Consciousness to these unconscious patterns, recognising them as distortions rather than truth and reconnecting with the Wholeness that has always existed beneath them.

What emerged for me through this experience was a profound understanding: we are the creators of our reality. Our collective Consciousness designed the mechanisms that are here for us to experience. *Yet, if we are the creators, why do we simultaneously feel like victims? What is it about what we have designed here that is so complex and perplexing for us?* From these questions, the true fracture emerged.

The Fundamental Fracture

We first feel a sense of wounding as we fracture from Source Consciousness at conception and begin our journey into a physical manifestation of individuality, duality and separateness. Your birth moves your energy and Consciousness from being deeply connected to the All to being limited to a three-dimensional existence. Our senses and nervous system are aching to resolve this split and find some safety and reconciliation in the physical world.

Here is how this cosmic fracture translates into our personal wounds: the moment we separate from Source, we experience the first trauma, the trauma of disconnection itself. This fundamental rupture creates an energetic template that manifests as specific wounds throughout our human experience. The Unloved Wound stems from this original abandonment of Source connection. The Unworthy Wound emerges from the contrast between our Divine perfection and our perceived human limitations. The Unknown Wound originates from the absence of the Source of knowing. The feeling of being unsafe arises from the radical sense of instability in the physical world. Each personal wound is simply a fractal expression of this primary separation.

Why Separation is Necessary for Physical Experience

It was a huge shift in awareness when I understood that the core fracture all humans have, is the separation from Source to have this dimensional experience. I saw how this pattern spiralled outwards in fractalising patterns that touched everything in existence. I knew this as a form of lived truth as I had the front row seat for the disorientating and chaotic journey from Source back to the earth during my out of body experience and reinception. The pure awareness I had maintained showed me how the arrival in this plane of existence forms the foundation of separation that ignites the patterns of separation or fractals that are at the heart of our Core Wounds.

But why is this separation necessary? In the unified field of Source Consciousness, there is no experience of individuality, no sensory perception, no linear time, no physical matter. To experience touch, taste, sight, sound and smell, to know love through relationships, to feel the satisfaction of growth and learning, to experience the joy of creation through physical form, Consciousness must create boundaries. It does so by designing us as a separate vessel of awareness.

The separation creates the very conditions that make experience possible. Without the boundary of individual consciousness, there would be no 'experiencer' to feel life. The fracture is not a mistake, it is the fundamental requirement for Consciousness to know itself through experience.

What we are here to reconcile is the subsequent unsafety we feel in being a Divine being having this physical experience. The Divine truth we know is the divinity of Source, the purity of energy, Consciousness and freedom that is the foundation of our essence. So claiming it and creating from it here is our mission.

The Interplay of Collective and Individual Consciousness

Our collective Consciousness, the unified field of all souls, designed this system of separation and return. Yet each individual Consciousness experiences this design as their personal journey. Think of it like a vast orchestrated symphony where each musician plays their individual part while contributing to the collective masterpiece. We are simultaneously the composers, the conductors and the individual instruments.

At the collective level, we chose to create a reality where Consciousness could experience itself through countless individual perspectives. At the individual level, we experience the full intensity of separation, challenge and awakening. This dual nature means we are both responsible for the design and genuine participants in its unfolding. We are not victims of a system imposed upon us, we are the system, experiencing itself from within.

You are a Divine being with deep roots to a vast understanding that is beyond the perception of your daily life at times. You are a being of pure Source, pure enlightenment, pure unconditional love, navigating the split into the expression of this life. For a moment I invite you to consider the implicit power your Consciousness holds in the co-creation and participation in the gift of life.

The Practical Path of Conscious Reconciliation

Knowing this journey also calls us individually into an evolutionary trajectory. You are here to become the embodiment of Source Consciousness within the cellular, physical body you exist in. So instead of taking the journey back to Source in death you are here to return home in your life. The true definition of Wholeness is realising this profound, complete and ultimate connectivity exists within us. You can access it here now. You do not have to wait. But you do have to release what blocks it. When our energy is circulating within us and not unconsciously investing in fractures all around us, we realise ourselves. We feel innately loved, as love is the fabric of existence. We feel innately worthy, as we are intrinsic to this creation. We feel innately known, as we are all knowing within this Consciousness. No gaps, no pain, no fear, no longing, no struggle, no isolation. Conscious completion and peace.

But how do we actually navigate this reconciliation? To begin I invite you to bring consciousness to the following key elements:

Conscious Awareness of the Inception Point: Begin by recognising that your human experience started with this fundamental fracture. In meditation, prayer or quiet reflection, connect with the moment of separation, as a sacred choice to be honoured. Feel both the loss of unity and the gift of individuality that this separation created. We will explore the pain here as a portal in coming chapters.

Recognising Fractal Patterns: Notice how your personal wounds mirror the original fracture. When you feel Unloved, recognise this as an echo of the original separation from Source. When you feel Unworthy, see this as the contrast between your human limitations and your Divine nature. When you feel Unknown, recognise this as you being the Source of all knowing. This recognition begins to dissolve the wound's power over you.

Embodied Connection: Practice bringing Source Consciousness and a sense of what I call, 'internal safety' into your physical form through conscious presence. Feel your Divine nature as the very essence of you expressing through your physical vessel.

The Ultimate Purpose

This entire journey from Source, to separation, to conscious return, serves the evolution of Consciousness itself. You are participating in the healing of the collective fracture. Each person who consciously navigates this return to Source while in human form contributes to the collective awakening of humanity.

The goal is to merge through our human experience bringing our Divine nature fully into our human form, creating a new expression of consciousness that honours both our infinite nature and our finite experience. We become bridges between heaven and earth, unity and individuality, the eternal and the temporal.

In this way, our personal healing becomes service to the whole and our individual awakening contributes to the collective evolution of Consciousness.

Understanding the Different Realities We Inhabit

To fully grasp the journey from wounding to Wholeness, we must first understand the different realities we inhabit, often simultaneously and unconsciously. These are not physical locations but states of Consciousness that define how we perceive and interact with everything around us. Each has its own energy, relationship to time and impact on our experience of being alive.

The Wound Reality: Living in Illusion

At its most basic, the 'Wound Reality' is the densest, default layer of reality manifested through our unconscious patterns. It includes the stories we make up in our heads and then mistake for truth. These are deeply ingrained narratives that form the foundation of our identity. They are the lens through which we interpret everything and challenging them often feels like a threat to our very existence.

Wound Reality is characterised by nervous system dominance, mental obsession, continuous judgment and a strange paradox: you may intellectually know that you are loved, worthy and known, yet you simply cannot experience these truths in your lived reality. This disconnect creates suffering that feels both inexplicable and inescapable.

This experience of Core Wounding is built into the design of human Consciousness. When our Consciousness moved from Source into a body, we experienced a fracture in our space/time continuum. Subsequently, the Wound Reality has a disturbing relationship with time; it constantly refers to past experiences to predict the future.

You know you are in Wound Reality when you find yourself using what you think happened in the past (filtered through your wounded perception) to project fear onto a future that has not yet occurred. In doing so, you strengthen the Wound Reality and remain caught in its wounded loop, missing the present moment entirely as you oscillate between past and future.

The Core Wound operates through specific energetic patterns that move in repeated, unconscious, fractalised designs. These patterns are based on our deepest sense of separation and our desperate desire to repair this separation through external connection and completion. Yet the very design of the wound ensures that this repair cannot happen externally. The Core Wound is programmed to perpetuate separation, so you can only resolve it internally.

The Critical In-Between Space: The Void of Transformation

Between the Wound Reality and the Wholeness Reality lies a space that is often overlooked in most healing modalities. I call this the 'In-Between Space' or the 'void'. This space is the quantum field itself – a realm you are always intimately linked to and co-creating with energetically. The In-Between Space is critical to your journey because it is impossible to move directly from wound to Wholeness.

You cannot simply leap from *I don't experience love* to *I love myself completely*, or from *I don't feel good enough* to *I know I am enough*. These statements might sound good in affirmations, but energetically, such a direct transition is not possible. This is because it has a dualistic relationship, trying for one by default implies the lack of the other. It is only when we dissolve the paradigm and come to our true nature that we realise that we are already that which we seek.

Your Consciousness has been operating from the unconscious space of the wound, designing your entire life through your repetitive thoughts, emotions and behaviours. Your world is a direct consequence of your attention to the wounded aspects. When you begin to change your internal operating system, you must enter a reality holding pattern – a state of nothingness where your old patterns can dissolve and new ones can form.

Developing a relationship with this Unknown is perhaps the most challenging and important work you will do. The basis of the In-Between Space is moving from the physical reality of being someone, somewhere, doing something, with someone, to being fully energetically self-contained in a state of being no one, nowhere, doing nothing, with no one (and subsequently realising you are everything, everywhere, in all time and connected to everyone).

This transition from wound to the In-Between Space will feel like dying if you do it properly. It is like energetically suffocating the wound that has lived in your nervous system, perceptual awareness and thought patterns your entire life. To go against these repeated reactions and programs feels like certain death and that is the strength of the wound's hold on you.

To give some perspective: you have been emanating the same reality your whole existence, from the moment of your Core Wound's formation. Entering the void is like entering rehabilitation, where you will absolutely see your 'wound addictions' flaring. You will process them and then you will rest back into nothing.

When you first rest in this space, it will feel uncomfortable and unfamiliar. You will explore 'being' rather than 'doing' in the deepest way possible. It is critical that you rest here until all the compulsions of the wound subside. This may take weeks, months or even up to a year. During this time, you will consistently peel back the layers of the wound, process them and rest into the quantum void of nothing; no one, nowhere, no space, no time.

The void is where your old identity, the one built around your wounds, begins to dissolve. The self you thought you were starts to fade away and a profound emptiness takes its place. This emptiness is a canvas upon which your true essence can begin to paint itself. As the wound-based identity loosens its grip, your essence begins to shine through.

This is why it is so critical to allow yourself to merge back with Source Consciousness: if you do not allow your Core Wound to become completely dormant in the void, it will continue to run your existence unconsciously. Only when your wound has come to complete rest can your Wholeness begin to inform the creation of your reality and this will look radically different from what motivated you from the wound.

The Wholeness Reality: Coming Home to Self

The Wholeness Reality is characterised by a deep inner knowing that you are complete in the now moment. This does not mean everything in your life is perfect or that challenges disappear. Rather, it means you are no longer defined or diminished by external circumstances. Instead, you use every situation as an opportunity to explore your own evolution.

This means that everything that happens around you becomes a reference point with which to explore more within you. So, instead of applying the old axiom that; *my thoughts create my reality,* you see everything around you as an extension of you and a powerful access point with which to know more of yourself. So whatever pattern or programs you become conscious of, then allows you to explore how that is designed within you. Then you see everything around you as connected to you and you feel sovereign and free in this reality.

In Wholeness Reality, separation no longer drains your energy and life force. When difficulties arise, you meet them with curiosity rather than reaction. You absorb these experiences into your Wholeness, responding from a fully empowered place of self-love, self-worth and self-knowing.

You become your own guru, teacher and guide, relying deeply on your innate wisdom to see things as they truly are, not as illusions of how you think they should be. This clarity of spiritual vision allows you to be present with all things, regardless of their apparent challenge or difficulty.

When you no longer seek external clarification, validation, love and attention, you naturally come home to give these things to yourself. You remember that you are a Divine being having a human experience and begin to access your multidimensional nature. You understand that you are Source, connected through all space and time and that the pattern of your Core Wound fracture is a gift, designed to bring you home to yourself in the most profound and powerful way.

Wholeness is the state of 'energetic self-sufficiency'. It requires the full reclamation of your energy from all patterns of unconscious separation. Reclaiming the energy invested in trauma, loops, triggers, pain and fear; and bringing all the energy back to within you. You become complete. In deep acceptance and reconnection of every part of you that has fragmented across space and time. You feel at peace and Whole and like you have arrived. This does not mean life does not keep happening and evolving you. It simply means that you get to be safe with all of it.

In Wholeness Reality, you embrace pain as your teacher, fear as a mechanism to free you from limitation and all moments as opportunities to experience the fullness of life. You fall madly in love with existence itself, knowing you have a place here and that you are witnessing yourself as the ultimate creator.

The movement from Wound Reality, to the In-Between Space to Wholeness Reality is a shift of Consciousness. As you shift through these understandings and embody them you will ultimately feel your relationship between yourself and reality as moving into a powerful partnership of creation. The coming chapter will give you a more in-depth understanding of the mechanism of the Core Wounding so you can begin to realise that the problem does not lie within you. It is a design function of humanity that you are here to witness and master within. Your birthright is to be free, to experience the gift of being alive, liberated in Wholeness.

CHAPTER THREE
The Core Wounds as Gateways

Once I began to realise my own brutal Unloved Core Wound, it was like a spontaneous revelation that others were also suffering from specific 'wound patterns'. The understanding of the three Core Wounds created a deep level recognition that energetic patterns create everything in our human experience.

I remember walking daily through the eucalyptus forest near the ocean, asking to be shown the design of the wounding. During one of these morning walks, a profound download laid the patterns out in front of my mind's eye. The recognition of my own wounding opened something within my Consciousness that allowed me to see these patterns operating everywhere around me. When I saw it, I could not unsee it. The patterns became as clear as day. Every interaction, every relationship dynamic, every societal structure seemed to be built around these three fundamental wounds. If these unconscious patterns were fuelling the design of humanity's separation, I felt a responsibility to keep diving deeper into their design.

This became an obsession of sorts, a relentless investigation into the mechanisms that keep humanity trapped in cycles of limitation and suffering. I began to observe vigilantly, both myself and others, questioning profusely: *What causes us to get confused about our core worth and meaning?*

In a sense, this understanding existed before me. Modalities have been looking at these patterns from the surface level for decades. Yet what remained hidden was the deeper mechanism of these patterns as the root of what separates us from Source, ourselves and ultimately a life we love. What I discovered was that these wounds are also responsible for making us susceptible to programming, conditioning and measures of domination and control. This occurs because the separation creates deep unconscious instability and unsafety. When we operate from these wounded states, we grasp at what we think will make us create safety around us, but at the expense of true safety and sovereignty within us.

This realisation shifted everything. I understood that working with these Core Wounds went beyond personal transformation. It was about humanity's liberation from the very mechanisms that keep us small, controllable and separated from our true power. The three Core Wounds are the foundation upon which all our limitations are built and understanding them is the key to reclaiming our sovereignty and our connection to Source.

With this overarching understanding of the journey from Source to duality and back again instilled within me, I knew I had to piece together the vital aspects of how wounding becomes embedded in our Consciousness. I understood that my childhood held keys to understanding how the perceptions about my separate self had been reinforced, so I felt drawn to explore this territory.

However, this exploration felt different from traditional inner child healing approaches. Rather than isolating those younger versions of myself as separate entities needing rescue, I wanted to understand something deeper: *How does the inner sensing or innocent aspect of our Consciousness initially attach to programs of limitation and survival? How does the pure awareness we are born with become filtered through patterns of separation?*

I began exploring how the specific imprints from caregivers and education had reinforced a limited version of my perception of reality and defined my place within it. This investigation revealed how my earliest experiences created the foundational perceptions that shaped everything that followed. The way I was held, spoken to, seen and responded to became my template for how I expected to be received by the world.

As I focussed on building a deep reconnection between my adult Consciousness and these younger aspects of myself, something profound began to shift. Rather than trying to heal my childhood wounds, I was reclaiming the Wholeness that had always existed beneath the programming. I began to see that the pattern of being Unloved existed more in an illusion zone than in truth and this recognition created radical levels of internal safety. Let us go deeper into this understanding together...

How Core Wounds Develop in Childhood

Our Core Wounds begin shaping our perception of reality from our earliest experiences. Each Core Wound functions as a reality-designing mechanism rooted in separation from self. As children we become increasingly conscious that we are separate from everything around us and we begin to feel the depth of pain present in this realm of experience.

Certain childhood experiences lead us to question whether we are truly loved in the way we long to be. Without consistent nurturing, validation, or acknowledgment, we begin doubting our inherent worth. If we were not seen, heard, or understood from a young age, we start questioning fundamental aspects of our existence:

✦ Am I truly known?
✦ Who in this world can truly meet my needs?

When we experience punishment, criticism and threats instead of security and reassurance, we fail to develop genuine inner safety. This pattern of separation begins forming the fundamental lens through which we perceive our external reality, creating the filters that will shape every subsequent experience.

From these early understandings, we begin developing intricate systems to manage our fear and pain. We create thought processes that attempt to make sense of our environment, emotional attachment patterns that help us navigate relationships and behavioural strategies designed to minimise threat and maximise safety. But at a fundamental level all of these create an interpretation of our experience that is not anchored in truth.

We attempt to relate to our external reality in ways that might ease our fear and avoid our pain. A child who feels Unloved might become exceptionally compliant, hoping that perfect behaviour will finally earn the love they crave or start to withdraw and distance themselves. A child who feels Unworthy might become an overachiever, believing that external success will prove their value or shut down and avoid trying for fear of failure. A child who feels Unknown might become hypervigilant about others' moods and needs, hoping that anticipating and meeting those needs will create the connection they desperately seek or become paralysed with anxiety.

Yet paradoxically, these very strategies, born from fear and pain, keep the wound cycling back on itself. The compliant child never learns to trust that they are loved for who they are, only for what they do. The achieving child never feels worthy of love without constant proof of their value. The hypervigilant child never feels truly seen because they are always focussed on seeing others.

Once these initial wound patterns are established, we become unconscious detectives, gathering evidence that confirms our deepest fears about ourselves and the world. Our developing minds begin to notice patterns that validate our core perceptions while filtering out information that contradicts them. The child with an Unloved Wound starts cataloguing every moment of perceived rejection while missing clear expressions of affection. The child with an Unworthy Wound begins collecting failures and criticisms while dismissing praise and accomplishments. The child with an Unknown Wound starts anticipating disasters and chaos while overlooking stability and predictability.

This evidence-gathering becomes increasingly sophisticated as we grow. We learn to interpret neutral events through the lens of our wound, transforming ambiguous situations into confirmation of our core perceptions. A delayed response becomes proof of rejection. A suggestion becomes evidence of inadequacy. A change in routine becomes a threat to security. Our perception becomes so filtered that we live in a reality specifically designed to validate our wounds.

Even more compelling is how we unconsciously seek out experiences and relationships that support our wound narrative. We gravitate towards people and situations that feel familiar, which often means recreating the very dynamics that wounded us originally. The Unloved Wound seeks partners who are emotionally unavailable. The Unworthy Wound chooses environments full of criticism and judgment. The Unknown Wound creates chaos and unpredictability. These choices feel like fate or coincidence, yet it is our unconscious mind's attempt to confirm what we believe to be true about ourselves.

Perhaps most devastating is our ability to dismiss or reinterpret positive experiences that contradict our wound story. Love offered freely gets explained away as pity or obligation. Success gets attributed to luck or lowered standards. Safety gets dismissed as temporary or fragile. Our wound becomes so invested in its own survival that it actively works against evidence of our inherent Wholeness and worth.

Family members unconsciously embody roles that sustain our separation from self, perpetuating our Core Wounds through complex relational dynamics. These relationships become powerful portals for accessing deeper Consciousness about ourselves and understanding the wound's intricate design. Understanding these dynamics allows us to see how our wounds were created by individual experiences and woven into the very fabric of our earliest relationships, creating the template for all relationships that would follow.

The Power of Imprints

Perhaps the most subtle yet profound mechanism sustaining our Core Wounds are the imprints we receive from others, especially our family. Imprints are mental patterns and internal voices that shape how we perceive ourselves and form our identity. These are the words, perceptions and perspectives that were repeatedly spoken over us, particularly during our formative years, that became interwoven with our own self-perception.

These imprints operate like a soundtrack playing continuously in the background of our Consciousness: *you're too sensitive; you'll never amount to anything; don't be so selfish; you need to try harder.* While these may have been spoken only occasionally, their impact was so significant that they became part of our internal dialogue, almost indistinguishable from our own thoughts.

What makes imprints so challenging is their stealth, we often do not recognise them as foreign to our true nature. We believe these voices are our own, that they represent objective truth about who we are. This inability to distinguish between our authentic voice and these implanted perspectives makes us vulnerable to the programs that keep us separate from ourselves.

Consider how these imprints reinforce our Core Wounds. The constant reminder to put others first maintains the Unloved Wound by teaching you to abandon yourself. The critical voice telling you that you are inadequate sustains the Unworthy Wound. The voice that questions your perceptions or dismisses your feelings perpetuates the Unknown Wound by disconnecting you from your inner knowing. To begin working with imprints, ask yourself:

✦ What recurring thoughts or 'truths' about myself feel heavy or constricting?

✦ Whose voice am I actually hearing when I criticise myself?

✦ What would I believe about myself if I had never heard these messages?

When you create space between yourself and these imprinted voices, you can begin to challenge them. You can recognise the pain of having adopted these voices to survive and navigate your early environment. As you bring Consciousness to these imprints, you can feel the pain they have caused, acknowledge their presence and begin the process of releasing them.

Most importantly, this awareness helps ensure you do not perpetuate these imprints by using these same voices with others, especially children, breaking the cycle of unconscious wounding that passes from generation to generation.

How Your Core Wound Creates Your Reality

As a child, you were energetically participating in the Core Wound separation pattern while overlaying mental constructs to make sense of it. This pattern both supports the wound and keeps you perpetuating its existence. All of this happened unconsciously, as you tried to navigate a world that felt overwhelming and uncertain. This could be a feeling of emotional or physical unsafety, a sense of needs not being met, isolation, fear, suppression, verbal or physical punishment or denial.

It is vital that we understand the life events that shaped us and the conclusions we drew about our Wound Reality. Once we gain clarity about these patterns, we can begin to collapse the wound pattern and reach Wholeness, we can reconnect with our soul's innate connection to Source.

Your emotional responses to the wound space likely involved some combination of suppression, repression or over-expression as you tried to avoid the associated pain and fear. Understanding your relationship with emotions becomes essential for liberation. It is powerful to reflect on how your emotional expression was met in your childhood home:

+ Were you shut down?
+ Were you shamed?
+ Were you ignored?
+ Were you punished or abandoned in some way for expressing any emotion?

The extent of this emotional management determines how deeply you store the cellular, emotional debris of the wound in your body.

Beyond your emotions, your nervous system itself becomes the home of your wounding. As you experience repeated moments of unsafety while in the wounded state, your autonomic nervous system begins to encode these patterns. Your body develops a sophisticated alarm system and constantly scans for threats based on previous painful experiences. This creates a physiological foundation for your wound patterns. This neurobiological adaptation gates your pain from being fully expressed and processed.

Instead of flowing through and releasing, emotional pain becomes trapped in your tissues, affecting your breathing patterns, muscle tension, digestive function and even immune response. Your body becomes the living archive of your unprocessed wounds. This is why authentic healing must include somatic awareness – bringing conscious attention to how these wounds live in your physical form, not just in your thoughts and emotions. We will delve into this more fully in the upcoming chapters on pain and fear.

Understanding Core Wound Energetics

Our wounds may show up in our bodies, but they are born in the invisible realm of energy, severing us from who we truly are. This rupture becomes a relentless inner voice whispering the same devastating lies: *You are Unloved. You are Unworthy. You are Unknown.*

These whispers drive us into survival mode. We constantly scan the world for someone or something to validate our existence, to prove we matter, to finally make us feel safe. But here is the cruel irony, the more desperately we seek acceptance outside ourselves, the deeper we sink into the very separation we are trying to heal.

We become addicted to the external search, forever chasing the next person, achievement, or experience that might finally fill the void. Yet each time we look outward, we reinforce the fundamental lie that we are separate, incomplete beings who must earn our place in the world. The seeking itself becomes the prison and we remain trapped in an endless cycle of longing, momentary satisfaction and inevitable disappointment.

To understand how wounds operate, we must recognise something fundamental about our nature: at the quantum level, what we perceive as solid matter emerges from dynamic energy fields. The space within our atoms is not empty, it is alive with quantum activity and pure potential. Meanwhile, every cell in your body communicates through bioelectrical signals, electromagnetic fields and quantum processes. Your thoughts, emotions and Consciousness operate through these energetic information systems before they manifest as physical sensations or actions. This means your energetic nature is the invisible architect of your visible experience, constantly creating your material reality from a foundation of pure potential and information.

When trapped in Wound Reality, we become completely absorbed with physical existence through our senses, fixating on the material world, the someones, somethings, somewheres and sometimes of our external experience. This creates a profound disconnect: as fundamentally energetic beings operating through dynamic quantum processes, we have become imprisoned by focusing solely on the physical manifestations while ignoring the energetic foundation that creates them.

How the Quantum Field Shapes Our Experience

The quantum field of Consciousness holds the All – all time (infinite time), all space (the building blocks for physical things), all frequencies (the full spectrum of emotional ranges and light frequencies from density to lightness) and all possibilities (an infinite field of potential). Our attention, how and where we focus our Consciousness, automatically brings energy into matter or potential into reality. Think of it this way: if we do not first observe something as energy, it will not manifest as matter. Our focus pulls potential out of the quantum field and makes it reality. But here is the crucial point: the baseline for creation in the quantum field is the Core Wound mechanism.

Our observation is largely unconscious and this unconscious patterning draws in the creation of our material reality. You will feel this in that you are consistently looking for the same areas of your life to complete and show you that you are wanted, enough and understood. As you are repeatedly looking for evidence that this is the case, you are in an ongoing relationship with this projection. It is a deeper design function that means we keep participating in similar relationships, work environments, physical illnesses, family dynamics, financial situations and unrealised purpose. The challenge is to bring awareness to the unconscious pattern. It is this pattern that is creating reality by default and with it, a sense that you are a victim to it, rather than the creator of it.

Let us dive more deeply into how the three Core Wounds are pathways to Wholeness. We will explore how these patterns are constructed and some of the more common aspects of their presentation in your life.

Unloved: The Portal to Self-Love

The Predictable Patterns of the Unloved Wound

The Unloved Wound creates distinct patterns in how people approach, maintain and exit relationships. These patterns often unconsciously recreate the very abandonment you fear.

This is a list of some of these, but you may experience others:

- **Attracting emotionally unavailable partners:** You gravitate towards people who cannot fully commit, are physically or emotionally distant, or require constant pursuit, recreating familiar dynamics of having to earn love.

- **Desperate clinging and inability to set boundaries:** You become anxious when partners need space, constantly seeking reassurance about the relationship, monitoring their every move and struggling to say no to their demands while panicking at signs of independence or withdrawal.

- **Testing love through drama:** You create conflicts or crises to see if partners will stay, pushing boundaries to confirm commitment, unconsciously sabotaging peace to prove the relationship can survive chaos.

- **Giving everything while neglecting your own needs:** You overextend yourself emotionally, financially, or practically while accepting minimal effort in return, abandoning self-care and personal needs because you believe you must earn love through constant sacrifice and service.

✦ **Difficulty accepting and trusting genuine love:** You question authentic affection, suspect ulterior motives when treated well, or feel uncomfortable with consistent kindness and care, often deflecting or arguing against expressions of love.

✦ **Losing identity to merge with others:** You abandon your own interests, opinions and goals to become what you think your partner, friends or others in your life want; shapeshifting to maintain connection at the expense of authenticity and personal boundaries.

✦ **Withdrawing and creating isolation:** You pull away from friends, family and potential partners when feeling vulnerable, decline social invitations, or avoid forming new connections, believing that staying alone prevents the pain of eventual abandonment, yet this isolation reinforces your perception that you are fundamentally unloved.

✦ **Pre-emptive self-sabotage:** You end relationships before you can be abandoned, pick fights when things get too good, or find flaws to justify leaving before being left, protecting yourself from anticipated rejection.

✦ **Tolerating poor treatment and boundary violations:** You accept behaviour from partners and family members you would never allow from friends, stay in situations where you are taken for granted, criticised, or neglected because any connection feels better than none, often justifying mistreatment as normal.

✦ **Post-breakup desperation and pursuit:** You are unable to accept endings gracefully, continuing to reach out long after relationships end, believing you can win love back through persistence, or entering rebound relationships immediately to avoid feeling unloved and alone.

Energy Depletion Through Over-Giving

'If I do not feed my energy into you, I will die'

With the Unloved Wound, you become an energetic fountain, constantly pouring love outward in a desperate attempt to secure connection. This intense overflow drives you to consistently overinvest in others, fuelled by the fear that if you do not fill every space with love, you will be abandoned forever.

You find yourself trapped in trying to secure something external to finally feel the connection you crave within. But no amount of external connection can satisfy this internal longing. The constant outpouring leaves you energetically depleted while simultaneously afraid to keep any energy for yourself, believing you must continue feeding it outward to survive.

The tragic irony? This very pattern destroys your capacity to receive love when it is offered. You miss the experience of true love: the love that exists within yourself.

The core fear driving this wound whispers: *I am not loved, so I do not exist.*

Yet seeking love externally will never feel safe or validating until you first anchor yourself in self-connection and discover the eternal nature of love within. When you travel back through the wound to Wholeness, you experience your own love as energetically self-sufficient. From this space, you meet all of life as the essence and expression of love itself. Your relationship with life transforms when you ask one simple question: ***is this loving to me?***

This becomes your compass for recognising whether you are investing all your energy outside yourself or maintaining energetic self-sufficiency. Let it become your prayer to yourself, to your highest internal connection to the Source of your love.

Unworthy: The Portal to Self-Worth

The Predictable Patterns of the Unworthy Wound

The Unworthy Wound manifests through behaviours that attempt to prove worth, while paradoxically reinforcing the perception that you are fundamentally flawed and do not deserve good things in life. The list below is a starting point and you may realise other patterns too:

+ **Overcompensating through achievement:** You become a high achiever from a desperate need to prove your worth rather than genuine passion. You collect degrees, certifications and accomplishments like armour, believing that accumulating enough external proof will finally make you deserving of love and respect, yet you never feel like you have enough.

+ **Self-sabotage when things go well:** You create problems or destroy good things when they arrive, unconsciously believing, *this is too good for me* and returning to familiar pain.

+ **Chronic people-pleasing:** You mould yourself into whatever others want, losing your authentic self while performing for acceptance, receiving hollow validation for your mask rather than your true self.

+ **Constant self-criticism, depreciation and comparison:** You have harsh internal voices that attack you before others can, manifesting as self-deprecating humour or pointing out your flaws when receiving attention. You measure yourself against others' achievements, income, appearance or status, using external benchmarks to confirm your inadequacy rather than developing internal worth.

- **Perfectionism as protection** - You use perfectionism to avoid criticism that would confirm your worst fears, believing mistakes are evidence of fundamental unworthiness rather than normal humanity.

- **Deflecting recognition and downplaying success** - When acknowledged for accomplishments, you immediately attribute success to luck, timing, or others' help while highlighting your own minimal contribution or mistakes made along the way.

- **Overworking and productivity addiction** - You believe your value comes entirely from what you produce, staying busy to avoid feeling worthless, equating rest with laziness and self-worth with output.

- **Chronic imposter syndrome and self-doubt** - You experience a persistent fear of being 'found out' as incompetent, despite evidence of competence, believing you have fooled everyone and that your success is undeserved or accidental. You constantly question whether you are on the right path and taking the right actions.

Energy Depletion Through Seeking

'If I do not have energy fed into me, I will die'

This wound operates like an internal void that drives a relentless pursuit of external validation. You constantly search for ways to have others' energy feed into you for survival, whether through approval from bosses, clients, friends, partners, children, or through achievements in career, finances, health and appearance.

The other side of this pattern shows up as avoidance, self-sabotage, or constant self-criticism that keeps you at arm's length from your own life. The core fear remains the same: if I do not receive acknowledgement and validation, I am not worthy enough to exist.

These external markers create a carefully constructed illusion where your sense of adequacy depends entirely on circumstances beyond your control. The wound convinces you that being enough is something you must achieve rather than something you inherently are. Each validation provides temporary relief before the hunger returns, demanding more proof of your worth.

You find yourself literally begging for scraps of approval, acceptance, or belonging to confirm your existence. This endless seeking creates a second-rate feedback loop where you have completely dismissed your own energetic currency in favour of others' responses. The exhaustion comes from being trapped in a cycle where your self-worth fluctuates with every external reaction.

The path to freedom involves becoming energetically self-sufficient. Instead of seeking completion outside yourself, you discover that your energy is sacred and meant to fuel your own experience. True liberation arrives when you realise your worth exists independent of external validation: you no longer need compliments, achievements, or others' approval to feel valuable. One powerful question to keep asking is: *am I honouring my intrinsic worth?*

This helps you recognise when you are giving your energy away versus maintaining your connection to your own internal energy source. The goal is keeping your energy focussed inward rather than constantly seeking validation from the world around you.

Unknown: The Portal to Self-Knowledge and Safety

The Predictable Patterns of the Unknown Wound

The Unknown Wound manifests through behaviours that desperately seek understanding, safety and knowledge while paradoxically creating more separation and uncertainty:

✦ **Constant need for verbal validation** - Endlessly trying to express yourself 'just right', seeking agreement with perspectives, ruminating and analysing every interaction to ensure you are heard and understood.

✦ **Over-explaining and repeating** - Telling the same story multiple times with different details, becoming frustrated when others do not grasp what you are trying to communicate, escalating efforts to be understood.

✦ **Hypervigilance about being misunderstood** - Scanning conversations for signs that others do not get you, becoming defensive when questioned, assuming others are judging or dismissing your viewpoint.

✦ **Withdrawal when not heard** - Shutting down or pulling away when feeling unheard, giving up on communication, retreating into isolation rather than continuing to try.

✦ **Obsessive worry and catastrophising** - Constantly anticipating worst-case scenarios, remaining in a state of tension waiting for disaster, draining energy into imagining everything that could go wrong.

✦ **Over-organising and controlling the environment** - Micromanaging details to create an Illusion of Safety, becoming anxious when plans change, needing everything in its proper place to feel secure.

✦ **Hypervigilance about others' safety** - Extending worry and control to family and friends, creating exhausting webs of concern, feeling responsible for preventing harm to others.

✦ **Information addiction and endless research** - Compulsively seeking external knowledge believing it will create certainty, investing heavily in courses, books and experts to find the 'right' answer.

✦ **Analysis paralysis** - Getting stuck in endless cycles of research and questioning, unable to make decisions without gathering more information, seeking the perfect understanding before acting.

✦ **Spiritual bypassing through seeking** - Using spiritual practices, teachers or modalities as another form of external seeking rather than trusting inner knowing and wisdom.

✦ **Feeling fundamentally Unknown by yourself** - Deep sense of not knowing who you really are beneath all the seeking, feeling disconnected from your own essence and authentic desires.

✦ **Difficulty trusting intuition and inner guidance** - Dismissing gut feelings in favour of external verification, doubting your own perceptions, needing others to confirm what you already sense to be true.

Energy Depletion through Seeking

'I stay lost in the Unknown or I will die'

The Unknown Wound has three fascinating aspects; you may resonate with one or all of these.

Unseen, Unheard and Misunderstood version: You desperately want others to meet you in deep understanding. There is a profound desire to have the people around you truly comprehend who you are through agreeing with your opinions and viewpoints, or simply by hearing you fully and grasping your essence. You might find yourself constantly trying to express yourself 'just right', seeking agreement with your perspectives or attempting to convince others of your way of seeing things.

This manifests as putting your energy into a middle ground space, waiting for it to be met. You focus all of your being on this connection, ruminating, questioning and analysing every interaction. It becomes an endless cycle of trying to find new ways to express yourself so others understand you, seeking validation through agreement or attempting to gain attention so you are fully seen and appreciated.

The more you want others to hear, understand and see you, the more you become addicted to investing your energy into these spaces. Paradoxically, the harder you try, the more unsatisfying, frustrating and consuming it becomes. You remain trapped in this middle ground, perpetually waiting for the understanding that feels just out of reach.

Unsafe version: This creates a desperate need to make everything as safe and secure as possible to prevent unknowable incidents from occurring. Your body remains in a constant state of tension, waiting for disaster to unfold. You might find yourself caught in cycles of worrying, overorganising, overthinking and overcompensating, trying to ensure that every experience feels safe and manageable.

This preoccupation often extends beyond yourself to include the safety and wellbeing of others, creating an exhausting web of vigilance and control. At the core of this wounding lies the greatest fear of all: death itself. There is a profound sense of separation from life that emerges from this preoccupation with avoiding death and uncertainty.

The pattern becomes all-consuming as you drain your energy into manipulating your environment, your thoughts and your behaviours to avoid confronting the fundamental uncertainty of existence. When reality refuses to provide the constant safety and predictability you crave, you experience a never-ending cycle of anxiety and avoidance.

This becomes the addiction: you are energetically drawn to preoccupy yourself with the very separation and instability you are trying to escape. The more you attempt to control the Unknown, the more trapped you become in its grip, perpetually focussed on the threat rather than the peace you seek.

Unknowing version: This drives a constant need to know everything. You energetically commit to seeking external knowledge, believing that accumulating enough truth and understanding will create the certainty and security you crave. You invest heavily in inquiry, putting all your energy into the external environment, hoping that knowledge will meet you halfway and provide the answers you seek.

There is a powerful illusion that somewhere in the endless information available, you will find the endpoint that brings complete understanding and safety. But in this three-dimensional reality of infinite knowledge, there is no such endpoint. You keep investing your energy outward into oblivion, searching for something that cannot be found externally.

The painful truth is that there is nothing to know in the way you are seeking and no way to know it all. The wound keeps you separate from your own internal knowing by convincing you that the answers lie somewhere outside yourself. You become trapped in an endless cycle of seeking, never recognising that what you are looking for has always existed within you.

This relentless trying to create external understanding and safety leaves you feeling completely Unknown, but the real issue runs deeper. It is not that you need others to know you better, it is that you feel fundamentally Unknown within yourself. You try desperately to shore up the external reflection of who you are while dismissing the vast certainty and safety that exists within your own connection to yourself.

In the remainder of the book you will often see the Unknown Wound split into these three versions.

The liberation from all Unknown Wound spaces comes through finally knowing yourself, finding the deepest security in fully seeing, hearing and understanding yourself at the core level. Your guiding question becomes: ***am I trusting my inner knowing?***

Supporting Mechanisms: Understanding What Keeps Us Wounded

Once you become conscious of your wounding, it is equally important to recognise the mechanisms that sustain and defend these patterns. From the initial formation of these programs, they perpetuate themselves continuously, often operating below your conscious awareness causing your entire reality to narrow into this singular focus.

Think of your wound patterns as wearing coloured glasses that you have forgotten you are wearing. If you have worn red-tinted glasses since childhood, you have come to believe the world simply is red. You do not question or notice it anymore, it is just your reality. Working with your Core Wounds is like finally removing these glasses and seeing the true colours of existence for the first time. The initial shock and disorientation gradually give way to wonder as you perceive the world without distortion and expand into an incredible sense of pure liberation. To be able to liberate we need to understand some of the secondary wound mechanisms that keep us unconsciously protecting our wounds. They are like the guards of the prison and keep us looping within the limited constructs. Realising they exist and questioning their role in your reality is crucial.

Victimhood: The Hidden Prison

When caught in victimhood, our lens often focuses sharply on the intense wrongdoing, betrayal and suppression we have experienced at the hands of others. The real challenge lies in investigating the paradigm of being a victim that supports this experience. Beneath the surface stories lives a mental, emotional and behavioural commitment to victimhood that we may not even realise we are making. ***Where do you still feel a victim of reality?***

Shame: The Self-Made Prison

Shame brings an unshakable feeling of wrongness that can feel completely debilitating. Here is what makes shame so powerful: to experience it, you must fully commit to being a victim. You must believe that what happened to you was significantly your responsibility, your fault and then take that perception deep into your being. The liberating truth emerges: you are not the victim but you have become the perpetrator against yourself. You have prosecuted yourself and built your own energetic prison of shame. ***What still gives you the feeling of shame?***

Judgment: The Illusion of Safety

The mechanism of judgment runs so deep because it is embedded in the very design of separation. Think about how we constantly categorise, mentally projecting arbitrary categories onto the things, people and experiences around us. This keeps us in a perpetual state of mental separation.

We have created an Illusion of Safety, taking stock and making moment-to-moment adjustments to improve our relationship with the external environment. But it is a zero-sum game, as we judge we separate from reality more and keep ourselves separate from the truth. ***How do you judge yourself and others?***

Blame: The Illusion of Control

One common spiritual misconception suggests that we create our own suffering. This is not exactly accurate. The mechanics of separation create our suffering, we did not bring this on ourselves, nor do we deserve to suffer. Our power instead lies in the story we tell about our suffering and how we relate to it.

We often despise our tendency to repeat dysfunctional patterns, convincing ourselves we are to blame for the suffering these patterns create for ourselves and others. But this viewpoint misses something crucial: these patterns emerge from the design of separation, not from our true nature. Every human being follows these patterns until they become aware of them. Remember this vital truth: no one consciously chooses this way of being, it is a mechanism of our Wound Reality. ***Who do you blame? Yourself or someone else?***

Guilt: The Self-Imposed Burden

Guilt operates as a peculiar form of self-punishment, different from shame in its focus. While shame says, *I am wrong*, guilt whispers, *I did wrong.* This subtle distinction creates a powerful trap. Guilt keeps us stuck in endless cycles of self-recrimination about past actions or inactions, convinced that carrying this burden somehow makes amends or prevents future mistakes.

Think of guilt as a heavy backpack you have chosen to wear.

You might believe carrying this weight keeps you 'good' or prevents you from making the same mistakes, instead it drains your energy and keeps you focussed on the past rather than present growth. The weight of guilt does not protect you or others, it simply perpetuates the wounded state. Liberation from guilt comes through understanding that nothing is a mistake, everything that happens is feedback for deeper alignment and growth. ***What have you not forgiven yourself for?***

The Chaos of Transformation

From our unconscious wound energetics, we have placed our attention on the quantum field in ways that have manifested all the aspects of our three-dimensional reality: our physical body, relationships, jobs, living situations, friendships, all these can be part of our unconscious wound creation.

When we enter the In-Between Space, we rewire our energetics and Consciousness to our Wholeness. This means there will be a period of chaos in your external world. Your internal reality will have shifted and will no longer be feeding the same quantum creation program externally. Things that your Core Wound would have energetically fed off are no longer relevant.

When you stay in the In-Between Space, change happens naturally. Some things will fall away; others will appear. This is not the time for concrete action or decision making, though you will be tempted as things start changing rapidly around you. Remember that quantum physics tells us that your attention (whether unconscious or conscious) defines your physical reality. You are changing your relationship with the quantum field and the quantum field is responding by changing your reality.

So sit tight. Stay in your energetic self-sufficiency and allow the external to shift, not from your doing, but from your being. Anything in your experience that causes pain in your participation with it needs to be physically released and you will learn to sit with the pain–fear relationship over and over again as you release the unconscious wounding and come to a point of stillness in your energetic self-sufficiency (there is more about this in coming chapters).

From this void, this sacred In-Between Space, you will begin to sense who you truly are, what you truly want and how you truly desire to show up in the world. Your essence is your true nature beyond the wounds of feeling Unloved, Unworthy and Unknown and it will begin to shine through like the sun emerging from behind storm clouds. This essence has always been there, but the density of your Wound Reality obscures it from view.

The Gift of Our Wounds

This journey asks for patience, commitment and profound self-compassion. As you work with these concepts, remember that you are participating in both personal and collective evolution. Every step you take towards Wholeness contributes to the expansion of human Consciousness itself. The void is not empty, it is the birthplace of your authentic self. It is the cocoon in which your transformation occurs, where the caterpillar of your wound-based identity dissolves into a primordial soup before reassembling as the butterfly of your essence-based being. This dissolution feels like death because, in many ways, it is a death. It is the necessary ending of the constructed identity that was never truly you, so your true self can finally emerge.

In this space between no longer and not yet, you learn to trust the process of becoming. You learn that identity is not fixed but fluid, not singular but multidimensional. You discover that the void, though terrifying to your ego, is actually the womb of your rebirth. Here, in the seeming emptiness, you are most full with possibility, ripening with potential, on the cusp of embodying the love, worthiness and knowing that have always been your birthright.

Practices for Working with Core Wounds

As you begin to recognise these patterns in your own life, here are some practices to help you engage with your Core Wounds as gateways to Wholeness:

Practice 1: Wound Awareness Journaling
Take a few minutes each day to reflect on your dominant wound pattern. Ask yourself:

- When did I feel Unloved, Unworthy or Unknown today?
- What triggered this feeling?
- Where did I feel it in my body?
- What did I do in response to this feeling?
- How did I direct my energy (outward or inward) when this wound was activated?

Simply observing these patterns without judgment creates space between you and the wound.

Practice 2: Energy Tracking
For one week, track your energy levels throughout the day. Notice when you feel depleted versus energised. What situations, thoughts or interactions correspond with each state? Pay particular attention to:

- Who or what situations consistently drain your energy?
- When do you feel yourself overgiving (Unloved Wound), seeking validation (Unworthy Wound) or trying to create certainty (Unknown Wound)?
- What happens when you consciously bring your energy back to yourself in these moments?

Remember, increasing Consciousness is the most powerful way to shift the pattern. Each time you bring awareness to a wound pattern, instead of automatically acting it out, you create new energetic possibilities.

CHAPTER FOUR
The Addiction to Your Wounding

When the reality of these wounds became clear to me, I started the work of returning to my Source nature. But this reunion proved challenging as yet another formidable force within reality's design emerged...

I discovered I was an addict. An addict to my Wound Reality. I was chemically dependent on the repetition of my wounded patterns, reactions, emotions and thought forms. I could tell myself I was a Divine being, but I truly could not feel it or live as it. An unconscious part of me was committed to the repetitive pain and fear of my wounds. I realised that as much as I did not like it, I was deeply reliant on it to create the known reality that I now see created an Illusion of Safety.

This chapter will examine how these 'wound addictions' shape your relationships, environments and perceptions, and why you may not have experienced lasting change if you have not recognised the attachment you have to the predictability of your wounding. Finally, we will glimpse the path towards liberation, through a radical new relationship with pain, fear and identity that transforms your entire experience of being human.

The Chemistry of Wounding

The harsh truth that we must face is this; your Core Wounds make you act like a person with an addiction. It is a fundamental reality that shapes every aspect of your existence. Like someone with a physical addiction to alcohol or drugs who craves their next fix. You are addicted to experiencing the separation of your wound and the energetics that support this separation. You structure your reality in repetitive patterns to know when, where and how you will get your next Core Wound hit.

The wound makes you addicted to your environment. You know the exact behaviours, thoughts and feelings needed to connect with reality in such a way as to get the predictable responses in your body and predictable responses from everything around you. You are such a powerful creator that you create a drug store all around you to get your addiction fed. Every relationship, job, living situation and daily routine becomes calibrated to deliver your preferred neurochemical cocktail.

Think of how the Unloved Wound might create a relationship where communication is just inconsistent enough to trigger abandonment panic, providing the familiar rush of cortisol followed by the relief of temporary reassurance. Or how the Unworthy Wound might design a work environment where praise is rare but criticism abundant, maintaining the motivation to overwork and dismiss self care. Or how the Unknown Wound might design a continual seeking of information through courses, while simultaneously creating the experience of not knowing enough. The drug store you have created does not look like a pharmacy, it looks like your life, carefully constructed to dispense exactly the neurochemical patterns your wound has become dependent upon.

You might resist this truth, thinking: *but I hate my wound and the way it makes me feel.* Yet the deeper truth is that you are craving it. You want it more than anything because it validates your energetic existence. This addiction has become so intertwined with your thoughts, emotions and behaviours that it literally supports all parts of your reality. Every thought pattern, emotional response and behavioural habit serves to maintain this wounded state.

This understanding explains why true change is so difficult to achieve. The addiction is not merely a habit or pattern we can modify through willpower or good intentions. It is woven into our deepest perceptions about who we are, forming the very foundation of our identity. To challenge the wound addiction is to challenge our entire sense of self and how we have learned to navigate existence. This is why conventional approaches to healing often do not move us beyond our loops and limitations. They do not recognise the depth and pervasiveness of this addiction, nor how completely it has hijacked our identity structure. When we understand that what we are really addicted to is a particular version of ourselves, the wounded self, we begin to grasp why transformation requires nothing less than a fundamental reimagining of who we are.

Your internal chemical domain influences your reality in profound and complex ways. You are, in essence, a walking chemical cocktail, ripe for stimulation. The external world provides hooks that activate and create deep-lasting chemical addictions, offering an illusion of control as you believe you can choose how to access your drug of choice. Each Core Wound seeks its own chemical comfort:

- The Unloved Wound seeks oxytocin (the love hormone creates connectivity and bonding) through desperate connection attempts.
- The Unworthy Wound craves dopamine (a hormone responsible for pleasure and satisfaction) through achievement and validation.
- The Unknown Wound chases GABA or gamma-aminobutyric acid (an amino acid that impacts on sleep, mood and anxiety regulation) through control and certainty.

The Primary Wound: Our First Addiction

We have already explored how at the heart of human suffering lies the primal wound of perceived separation from Source, from the infinite, from Wholeness, from the Divine. It is the first fracture that creates all other fractures, the original split that makes all other splits possible.

This wound manifests as a profound sense of abandonment, a feeling of being cast out from paradise, cut off from our essential nature. It is the existential loneliness that no relationship or achievement can fully heal, the gnawing sense that something fundamental is missing.

From this primary separation, our three fundamental wounds emerge. These wounds form the foundation of human suffering and give rise to all our addictive programs:

+ The Unloved Wound (Abandonment)
+ The Unworthy Wound (Inherent Defectiveness)
+ The Unknown Wound (Powerlessness and Uncertainty)

Each of these wounds creates its own unique addiction pattern, its own desperate search for relief that ironically deepens the very wound it seeks to soothe. Below are a few case studies of the design of this addiction, yet your circumstances will be unique to you and your programming. Let them become a spring-board for greater revelation and awareness.

The Unloved Wound's Desperate Dance

The addiction of the Unloved Wound creates perhaps the most heartbreaking dance with reality. Consider Sarah, whose story illustrates the devastating cycle of this wound. She constantly checks her phone, her heart racing every time it lights up. In the morning, she wakes up already craving connection, scanning her messages before she is even fully conscious. By mid-morning, she has crafted careful texts designed to elicit responses that prove she matters; when the response does not come quickly enough, her body floods with cortisol, triggering the familiar panic of abandonment.

The physical sensations are unmistakable, a hollow ache spreading through the chest, a tightening of the throat that makes it difficult to swallow, a restless energy that makes sitting still nearly impossible. The mind races with possibilities: *did I say something wrong? Are they with someone else? Do they still care?* The body becomes a tuning fork, vibrating with anxiety and longing, unable to settle until the next dopamine hit of connection arrives.

"I know it's destroying me," Sarah shared, "but I can't stop. Even when I try to pull back, to give myself space, the anxiety becomes unbearable. I find myself creating dramas just to feel something, anything that proves I exist in someone else's world." She creates elaborate scenarios to test whether people truly care about her, all while telling herself she is just being 'careful' or 'protective'. But the truth is, she is seeking her next hit of validation, of proof that she matters.

Like any addiction, Sarah's pattern follows a predictable cycle: the initial craving for connection, the brief high of receiving attention, the inevitable crash when the attention fades and the desperate seeking that begins again. Each cycle deepens the wound, confirming her core perception that love is scarce and must be constantly pursued.

The Unloved pattern becomes a sophisticated drug seeker, creating intricate scenarios to prove its core perception: that love is limited, conditional and must be earned through specific behaviours or achievements. Like a person with an addiction knowing exactly where to find their dealer, you know how to create situations that will give you your next hit of abandonment, separation or rejection.

Your body becomes exquisitely tuned to this dance, addicted to the oxytocin surge of momentary connection followed by the cortisol spike of inevitable separation. You find yourself in relationships with unavailable partners, not because you are unlucky in love, but because your addiction demands the familiar pattern of reaching for what cannot be fully grasped.

This wound touches our deepest fear, that we will be left alone, unsupported and uncared for. It is abandonment on our deepest physical, emotional and spiritual levels. This wound creates a complex web of programs that profoundly impact our relationship with ourselves and others. At its core, it generates intense fears around attachment and dependency, leading us to either cling desperately to relationships or avoid them entirely.

The fear of intimacy becomes a constant companion, creating an invisible barrier between ourselves and others, even when we long for connection. Many develop patterns of excessive self-reliance, building fortresses of independence that protect them from the possibility of abandonment while simultaneously keeping out the very connection they crave.

The Unloved Wound creates a pattern of abandonment that manifests in paradoxical ways through our behaviour. Some become the person who never allows anyone to get close, maintaining careful emotional distance while longing for connection from afar. Others transform into those who cannot let go, holding onto relationships well past their natural conclusion, driven by the terror of being alone. The chronic people-pleaser emerges as another manifestation, constantly working to earn love and prevent abandonment through endless accommodation of others' needs. And then some become the fiercely independent loner, wearing their self-sufficiency like armour, convincing themselves they need no one while nursing a deep, unacknowledged hunger for connection. All these manifestations stem from the same Unloved Core Wound, just expressed through different programs.

The Unworthy Wound's Endless Striving

The Unworthy Wound creates an addiction to external validation so profound that it reshapes your entire reality. Think of Michael, whose story reveals the relentless cycle of achievement addiction. He has achieved everything society claims should make him feel worthy: the prestigious career, the overflowing bank account, the peer acclaim, all the external markers of success. Yet each accomplishment feels hollow, driving him towards the next goal, the next validation, the next temporary hit of worth.

In his body, the Unworthy Wound creates a constant state of tension, his shoulders perpetually raised towards his ears, jaw clenched even in sleep and his stomach knotted with acid. The sensation is one of perpetual insufficiency, a physical emptiness that seems to hollow out the centre of the chest, creating a vacuum that no achievement can fill. At night, his mind races with lists of uncompleted tasks and future goals, while his body lies rigid with the tension of unrealised potential.

"It's like being on a treadmill that keeps speeding up," Michael explains. "I'll set a goal, meet a partner, buy the house, get the recognition and be convinced that this time it will finally be enough. When I achieve it, there is this brief moment of euphoria, this hit of satisfaction. But within days, sometimes hours, the emptiness returns and I'm already scanning for the next target, the next achievement that might finally prove I'm enough."

The cycle is exhausting yet seemingly inescapable: the initial rush of setting a new goal, the adrenaline of pursuit, the dopamine hit of achievement and the inevitable crash that sends him searching for the next fix. Even his moments of rest are contaminated by anxiety, his mind already racing towards the next proof of worth.

This pattern becomes a relentless taskmaster, never allowing rest or satisfaction. Like a gambling addict convinced the next bet will finally bring the big win, you constantly strive for the next achievement, the next recognition, the next proof of your value. Your nervous system becomes so dependent on this cycle that moments of rest feel like failure.

Your body craves the dopamine surge of achievement, creating a chemical dependency that drives you further into the pattern. You structure your entire life around opportunities for validation, turning every interaction into a performance, every relationship into a stage for proving your worth.

This wound touches our fundamental sense of value and right to exist. It manifests as a deep-seated perception that we are somehow inherently flawed or defective, creating a perpetual sense of inadequacy that no external achievement can fully resolve. From this wound emerges an intricate tapestry of compensatory behaviours and self-protective mechanisms. Perfectionism becomes a constant drive, pushing us towards ever-higher achievements in an attempt to prove our worth. Yet no accomplishment ever feels quite sufficient, as the wound continues to whisper its message of fundamental unworthiness.

Self-sabotage often emerges as a paradoxical protection mechanism; if we are going to fail anyway, it is better to do it on our own terms. This pattern can become so subtle and ingrained that we mistake it for bad luck or circumstances beyond our control. Chronic comparison to others becomes a habitual lens through which we view life, constantly measuring ourselves against an impossible standard and always finding ourselves wanting. Imposter syndrome takes root deeply, creating a persistent fear that, at any moment, others will discover the truth of our unworthiness. These patterns weave together to create a state of perpetual striving and insatiable addiction, never allowing us to rest in the simple truth of our inherent value.

The Unknown Wound's Compulsive Seeking

The Unknown Wound creates perhaps the most subtle yet pervasive addiction, a desperate seeking of certainty and understanding that shapes every engagement with reality. Consider Jemma, whose story illuminates the exhausting cycle of seeking understanding. She spends countless hours analysing every interaction, every relationship, every possibility, caught in an endless loop of trying to make sense of her world.

Physically, this wound manifests as a persistent buzzing in the nervous system, a subtle but unrelenting vibration that prevents true rest. The chest tightens, the breath becomes shallow and rapid and the eyes dart constantly, scanning for threats or inconsistencies. Sleep becomes elusive as the mind refuses to quiet its endless cataloguing of possibilities and dangers. The body itself becomes a terrain of hypervigilance, unable to settle into the present moment because it is constantly bracing for what might come next.

"I can't just experience life," Jemma confessed. "Every conversation becomes a puzzle to solve, every relationship a mystery to decode. I tell myself I'm just being thorough, trying to understand, but the truth is, I'm addicted to the brief relief that comes when I think I've figured something out. Then a new uncertainty arises and the cycle starts again. It's like my mind is a detective that can never rest, always searching for the next clue, the next piece of understanding that might finally make me feel safe."

The pattern follows a familiar addiction cycle: the anxiety of uncertainty triggers intense analysis, leading to a moment of apparent clarity that brings temporary relief. But this relief is quickly shattered by new unknowns, sending her back into the spiral of seeking. Each cycle reinforces her core perception that she must understand everything to be safe, driving her deeper into the pattern.

This pattern turns life into an endless puzzle to solve, each piece promising the certainty you crave. Like an information addict constantly seeking the next piece of data, you find yourself compulsively trying to make sense of everything around you. Your nervous system becomes dependent on the GABA release that comes with momentary understanding, driving you further into the pattern of analysis and control.

This wound relates to our relationship with personal power and agency. It stems from early experiences of helplessness and creates programs around control and manipulation, victimhood mentality and difficulty setting boundaries. The wound of powerlessness often creates a pendulum swing between excessive control and micromanagement and complete abdication of responsibility.

The Reality Creation of an Addict

Consider this profound realisation from one of my clients. "I see where I do this to myself. I attach to expectations. I attach to loyalty to and from others. I attach to drama. I attach to putting myself through hell. It's me. It's not the situation. It's not what was said. It's what I do in my head that's the issue."

This moment of truth can begin transformation; when we recognise that we are not victims of our reality but unconscious creators of it.

Counterintuitive Manifestations of Wound Addiction

What makes wound addiction particularly insidious is how it can manifest in ways that seem completely disconnected from the original wound pattern and at times almost contradictory. These alternate survival modes need careful consideration also:

The "Self-Actualised" Unloved: Someone with this wounding appears to be the epitome of self-sufficiency and independence. Maybe living alone, travelling solo and priding yourself on 'not needing anyone'. Friends admire your freedom and autonomy. Yet beneath this carefully constructed persona lies a profound Unloved Wound. Your independence has become a protective strategy against the pain of abandonment. By needing no one, ensures no one can leave you. The apparent freedom is actually a prison of isolation, constructed by your wound addiction.

The "Humble" Unworthy: This creates a pattern of deflecting compliments, minimising your achievements and always emphasising flaws and mistakes. Many mistake this for humility or spiritual advancement. In reality, this behaviour stems from the Unworthy Wound. By pre-emptively acknowledging your unworthiness, you attempt to control the narrative and protect yourself from others' judgment. What appears as spiritual virtue is really a sophisticated manifestation of wound addiction.

The "Spontaneous" Unknown: This pattern presents itself as being free-spirited and spontaneous, changing plans at the last minute and refusing to be 'tied down' by schedules or commitments. While this appears as liberating flexibility, it is actually driven by the Unknown Wound. The unpredictability allows the person carrying this wound to avoid the vulnerability of committing to a direction that might reveal uncertainty. The apparent spontaneity is a control mechanism that prevents true surrender to life's natural unfolding.

These counterintuitive expressions reveal how wound addiction can disguise itself as positive traits, spiritual advancement or cultural ideals, making them particularly difficult to recognise and address. The addiction can be hidden in what we consider our strengths and virtues not just in our suffering. The telling factor is if it continues to separate us from ourselves and increases our survival patterns to the external reality.

Secondary Wounds and Their Addictive Patterns

Beyond our three primary wounds of being Unloved, Unworthy and Unknown, several secondary wounds create their own distinctive addiction patterns. They are secondary as they blend elements of the primary wounds so; betrayal is Unloved and Unworthy, rejection is Unworthy and Unknown, feeling unwanted is a blend of all three. There are also others not mentioned here that you may experience in your own life and I invite you to explore their design.

The Betrayal Wound

The 'Betrayal Wound' affects our ability to trust life itself, creating a fundamental suspicion of reality that colours every experience and relationship. It instils a deep-seated vigilance that keeps us perpetually on guard, scanning for potential threats and betrayals. This hypervigilance manifests as chronic anxiety, a constant state of alert that exhausts our nervous system and depletes our capacity for joy and spontaneity.

The Betrayal Wound creates intricate and often self-defeating patterns in our relationships. We might find ourselves constantly testing people, creating small challenges or trials to prove their loyalty, unknowingly pushing away the very connection we seek. Some of us learn to betray others first, a pre-emptive strike born from the certainty that betrayal is inevitable. We might build elaborate emotional walls, carefully constructed barriers designed to prevent hurt but which ultimately prevent love as well.

The addiction pattern here involves the adrenaline rush of vigilance followed by the temporary relief of detected 'threats' that confirm our worldview. The betrayed becomes addicted to the very suspicion that prevents connection.

The Rejection Wound

The 'Rejection Wound' relates to our fear of not being accepted or welcomed. It creates programs around social anxiety and withdrawal, excessive conformity, fear of self-expression and people-pleasing behaviours. It can look like shapeshifting to fit the environment; different personalities for different friends, different voices for different situations. The fear of rejection is so big, that you reject your authentic self first.

The addiction pattern here involves the temporary relief of acceptance gained through self-rejection, followed by the inevitable emptiness that comes from abandoning oneself, creating a craving for more external acceptance.

The Unwanted Wound

This wound strikes at our most fundamental need to belong and be welcomed into existence itself. It creates a deep programming that we are a burden, an inconvenience, or simply too much for others to handle. This wound instils the devastating perception that our very presence is problematic and that we must somehow earn our right to take up space in the world.

The 'Unwanted Wound' manifests as a persistent sense of being an outsider, even in intimate relationships and familiar environments. We might find ourselves constantly apologising for existing, minimising our needs or making ourselves smaller in every possible way. This wound creates patterns of self-erasure where we habitually put ourselves last, cancel our own plans to accommodate others and struggle to assert any preferences or boundaries.

Those carrying this wound often develop an extraordinary ability to read rooms and adjust their energy to what they perceive others want, becoming chameleon-like in their desperate attempt to be acceptable. We might overcompensate by becoming indispensable, working overtime to prove our value through endless giving and service. Alternatively, some withdraw completely, isolating themselves to avoid the painful confirmation that they truly are unwanted.

The Unwanted Wound creates intricate relationship patterns where we either cling desperately to anyone who shows us attention, accepting treatment that confirms our unworthiness, or we pre-emptively distance ourselves from others to avoid the inevitable moment when they discover we are too much and leave. We might find ourselves in relationships where we do all the initiating, all the giving, all the emotional labour, while constantly fearing that we are overwhelming or burdening the other person.

The addiction pattern here involves the temporary relief of being needed or useful, followed by the crushing realisation that our value depends entirely on what we provide rather than who we are. This creates a relentless cycle where we must constantly prove our worth through performance, sacrifice and self-denial, all while the Core Wound of being fundamentally unwanted remains untouched.

The Unwanted Wound also manifests in our relationship with success and visibility. We might sabotage opportunities that would put us in the spotlight, believing deep down that increased visibility will only lead to increased rejection. Or we might achieve great things while feeling like frauds, convinced that if people really knew us, they would see that we are undeserving.

This wound creates a particular sensitivity to being excluded, overlooked, or forgotten. A cancelled invitation, an unreturned message, or being left out of plans can trigger devastating emotional responses that seem disproportionate to the situation but are actually touching the core perception that we are fundamentally unwelcome in this world.

At this point you may have a clear concept of how the wounds show up in your life and feel a discomfort in having realised them more fully. Sit tight as we are only just beginning the unravelling of the wounded design. There is a path through and there is a life of peace, connection and Wholeness awaiting you.

The Three Pillars of Reality Creation and Their Long-Term Consequences

Through the lens of addiction, we can better understand how our wounding shapes our reality creation. These three spaces define how our addictions become the cornerstone of our unconscious choices, creating consequences that extend far beyond momentary discomfort, establishing long-term challenges that shape our entire lives.

1. Relationship Dynamics: The Wound Bond

This internal disconnection also creates ramifications for our relationships. We form unconscious agreements with others to maintain familiar patterns of pain. We become emotionally addicted to predictable cycles of hurt because the known suffering feels safer than the unknown possibility of genuine connection. Our nervous system is attuned to ancient survival mechanisms and develops hypervigilance around specific emotional threats, constantly scanning for the repetition of our original wounding.

In these dynamics, we unconsciously seek out people who will confirm our deepest fears about ourselves, then judge them for the very characteristics we have adopted to survive. We project fixed identities onto them, casting them as the perpetrator to our victim, which gives us permission to show up in our most wounded, reactive ways. The cruel irony is that we often take on the exact behaviours that hurt us most, becoming the very thing we claim to despise, while remaining blind to our own role in perpetuating the cycle.

These 'wound bonds' operate like emotional addictions across what could be called 'fractal patterns', the same core pain playing out with different characters throughout our lives. From parents to partners to children, the essence remains identical: we feel an immense sense of separation both from others and from ourselves. We develop predictable thought forms, behaviours and emotions connected to our survival patterns, creating what feels like being on a relationship treadmill where different attempts to change yield the same painful results.

The addiction mechanism runs deeper than we realise. We know exactly how to trigger the other person to get our familiar dose of rejection, abandonment or betrayal. We become hypervigilant to threats that confirm our unworthiness, scanning for evidence that we are not loved, not heard, seen, understood or even safe while simultaneously creating the very separation we fear. We fix the other person's identity through our judgments, which allows us to fix our own identity. We create a sophisticated dance of mutual unconsciousness that feels both inevitable and impossible to escape.

Within these patterns, we develop two primary survival strategies: attack and withdrawal. We learn to move forward aggressively through argument, control, defensiveness, or anger, while also mastering the art of retreat through distance, isolation and emotional unavailability. These become our unconscious methods of managing the perceived threat, yet they ensure we remain trapped in the very separation we are trying to heal.

The most devastating aspect of wound bonds is how they operate in a holographic reality where we literally create what we expect to experience. The more we witness separation and lack of safety, the more we perpetuate it. We project our programs of separation onto relationships, then develop survival-based hypervigilance within those very relationships. We become so invested in seeing others as fixed in their problematic identities that we miss how we are using their perceived flaws to justify our own unconscious, addictive patterns of being.

This creates a closed loop where both parties unconsciously collude to maintain known pain rather than risk the vulnerability required for authentic connection. We are all acting as both victim and perpetrator, though we rarely see our own perpetrator aspects because acknowledging them would threaten our fixed identity as the wounded one. The shame and guilt that arise when we glimpse our own unconscious behaviours only serve to deepen our self-betrayal, creating another layer of internal separation that mirrors the external dysfunction.

The long-term consequence of unconscious relationships extends far beyond individual pain. These patterns become the template through which we approach all connections, creating a reality where genuine intimacy becomes impossible. We live in constant fear of being truly seen, while simultaneously desperate for the very connection we are systematically destroying. The wound bond becomes our primary model for love, teaching us that suffering and connection are synonymous, that drama equals depth and that peace must be inherently boring or dangerous.

2. Perceptual Filters: From Bias to Purpose Distortion

Our wounds filter our perception, causing us to notice evidence that confirms our core perceptions while filtering out contradictory information. This creates a selective attention system that operates below conscious awareness, ensuring our reality consistently matches our wounded expectations.

The Unloved Wound notices every moment of disconnection while missing genuine offers of love. When someone shows affection, it might be dismissed as pity, obligation or temporary kindness that will inevitably disappear. Every slight delay in response, every moment of distraction, every normal human boundary becomes evidence of rejection and abandonment. Meanwhile, genuine gestures of care, consistent presence and unconditional acceptance remain invisible or are reinterpreted through the lens of separation.

The Unworthy Wound catalogues every mistake while dismissing accomplishments. Successes are attributed to luck, timing or other people's contributions, while failures are seen as evidence of fundamental inadequacy. This wound creates a mental filing system that carefully preserves every criticism, every moment of falling short, every comparison that highlights insufficiency, while actively discarding praise, recognition and evidence of competence and value.

The Unknown Wound notices every unexpected change and fears the worst while missing patterns of consistency and safety. This wound scans for threats, interpreting neutral events as potential dangers and assuming the worst possible outcomes in ambiguous situations. It becomes hyper-attuned to signs of instability while remaining blind to the reliable patterns, the consistent support systems and the evidence that life is generally predictable and safe.

Perhaps most devastating is how this perceptual bias hijacks our authentic life purpose. The gifts we came to share become corrupted by wound patterns, twisted into expressions of limitation rather than expansion. Our natural talents become vehicles for wound addiction rather than authentic self-expression.

Natural healers become codependent through Unloved Wound patterns, using their gifts to create the illusion of being needed rather than offering genuine service. They might attract clients who become dependent on them, or find themselves seeking affirmation than providing genuine transformation.

Brilliant creatives become blocked by Unworthy Wound perfectionism, spending years paralysed by the fear that their work will reveal their inadequacy. They might create obsessively and then destroy their work or never share their gifts because nothing feels good enough. The creative impulse becomes distorted into a desperate attempt to prove worth rather than an expression of authentic inspiration.

Visionary leaders become controlling through Unknown Wound fear, using their natural ability to see possibilities to manipulate outcomes and avoid uncertainty. Their vision becomes distorted by the need to control every variable, creating rigid systems and structures that stifle the very innovation and flow they were meant to facilitate.

Decades pass as we live wound-driven versions of our lives rather than authentic expressions of our essence. We might achieve external success while feeling empty inside, or we might sabotage opportunities that would allow our gifts to flourish because they threaten the familiar identity of limitation. The question eventually arises: *whose life have I been living?* The answer, painfully, is that we have been living our wounds' life rather than our own.

3. Generational Legacy: From Personal Pain to Collective Transmission

If left unaddressed, our wound addiction becomes our legacy. We pass these patterns to our children, colleagues and communities, extending the addiction cycle into future generations. The wounds we carry become the wounds we unconsciously inflict, creating intricate systems of intergenerational trauma that can persist for decades or even centuries.

Children absorb our wound patterns through mirror neurons, energetic transmission and learned behaviour. They watch how we handle stress, how we relate to ourselves and others and how we navigate the world. Our unhealed wounds become their template for what relationship, success and safety look like.

A parent with the Unloved Wound might unconsciously create children who feel they must earn love through performance, behaviour, or caretaking. The child learns that love is conditional, unpredictable and must be constantly sought rather than trusted as a given. They might develop their own Unloved Wound or compensate with Unworthy patterns, learning to be perfect to ensure they receive the love that feels uncertain.

A parent with the Unworthy Wound might unconsciously create children who feel they are never enough, constantly pushing for higher achievements while never celebrating what is. The child learns that their value is tied to external accomplishments and that rest, play and simply being are inadequate. They might internalise the same Unworthy patterns or rebel with Unknown Wound chaos, rejecting all systems and structures that feel demanding.

A parent with the Unknown Wound might unconsciously create children who feel the world is unsafe and unpredictable, requiring constant vigilance and control. The child learns that peace is impossible, that relaxation is dangerous and that they must always be prepared for the worst. They might develop the same hypervigilance or compensate with Unloved patterns, seeking relationships that provide the stability and safety they never felt with their parents.

Colleagues and communities also absorb our wound patterns through the culture we create and the standards we normalise. Organisations led by people with unhealed wounds often perpetuate those same patterns throughout their systems. The Unloved Wound creates cultures of emotional deprivation and competition for limited attention. The Unworthy Wound creates cultures of perfectionism and criticism where mistakes are unacceptable. The Unknown Wound creates cultures of hypervigilance and control where innovation and trust are impossible.

The stakes of this work extend beyond personal healing to our collective evolution. Every pattern we transform creates new possibilities for ourselves and for all those we touch. When we transform our wounds, we break the transmission cycle and create space for healthier patterns to emerge in our relationships, families and communities.

When we choose to work with our wounds, we stop the transmission cycle to those we love and future descendants. We become the generation that says: this pattern ends with me. We create new possibilities for how love can be expressed, how worth can be experienced and how safety can be cultivated from within, rather than grasped from external sources.

When we live from our wounds, we experience only a fraction of our potential for joy, love, creativity and contribution. We settle for survival when we were designed for thriving.

This understanding raises the stakes of our healing journey from self-improvement to the essential reclamation of our of Wholeness. This is about reclaiming our authentic self, our true purpose and our capacity to love and be loved without the filters of our wounds. It is about stepping into the life we came here to live rather than the life our wounds have created as a substitute.

The Wound–Program Connection

Understanding how wounds create addictive programs is crucial for liberation. When you understand this then you can start to be aware of the choice you have at every moment. Without this you move through life in default patterns that keep you trapped in a reality you unconsciously reinforce. This sophisticated process begins when a triggering event touches the wound, immediately activating pain and fear that sends the entire system into protection mode. In this vulnerable moment, something profound occurs beneath our awareness, the mind rapidly develops a strategy designed to avoid experiencing this pain again, creating a false safety that confirms the known.

What follows is the formation of behaviours and perceptions that crystallise around this protective strategy. These responses, born from our deepest fear of re-experiencing the wound, gradually become automated and unconscious, operating like invisible software running in the background of our lives. The program appears to work, at least temporarily, providing relief from the immediate discomfort and creating an apparent solution to our suffering.

This temporary success becomes the hook that reinforces the entire program. Each time we unconsciously run this protective sequence, we strengthen the neural pathways and emotional patterns that sustain our addiction to the wound itself. The original pain remains untouched beneath these layers of protection, while the program grows stronger and more automatic with each repetition.

This creates a self-perpetuating cycle that operates largely beneath conscious awareness. It is a sophisticated system where the very strategies we have developed to avoid our wounds become the mechanisms that keep us bound to them. The programs promise momentary freedom from pain while actually ensuring our continued relationship with the underlying wound, creating an addiction to the very patterns that maintain our separation from Wholeness.

The Path to Freedom: Recovery and Integration to Wholeness

The journey of transformation begins with radical honesty about our addiction, but traditional approaches to addiction recovery often fall short when applied to our wound patterns. Conventional methods like behavioural modification, willpower or substituting 'positive' patterns for negative ones may provide temporary relief but rarely address the deeper mechanisms at play.

Jean, who committed to unravel her Unloved Wound patterns, shares, "I tried everything, self-help books, affirmations, therapy, even addiction recovery programs. They all helped temporarily, but the patterns always returned. The turning point came when

I realised my symptoms were not problems to fix but doorways to something deeper." What makes wound addiction uniquely challenging is that it is woven into the very fabric of our identity and nervous system. It is a fundamental orientation to reality itself. This is why the path to genuine freedom requires something more radical than conventional approaches.

In the chapters ahead, we will explore the four critical gateways to dismantling wound addiction at its source:

- **The Engagement with Fear:** How fear maintains the addiction cycle and how working directly with fear creates new possibilities for liberation (Chapter 7).
- **The Relationship to Pain:** How our avoidance of pain perpetuates addiction and how a transformed relationship with pain becomes a primary pathway to freedom (Chapter 8).
- **The Collapse of Identity:** How the addicted identity structure must ultimately dissolve for true freedom to emerge and how to navigate this profound transformation safely (Chapters 9 & 10).
- **The Integration of Wholeness:** This is the essence of accepting all aspects of your journey, all aspects of yourself, your past, your present, your future, the Unknown and the Known. In Wholeness you move from a Consciousness of separation and victimisation to connectivity and peace (Chapters 11 & 12).

These approaches operate at a fundamentally different level than traditional recovery methods, addressing not just the symptoms of wound addiction but its very foundation in our Consciousness.

The journey involves creating new chemical and energetic pathways within. Through consistent awareness and conscious engagement with our patterns, we begin to establish new neural pathways that are not dependent on our wound addiction and most importantly, are underpinned by a new Consciousness. Jenny found this revolutionary, "Learning that I could recognise my addiction patterns without being controlled by them, that I didn't need to follow the familiar cycle to feel secure, changed everything."

The Paradox of Healing

Here, we encounter a fundamental paradox: true healing comes not from trying to heal, but from fully embracing what is. This paradox requires us to drop the healing agenda entirely. When we stop trying to fix or change ourselves, when we end the internal war with our experience, we create space for natural transformation to occur. The very effort to heal often reinforces the idea that something is broken, perpetuating the wound itself. Instead, as we allow everything its place and trust the intelligence of life's process, a different kind of healing emerges.

This approach invites us to embrace Wholeness by recognising that nothing is actually broken in the first place. What we have labelled as wounds are in fact doorways to depth, invitations to a more authentic engagement with life. Pain serves a sacred function in this framework, not as something to transcend or eliminate, but as a messenger guiding us towards greater integration. As we trust the process of life itself, surrendering our need to control the healing journey, we discover that the very things we have been trying to heal reveal themselves as pathways to the Wholeness that was always present beneath our addiction to separation.

The Ongoing Journey

In all honesty, there is no perfect state where wounds never arise or triggers never activate. Instead, it is about developing a new relationship with our human experience. We learn to recognise when we have slipped into separation Consciousness and know how to return to Wholeness.

The patterns we have discussed, the seeking of external completion, the addiction to familiar pain, the investment in systems that do not serve us, may still arise. But now we can see them for what they are: invitations to remember our truth, to choose again, to create differently.

This journey requires us to face the inner truth that we are not just healing behaviours or patterns, we are dissolving an identity structure that has organised our entire reality. The wound addiction has created a self-concept so pervasive, that challenging it feels like challenging our very existence. This explains why transformation can feel so threatening and why the death-like withdrawal is the experience of an identity structure beginning to dissolve.

Remember, you stand at the threshold of a new way of being. The understanding you now hold can transform every aspect of your life, if you choose to live from it. It is about engaging with a heightened Consciousness towards your whole human experience, bringing more creativity, more curiosity, more connection. As we continue this journey together, we will explore exactly how to work with the nervous system, pain, fear and identity to create the space where genuine transformation becomes inevitable.

Looking Ahead: The Nervous System's Role

While this chapter has explored the nature of wound addiction and its patterns, we have only touched the surface of understanding why these patterns are so difficult to break. To go deeper, we must examine the sophisticated biological mechanism that maintains these addictions: our nervous system.

Our nervous system is actively preserving our patterns. The same system designed to keep us alive has been hijacked by our Core Wounds, turning our biology into the perfect delivery system for our addiction. Every trigger, every emotional response, every behavioural pattern is supported by intricate neurological processes that have been refined through years of repetition.

However, before we dive deeper I invite you to take a pause, and integrate and reflect on the concepts and awareness that are coming into Consciousness. This book covers a lot of ground, so I invite you to take a moment and consolidate what we have covered before moving forward. There is no rush in your relationship with Consciousness, everything has its own Divine timing.

Part II

CHAPTER FIVE
Unifying Your Fragmented Self

As I began to unfold my relationship to my wound addictions, I became very conscious of exactly how they came into being. I would be feeling connected, centred and in my Wholeness and suddenly I would step on a land mine in my life and in a split second everything would implode. The fabric of my connected reality would rupture, my addiction would kick in and drag me straight into my Wound Reality.

It was then that I discovered the mechanism of the 'trigger'. A trigger is what pulls you into unconscious thoughts, behaviours and emotions that feel inescapable. These design reality in such a powerful way that it makes your life a battlefield littered with invisible mines waiting to go off.

So I slowed right down and began to examine this construct. I realised there is a moment that exists between stimulus and response, a microsecond of pure potential. Instead of allowing this space to be hijacked by past wounds, I realised that this was a portal of multidimensional access and creation that had been largely overlooked.

This insight transformed my experience rapidly. Rather than accepting the pattern of being triggered, I dove deep to the root of these moments to reshape my inner landscape and engage differently with the world around me. This felt like awakening from a dream. I was shifting from being a passive observer to an active participant in my own life.

This chapter will take you through recognising how your triggers contain activation patterns, how these can be converted into conscious 'choice points', and the vital work of reclaiming the trapped fragmented aspects of yourself.

Understanding the Trigger Point and Your Wound Reality

A 'trigger point' is an access point in reality where you become hooked into an unconscious mode of operating. It is where something in your external environment; whether it is seeing people act in certain ways, receiving a particular message or witnessing specific events, activates a familiar pattern stored in your nervous system. This external stimulus ignites an existing program within you, launching you into an automatic, unconscious response.

The moment you enter this triggered state, your nervous system takes over from a survival perspective. You become caught in the illusion that you exist solely in the physical world and must maintain certain external conditions to remain safe, so these triggers ultimately send you into hyperdrive. You have shifted into 'wound mode'. In this survival Consciousness you forget the truth; that you are an infinite, eternal, Divine being having a human experience and that nothing external can truly impact your essential nature.

Instead, we desperately attempt to manage the trigger from this unconscious space, but our management strategies simply repeat the same thoughts, feelings and behaviours that are rooted in our original wounding. This creates a feedback loop with the external reality, trapping us in repetitive cycles of reaction and re-creation of the same painful dynamics.

We are often advised to simply stop mid trigger and regulate. I do not find this successful as the loop that has been initiated must complete itself. There is no purely conscious way to end the loop through force or mental effort, you would be fighting against the natural force of duality itself. A little bit like trying to eject from the roller coaster ride. So instead of trying to re-orientate yourself mid trigger, let the loop complete while witnessing it consciously. The path forward requires massive levels of Consciousness around when the trigger is next activated. Staying completely present with the experience as it begins, eventually allows you to transform the trigger point into a choice point.

The Eternal Nature of Triggers

It is crucial to understand that triggers are not isolated incidents happening only in this moment. A trigger may feel relevant to your current circumstances, with the illusion that if you just get past this particular challenge, it will be over. However, this perception is limited to three-dimensional thinking.

The truth is that this moment is connected to all moments. It is multidimensional. Every trigger has its foundation in the fracture of an original wound and the initial energetic pain is being repeated across time. When we only try to manage the trigger from our perceived 'now', we severely limit our capacity for healing and transformation.

Instead, we need to merge through space and time with the earliest memory of the trigger. For some, this will trace back to childhood experiences; for others, it may reach into other lifetimes or generational patterns. The trigger maintains an energetic hook through space and time to its beginning point, reverberating consistently outward from that original fracture.

Recognising When You Are in a Trigger Point

Learning to recognise when you are in a trigger point is essential for transformation.

+ Your body often signals this state through physical tension, shallow breathing, racing heart, feeling hot or cold, digestive upset or sudden fatigue as your nervous system activates its survival responses.

+ Mentally, you might notice obsessive thinking, catastrophising, black-and-white thinking, inability to see options, feeling like you 'know' what will happen or mental loops that feel impossible to break.

- ✦ Emotionally, triggers create intensity that feels disproportionate to the situation, sudden rage or despair, feeling like a child, overwhelming fear or emotional numbness and disconnection.

- ✦ Behaviourally, you might find yourself engaging in reactive communication, withdrawing and isolating, seeking validation or control, engaging in addictive behaviours or doing things that later feel 'not like you'.

The key insight is that triggers often make you feel and act like the age you were when the original wound occurred, regardless of your actual age now. This is why a successful adult might suddenly feel like a powerless child when criticised or why someone confident in most areas might become desperately insecure in romantic relationships.

Growing Parts of Self Up: Understanding Cellular Memory

So where do these triggers originate? Often parts of ourselves become crystallised in pain, like amber preserving ancient fragments, keeping them suspended in time rather than allowing them to transform and integrate. The unfelt pain causes these aspects of ourselves to become stunted and developmentally frozen, even as other parts of us continue to grow. This pain imprint penetrates deep into our cellular foundation.

Every cell in your body carries memory far stronger than mental memory, cellular memory records and stores experiences across space and time. This cellular memory unconsciously informs your entire system, influencing your behaviours, perceptions, interactions and preferences. You can often trace these patterns back to specific periods in your life and explore where the core pain was initiated and at what developmental level it sits in your cellular memory.

Developmental Stages of the Three Core Wounds

The three Core Wounds - Unloved, Unworthy, Unknown (unseen/unheard, unsafe and unknowing versions), form at different developmental stages, creating the foundation for all future triggers and patterns. Understanding how these wounds develop helps us recognise their expressions in our adult lives and begin the work of healing them at their source.

I invite you to go on a life review with these words, feeling into any sensations or memories that arise when you read about these unique stages. When we increase Consciousness, we begin to connect the dots between recurring experience and we gain access to the design of the patterns. This creates the foundation for real shifts.

Infancy and Early Childhood

Many of our basic survival programming stems from unmet needs in our earliest years. The fundamental requirements for being fed, sleeping peacefully, feeling held and experiencing safety form the foundation of our nervous system's approach to life. When these needs are not adequately met, the Core Wounds begin to form, creating ongoing unconscious patterns that will be triggered throughout life. While reading this section become attuned to any emotion or reaction that arises in the body, it is a sign for deeper exploration.

The Unloved Wound develops as emotional needs emerge alongside physical ones. When an infant's bids for connection, comfort and attunement are consistently missed or rejected, they begin to form the core perception that they are not worthy of love or that love is conditional and unreliable. A baby who is fed and kept physically safe but receives little warmth, eye contact or emotional responsiveness learns that love is scarce and they must be diligent to receive even small amounts of affection. Children who experience early abandonment, whether through death, divorce or emotional unavailability, develop the deep cellular memory that love is temporary and people will inevitably leave.

The Unworthy Wound often forms alongside the Unloved Wound but has a particular quality of shame and defectiveness. A child who is consistently treated as a burden, whose needs are met with irritation or resentment or who receives the message that their very existence is problematic develops the core perception that they are fundamentally flawed and do not deserve good things. This wound deepens when children are made to feel responsible for their parents' struggles and when their natural developmental needs are treated as selfishness or demanding behaviour.

The Unknown Wound (unseen/unheard version) begins to form as children develop language, self-awareness and when their authentic self is consistently misunderstood or rejected. A child whose emotional expressions are labelled wrong, whose natural personality is criticised or whose interests and preferences are dismissed, learns that who they really are is unacceptable. This creates a split between their true self and the self they present to the world, leading to the core perception that no one can truly know or accept their authentic nature. This misunderstanding deepens as children attempt to communicate their inner world and have their experiences constantly invalidated, minimised or reinterpreted by caregivers. A child who is told they are being too sensitive when they are hurt, that they are making things up when they report problems or that their perspective on events is wrong, develops the core perception that their inner reality is invalid and that others will never truly understand their experience.

The Unknown Wound (unsafe version) forms earliest, often in the womb or first months of life when our basic survival needs are threatened or unpredictably met. A baby whose cries for food or comfort are consistently ignored develops the cellular perception that the world is unreliable and dangerous. Infants who experience feeding difficulties, medical procedures or early separation from their mother encode deep messages that they cannot trust their environment to support their survival. Babies born into chaotic households where parents are fighting, struggling with addiction or dealing with mental illness develop nervous system patterns of hypervigilance alongside the core perception that safety is an illusion.

The Unknown Wound (unknowing version) begins to form in early childhood when a child's natural curiosity and questions about the world are met with dismissal, shame or punishment. A child who asks "why" repeatedly only to be told "because I said so" or "stop asking so many questions", learns that their innate drive to understand is problematic. This wound deepens when children are given inconsistent or confusing information about their reality, when their observations are dismissed as wrong or when family secrets create an atmosphere where seeking truth feels dangerous. Children who grow up in environments where asking questions leads to anger, where seeking understanding is met with ridicule or where uncertainty is treated as a personal failing, develop the core perception that not knowing is dangerous and that they must accumulate external knowledge to feel secure. This creates a compulsive need to research, analyse and seek certainty from outside sources rather than trusting their own inner knowing.

Teenage years

Adolescence brings intense activation of all the Core Wounds as teenagers navigate the complex process of individuation while still being dependent on their families. The teenage years are when these wounds often become most visible and problematic, as the young person's developing identity clashes with family systems and social pressures. Take a moment to attune to what your teenage years really felt like for you and what you felt you had to survive.

The Unloved Wound becomes particularly acute in teenage relationships as young people seek love and acceptance outside their families. Adolescents who experience romantic rejection, social exclusion or conditional love from peers often have their core Unloved Wound deeply reinforced. Those whose emerging sexuality or identity expression is met with disapproval or rejection learn that love is only available if they hide essential parts of themselves. In friendships, experiences of intense loyalty bonds, sudden betrayals and painful bullying from social groups create some of the most formative experiences around lovability.

The Unworthy Wound often intensifies around academic performance, achievements and social status during the teenage years. Adolescents who struggle in school, fail to meet expectations or do not fit into valued social groups often experience crushing shame that reinforces their core perception that they are fundamentally defective and do not deserve success or happiness. This wound is particularly activated by comparison with peers and the pressure to excel in multiple areas.

The Unknown Wound (unseen/unheard version) becomes especially painful during identity formation as teenagers struggle to understand and express who they are. Adolescents whose authentic self-expression is met with criticism, whose interests are dismissed as phases or whose emotional world is consistently invalidated learn that their true nature is problematic and must be hidden. This creates immense internal pressure and confusion about their authentic identity. The misunderstanding often reaches its peak during the teenage years as young people desperately seek to be understood while simultaneously feeling alien to the adult world. Teenagers whose emotional intensity is pathologised, whose perspectives are dismissed as immaturity or whose struggles are minimised, develop the deep perception that no one can truly comprehend their experience. This wound is particularly activated by well-meaning adults who try to fix or advise without first seeking to understand.

The Unknown Wound (unsafe version) in teenagers often manifests around issues of autonomy and control. Adolescents whose attempts at independence are met with harsh punishment, threats or emotional withdrawal learn that expressing their true selves brings danger. Those who experience bullying, social rejection or peer cruelty have their basic unsafe wound reactivated, confirming their perception that the world is hostile and unpredictable. Teenagers who live in unstable home environments or witness violence develop complex survival strategies that keep them in chronic hypervigilance.

The Unknown Wound (unknowing version) becomes particularly intense during adolescence as teenagers face overwhelming uncertainty about their future, identity and place in the world. Adolescents who ask deep questions about meaning, purpose or their life direction but receive dismissive responses like, "you'll figure it out" or "just focus on your grades", learn that their existential uncertainty is a personal failing rather than a natural part of development. This wound deepens when teenagers are pressured to make major life decisions about tertiary education, career paths or their future, without adequate support for navigating uncertainty. Their questions about life's bigger mysteries are met with rigid religious dogma, cynical dismissal or adult anxiety that they must have everything figured out to be acceptable. The wound is particularly activated by well-meaning adults who respond to teenage uncertainty with platitudes or pressure rather than acknowledging the profound courage it takes to face life's unknowns.

Adulthood

Understanding how the three Core Wounds developed helps explain why certain situations trigger us so intensely as adults. The triggers are not really about the present moment, they are about the unhealed Core Wounds from these earlier developmental stages. When you are triggered as an adult, you are often not responding to the current situation; you are responding from the wounded part of yourself that formed during these crucial developmental periods.

The Unloved Wound creates triggers around rejection, abandonment or any situation where love feels conditional or threatened. A partner being distant, friends making plans without you or criticism from someone important can activate the core perception that you are unlovable or that love is temporary and unreliable. This wound often drives people-pleasing, codependency or desperate attempts to secure love and approval. In professional settings, it may manifest as taking work feedback personally, feeling devastated by criticism or overworking to gain approval from colleagues or supervisors.

The Unworthy Wound creates triggers around a sense of a lack of success or recognition. Paradoxically, receiving opportunities for advancement, compliments or abundance can also trigger the core perception that you do not deserve good things. This wound often manifests as self-sabotage, imposter syndrome or the inability to receive or enjoy positive experiences. Adults with this wound may find themselves downplaying achievements, feeling anxious when things go well or unconsciously creating problems when life becomes too good.

The Unknown Wound (unseen/unheard version) creates triggers around being seen, understood or expressing your authentic self. Situations where you need to share your true thoughts or feelings, where your individuality is highlighted or where intimacy requires vulnerability can activate the core perception that your authentic self is unacceptable. Conflicts where your viewpoint is dismissed, situations where you feel unseen or unheard, or interactions where others make assumptions about your experience can activate the core perception that no one can truly understand you. This wound often manifests as isolation, anger or giving up on being known.

The Unknown Wound (unsafe version) creates triggers around anything that threatens your sense of security or control. Financial stress, relationship conflicts, health concerns or unpredictable situations can activate the deep cellular memory that the world is dangerous and you cannot trust your environment to support you. This often manifests as anxiety, control issues or the need to create rigid structures to feel secure. Adults with this wound may become hypervigilant in new environments, struggle with change even when it is positive or develop elaborate safety protocols that limit their life experiences.

The Unknown Wound (unknowing version) creates triggers around uncertainty, decision-making or facing situations without clear answers. Major life transitions, career changes or any circumstance where you do not have complete information can activate the core perception that not knowing is dangerous and must be avoided at all costs. This may manifest as analysis paralysis, compulsive research or seeking excessive advice from others before making decisions. Adults with this wound often struggle with life's natural uncertainties, becoming overwhelmed when they cannot predict outcomes or control variables.

It is important to recognise that these wound patterns can vary significantly based on cultural background, socioeconomic factors, family structure and individual resilience. Some adults may have one dominant wound while others experience multiple wounds intensely. The manifestation of these wounds can also shift throughout different life stages, relationships and circumstances, creating a complex and ever-evolving landscape of triggers and responses.

The Cellular Search for Unity

With each developmental stage, these Core Wounds become imprinted in our cellular memory, creating patterns of separation from our Wholeness. The survival strategies we develop around each wound keep the pain at the centre of our cellular experience while seeking external resolution to internal fractures.

Our cells are inherently seeking unity and unification; they want Wholeness with the entire system. However, until we develop Consciousness and awareness of how these wounds impact us and we can viscerally release the pain they carry, they continue to unconsciously inform patterns of separation and reactive behaviour.

The infant, child and teenage aspects of ourselves that carry these wounds all need to be integrated back into our Wholeness, with safety created around them to support this integration. Each Core Wound needs to be honoured and used as a portal of reunification back to the unity of self, moving beyond the patterns of separation they have created.

The Holographic Nature of Self-Treatment

Understanding the 'holographic principle' is crucial: how you treat the wounded parts of yourself becomes the template for how you experience being treated by others and how you treat others. This operates at the level of Consciousness itself, where your internal reality creates the template for all external experiences. The holographic principle suggests that every part contains the whole, meaning that your relationship with your wounded parts is simultaneously your relationship with your greater self. When you are harsh, critical and rejecting towards your own pain, this creates a vibrational frequency that unconsciously attracts that same treatment from others. You become a magnet for criticism, rejection and harshness because that is the frequency you are broadcasting through your self-treatment. More subtly, you will find yourself being harsh towards others' vulnerability, often without conscious awareness, because that is the program running in your system.

This manifests in countless ways throughout daily life. If you shame yourself for feeling unloved, you will unconsciously attract partners who shame your need for connection. If you judge your own unworthiness, you will find yourself in relationships and situations where your value is questioned or dismissed. If you criticise yourself for not knowing something, you will attract teachers, colleagues or friends who make you feel stupid or inadequate for your questions or uncertainty.

The holographic nature extends beyond interpersonal relationships into every area of life. Your relationship with your wounded parts becomes the default pattern for how you relate to your body, your work, your finances and even your relationship with the Divine. If you treat your wounds as enemies to be conquered, you will find yourself in constant battle with life circumstances. If you abandon yourself when you are struggling, you will create situations where others abandon you during difficult times.

Conversely, when you develop genuine compassion, understanding and acceptance for your wounded parts, you naturally begin to experience more compassion from others and extend more understanding to those around you. This shift happens automatically, through the natural law of resonance. As you hold your own pain with tenderness, you become capable of recognising and holding others' pain with the same quality of presence.

The transformation is often remarkable in its simplicity. When you stop judging your Unloved Wound for its desperate seeking of connection, you stop attracting avoidant partners and begin to notice the genuine love that was always available. When you cease criticising your Unworthy Wound for its need for validation, you stop attracting critical environments and begin to see your inherent value reflected in others' responses to you. When you embrace your Unknown Wound's uncertainty with curiosity rather than fear, you stop attracting chaotic situations and begin to trust the intelligence of the Unknown.

This holographic principle explains why external change without internal transformation rarely creates lasting shifts. You might leave a partner only to attract another one or change jobs to escape a harsh boss only to find similar dynamics in the new workplace. The external pattern persists because the internal template remains unchanged.

The template of radical self-acceptance becomes your new program of reality, creating a positive feedback loop in all your relationships. As you develop a compassionate inner voice, you begin to hear more compassionate voices in your external world. As you learn to comfort yourself in moments of pain, you attract and notice others who offer genuine comfort. As you become curious about your own patterns rather than judgmental, you attract relationships where your growth is supported and celebrated.

This is why inner work is never just personal, it ripples out to transform every relationship and interaction in your life. Each moment of self-compassion you cultivate becomes a gift to every person you encounter, as you can only give to others what you have learned to give to yourself. The wounded parts of yourself become gateways to your own healing and to contributing to the healing of the collective human experience.

The holographic nature also reveals why healing happens in layers and spirals rather than linear progression. As you develop greater compassion for one aspect of your wounding, it naturally expands to encompass other wounded parts, creating ripple effects throughout your entire system. A breakthrough in accepting your Unloved Wound might simultaneously shift your relationship with your Unworthy Wound, as the template of self-acceptance penetrates every aspect of your inner landscape. Allow this understanding to create a deeper commitment to the power of your inner work.

The Journey of Reclamation: Taking the Train Back Through Time

Finding and integrating these uncared-for parts is fundamentally about reunifying yourself into Wholeness. Imagine taking a train back along your personal timeline, stopping to pick up all the separated, lost and abandoned versions of yourself that have been left behind in moments of pain and trauma. This is a multidimensional movement which means you access past versions as if they are here now, because in truth they are alive in your body as much now as in the temporal past.

This journey of reconciliation requires you to merge through space and time with the earliest memory of each trigger, which takes you back to the original fracture. The work involves reconfiguring your understanding of that experience from a soul perspective, this means seeing the truth of Wholeness beyond the illusion of the wound and rewriting the sense of being wronged or a victim.

The essential elements of this inner work involves deeply seeing, hearing and feeling the pain that you experienced with complete compassion for yourself. This means moving beyond the story of what happened to the pure felt experience of that younger part of you. You learn to love yourself deeply in all moments of evolution, recognising that every response you had was an attempt to survive and cope with circumstances beyond your control. You begin advocating for yourself when you did not have the support in the moment to protect or speak up for yourself. This might involve telling that younger part what they needed to hear or imagining yourself intervening in the situation. You practice seeing through illusion to honestly be with what is, moving past the stories and interpretations to the core emotional and energetic experience.

Finally, you learn to meet your own unmet needs, if you were Unloved, you love yourself; if you felt Unworthy, you learn to value yourself; if you felt Unknown, you take time to truly know yourself; if you felt unsafe, you create safety within yourself; if you felt misunderstood, you learn to understand and validate your own experience.

What Integration Actually Looks and Feels Like

Many people wonder what successful integration feels like, so they know what they are moving towards. Integration creates an internal connection where all parts are known, accepted and valued; it does not eliminate the wounded parts or pretend the pain never happened.

Signs of successful integration include a growing sense of internal peace where the constant inner critic or anxious voice quiets down and you experience more moments of genuine inner calm and self-acceptance. You develop better emotional regulation where triggers still happen, but they are less frequent and less intense. When they do occur, you recover more quickly and do not get stuck in loops. Your relationships become more authentic because you are more genuine and you are not constantly managing or hiding parts of yourself. You find you start to attract people who can appreciate your Wholeness. Energy that was tied up in managing wounds becomes available for creativity, passion projects and authentic self-expression.

With less internal noise from wounded parts fighting for attention, you can more easily access your inner wisdom and guidance. As you develop genuine compassion for your own wounds, you naturally extend more understanding to others' struggles and reactions. You see them as simply acting out their unprocessed wounded parts. Perhaps most importantly, you find yourself responding to life from conscious choice rather than unconscious compulsion, where the wounded parts inform you but do not control you. You can see them, feel them and understand them but they are no longer dominating your experience. Integration does not mean you never feel pain or never get triggered, it means you have a healthy, conscious relationship with all parts of yourself, including the wounded ones.

A Practice for Integration: Meeting The Isolated Parts of Self

To begin connecting with and integrating your wounded parts, create a safe space where you will not be interrupted. You might like to journal through the stages or simply visualise. There is also a meditation in the resources you can find at the front of the book to guide you through this process.

1. Identify a recent trigger and ask which of the three Core Wounds got activated: did you feel Unloved, Unworthy, Unknown (unseen/unheard, unsafe or unknowing versions)?
2. Notice what age this part feels like and what they are experiencing. Visualise or simply sense this part of yourself, seeing them clearly, their age, appearance and emotional state.

3. Then move your full adult Consciousness back through space and time to be with this part of self in full presence.
4. Visualise entering the space and introducing yourself as the future version of yourself that has come back to be with your younger version.
5. Listen to this version of yourself without trying to change or fix anything, simply attune to what is painful for them.
6. Ask what they need from you right now. It might be acknowledgement, protection, love or simply to be seen and heard. Attune to them and give them what they are asking for.
7. Let this part know they do not have to carry their pain alone anymore and invite them to remain connected to your conscious adult self, while also honouring their experience and wisdom.

Keep showing up and reconfiguring the experience for your younger self, building a pattern beyond the separation that you have accepted as the default of your life. Making yourself feel deeply, internally safe. Practice this regularly with different versions that arise through your triggers, gradually building a conscious, loving relationship with all aspects of your younger self and addressing each of the three Core Wounds as they surface.

Working with Resistance to Integration

As you begin this work of integration, you will likely encounter significant resistance. This resistance is natural and protective. Common forms of resistance include fear of the pain, where you might think that if you really feel this, it will destroy you. I want to remind you that the pain you are afraid of feeling is pain you are already carrying and conscious feeling leads to healing and release. We will cover the pain more comprehensively in Chapter 8.

You might find yourself minimising the impact with thoughts like, *it wasn't that bad* or *others had it worse*, but this bypassing keeps you from accessing and transforming the wound. Self-judgment often arises with thoughts like, *I should be over this by now* or *this is weak*, but these judgments are often internalised voices from others and keep you from the compassion needed for healing.

Fear of change can manifest as, *if I heal this, I won't be me anymore*. This reflects the fear that healing will fundamentally change your identity and you will no longer be able to tolerate present circumstances and need to change. Finally, loyalty to family or caretakers can make healing feel like betrayal of those who wounded you, especially if they were doing their best within their own limitations. However, what I want to offer is that your healing is connected to the healing of everyone around you. As you change, timelines change and you meet other versions of those around you.

Overall, when you encounter resistance, meet it with curiosity and compassion rather than force. The resistance itself is a part that needs understanding and integration and pushing against it often strengthens it.

The Path Forward: Trigger to Choice Point

The journey from trigger point to choice point, supported by the ongoing work of healing the Core Wounds and integrating fragmented parts of self, is perhaps the most important work you can do. It is the difference between unconsciously repeating old patterns rooted in feeling Unloved, Unworthy, Unknown and consciously creating new realities from a place of Wholeness.

Remember, you are the greatest balm for your experience of energetic separation. You are the one with the medicine you seek. You are also the one who can stop the fracturing outward into wound space and instead develop the deep inner bond of Wholeness. The multiple versions of yourself that carry these Core Wounds will reveal themselves through the triggers in your daily experience. Each trigger is simply an indication of energetic misalignment and an invitation to reclaim another abandoned part of yourself.

The parts of you that feel Unloved, Unworthy, Unknown are aspects of your Wholeness to be reclaimed. They carry medicine, wisdom and gifts that can only be accessed through integration rather than rejection. Through this conscious work of recognition, integration and choice, you transform from a collection of wounded, reactive parts into a unified, whole being capable of responding to life from love rather than fear, from truth rather than illusion, from choice rather than compulsion.

The Choice Point: Moving from Closed to Open Reality

The relationship to my triggers opened me to an incredible new awareness about the energetic commitment I had to my predictable reality. When I began to understand that the most powerful currency I have is the current of my energy, I could see that mastering my energetic relationship to reality was critical. I realised I must withdraw the energetic resources that would typically fuel my management strategies, hypervigilance or reactive responses and bring all those resources back into my body through 'energetic reclamation'. (I will cover this comprehensively in Chapter 11).

Your triggers capture and control your energy. They hold your energy hostage to what is outside your sphere of control. The choice point represents the moment when you reclaim your energy from the predictable trigger and you move from a closed reality to an open reality. It is when you develop enough Consciousness to formulate an alternative response to the triggering experience, because your energetic resources are connected to your inner being. The profound irony of reaching a choice point is that instead of doing more, you need to do nothing.

Recognising When You Have Reached a Choice Point

When you successfully shift into a choice point, you will notice distinct changes in your internal experience. You feel an inner calm, even if the external situation has not changed and you feel more peaceful and centred within yourself. Your perspective expands and you can see options and possibilities that were not visible when you were triggered. Instead of feeling certain about negative outcomes or other people's motives, you become genuinely curious about what will unfold. You are able to hold compassion for yourself and others involved, seeing everyone as doing their best from their level of Consciousness.

It is up to you in all cases, if you respond to any of these triggers as if the feared outcome has already occurred, you are unconsciously creating that timeline. If you sit back and witness the unfolding, you will see what is actually true. When you operate from choice point rather than trigger point, you will discover that reality, when you are not in fear or survival mode, is incredibly loving. It does not want you to have anything less than a benevolent experience, though it simultaneously wants to evolve you and show you where you need to know more about yourself.

The Choice Point Process

The moment you recognise you are triggered, you have access to a choice point, a space between the stimulus and your response where conscious transformation becomes possible. This process involves three essential steps:

1. Recognise the Wound Pattern: Instead of being swept away by the emotional intensity, you pause to identify which Core Wound has been activated.
+ Are you in the Unloved Wound's fear of abandonment?
+ The Unworthy Wound's spiral of inadequacy?
+ Or the Unknown Wound's anxiety about understanding, safety or certainty?

2. Reclaim Your Energy: Rather than trying to control the external situation or fix what triggered you, you bring all your energetic resources back to yourself. You ground in your physical presence and recognise that the intensity you are feeling comes from past experiences rather than present reality.

3. Witness the Original Imprint: From this centred space, you can trace the trigger back through time to earlier experiences where this pattern was formed. You witness these original wounds with compassion; understanding that your nervous system learned these responses as survival mechanisms that once served you, but may no longer be necessary.

This approach transforms triggers from unconscious reactions into conscious opportunities for reclaiming parts of yourself that have been trapped in past trauma. Each trigger becomes a doorway back to Wholeness, allowing you to respond from your authentic self rather than react from your wounded programming.

When you consistently practice meeting triggers at the choice point, something profound shifts. You stop being at the mercy of external circumstances and begin operating from internal sovereignty. The trigger loses its power to hijack your nervous system because you are no longer unconsciously seeking safety through controlling outcomes or people's responses. Instead, you have learned to find safety within yourself, regardless of what is happening around you. This work is truly life changing.

I finally had access to the underdeveloped, separated parts of me that were crying out for support through every trigger. Applying deep presence and Consciousness was the most emotionally soothing thing I could ever do. Learning to really be present and create safety for that separated, disconnected part was like a light was shining through me and all around me.

My whole perception of reality shifted. I realised everything was happening in response to my imprint on reality and that imprint largely came from this unconscious pattern within me. So when I paused and truly explored and questioned and went deeper within myself, I began to see and feel things that showed me, it was me. That I could move my automatic response into a conscious space. From there I could also discern so powerfully what was not ok for me.

Moving out of being triggered gave me greater access to my values and internal alignment. So I politely left relationships, situations and experiences that no longer served me. If I had not gone deeper I simply would have accepted these spaces as the status quo and remained hooked into the matrix of triggers.

From here we will move back into understanding the deeper role your nervous system plays in perpetuating your Wound Reality below your conscious control. This is about becoming intimately acquainted with its limitations. This may just be your missing piece as to why you have tried to heal with other modalities and it simply has not landed on a deeper level. I believe by understanding the neurobiological basis of our addiction, how completely it has colonised our sense of self, we gain access to the territory where true liberation becomes possible.

CHAPTER SIX
Freeing Your Nervous System

Do not get me wrong, as I was reorienting my life after my out of body experience, I tried all the methods, therapy sessions, self-help books and meditation practices, to find peace. But it felt inadequate and not comprehensive enough to find the path through. I found myself repeating the same painful patterns, as if some invisible force kept pulling me back into familiar territory.

So, I began asking myself; *what if the very system designed to protect me had become the architect of my suffering?* I discovered that this invisible force was not a character flaw or lack of willpower...it was my nervous system.

I realised it was operating with the precision of a master strategist and the speed of lightning, maintaining my wound patterns at a level far below conscious awareness. I realised that my nervous system had become so sophisticated at protecting me from perceived threats that it was actually creating the very experiences I was trying to heal. This revelation changed everything and now I will share it with you, as it might be the missing piece in your own transformation.

The Hijacking of Your Biology

Your nervous system has been exquisitely trained by your Core Wounds to maintain states of survival that once served you but now imprison you. Like a security system that never received the all-clear signal, it continues to sound alarms and activate defenses against threats that may no longer exist. Every cell in your body has learned to anticipate danger, seek validation or prepare for abandonment before your mind even registers what is happening.

Your wound patterns are encoded in your neural pathways, written into your muscle memory and stored in your cellular intelligence. They operate through intricate networks of hormones, neurotransmitters and electrical impulses that create your reality from the inside out, generating the very thoughts, emotions and behaviours you are trying so hard to change.

Modern neuroscience confirms what contemplative traditions have long understood: repeated mental and emotional patterns create physical changes in brain structure and nervous system functioning. Every time you react from your Core Wound, you strengthen the neural pathways associated with that pattern, making it more automatic and requiring less conscious activation. Over decades, these pathways become superhighways of reactivity, while alternative responses remain underdeveloped, like rarely travelled back roads that have grown over with weeds.

We are born into a pre-prepared field of energetic information, our cellular programming directly connected to our ancestral lineage and the continuation of patterns of survival. This biological entrenchment explains why most approaches to healing may not get deep enough. Cognitive understanding, positive intentions, even behavioural modifications rarely penetrate to the level where the pattern is maintained: in the very structure and functioning of your nervous system.

The Threat–Response System: Your Wound's Guardian

At the core of this neurobiological prison lies your threat–response system, an ancient survival mechanism exquisitely designed to protect you from danger. This system has learned to deploy two primary strategies to maintain your organism's safety: over-activation and suppression. Over time your nervous system has perfected both responses to navigate what it perceives as a threatening world.

Over-activation floods your system with energy, stress hormones and heightened alertness. It is your body's way of mobilising all resources to meet perceived danger. Suppression does the opposite, shutting down energy, numbing sensation and creating disconnection. It is your system's strategy for surviving overwhelming circumstances by essentially 'going offline'. Neither response is inherently pathological; both represent sophisticated survival strategies that your nervous system has carefully cultivated based on your interpretation of your lived experience.

These trained behavioural and emotional responses operate with remarkable precision. Your system has learned exactly when to activate, when to suppress and how intensely to deploy each strategy. What appears to be dysfunction in reality is your nervous system demonstrating its mastery of survival.

However, your Core Wound hijacks this system, creating a distorted perception of threat that keeps your biology locked in these survival strategies regardless whether there is true physical danger or not. The system continues to deploy over-activation or suppression based on old programming, maintaining patterns that once served you but now limit your capacity for full engagement with life.

When your nervous system is truly at peace, neither over-activated nor suppressed, it becomes part of an integrated system where all aspects of your being work in harmony. In this state, you exist in connected Consciousness, able to respond freshly to each moment rather than react from old survival programming. This integrated state represents evolution beyond the need for constant vigilance, allowing your full potential to emerge naturally.

How Your Nervous System Evaluates Safety

To understand how completely your Core Wound has colonised your biology, we must understand that your nervous system is constantly, unconsciously evaluating the safety and danger in your environment. This is a biological process, happening automatically and continuously without your conscious awareness.

Your Core Wound fundamentally distorts this process, creating false threat assessments that keep your system in perpetual protection mode. This is because it is looking for an Illusion of Safety: a sense that things are safe because they are familiar and the outcome is predictable, even if you do not desire to continue within that pattern.

Jenny, whose primary wound was unworthiness, described this distortion vividly. "My body would respond to the slightest hint of criticism as if I was being physically attacked. I could feel my chest tighten, my breathing become shallow, my vision narrow. My thinking would become rigid and defensive and I'd either withdraw completely or counterattack. All this would happen before I even had a conscious thought about what was happening."

This distorted perception creates a self-reinforcing loop: the wound-distorted lens perceives threat where none exists. The sympathetic nervous system activates in response to the perceived threat. The physiological activation creates sensations that 'confirm' the threat is real. The wound pattern receives neurobiological reinforcement. The pattern becomes more deeply encoded in the nervous system.

This process happens so rapidly and automatically that by the time you become consciously aware of your reaction, your biology has already committed to its protection response. This explains why even when you intellectually understand your patterns, you may still find yourself helplessly caught in them; your biology has already initiated its programmed response before your conscious mind can intervene.

The Neurobiological Signatures of Core Wounds

Each Core Wound creates distinctive patterns of nervous system dysfunction, with characteristic oscillations between activation and shutdown states. Understanding these biological signatures reveals why certain triggers consistently produce the same responses, regardless of your conscious intentions. Below I have listed only a few of the ways in which this can show up in your biology. Before you read on, I invite you to sit with a journal and become aware of the ways your body automatically responds to the perception of a threat to your wound. If it is difficult to identify, take a few days to consciously witness your reactions. This will truly support you to sink deeper into this material. Remember, numbing out and shutting down is also a nervous system response.

The Unloved Wound State

The nervous system of someone with an Unloved Wound oscillates between two distinct states. In over-activation, the system floods with desperate connection-seeking energy. Your heart rate and blood pressure elevate as if preparing for battle, while your breathing becomes shallow and rapid. Muscle tension grips your chest and throat; the very areas associated with expression and connection. Your digestive system disrupts with butterflies and nausea, while your startle response becomes hypersensitive to any hint of disconnection. Sleep becomes elusive as intrusive thoughts about abandonment or loneliness cycle through your mind.

When this activation becomes overwhelming, your system flips into protective disconnection. Here, emotional numbing and flatness replace the desperate seeking. Your body feels physically heavy and fatigued, as if weighed down by invisible stones. You dissociate from bodily sensations, your breathing becomes restricted and your digestive system slows to a crawl. Cognitive flexibility disappears, leaving you trapped in rigid patterns of thinking.

Olivia describes this oscillation. "When my abandonment fears were triggered, my body would go into this frantic, desperate state and I was physically unable to sit still. But if the rejection actually happened or became too overwhelming, I'd flip into this deadened state where I felt nothing at all. My body would feel heavy, my mind foggy. It was like I'd disappeared from myself."

The Unworthy Wound State

The Unworthy Wound creates a relentless oscillation between proving and collapse. In chronic activation mode, your body becomes a machine that cannot rest. Persistent muscle tension grips your jaw, shoulders and back, creating a fortress of effort around your core. Your breathing restricts to the upper chest, never allowing the deep belly breaths that signal safety. Digestive issues emerge from chronically suppressed parasympathetic function, while sleep becomes another arena of performance anxiety with difficulty 'turning off' even when exhausted.

Elevated cortisol courses through your system as you maintain hypervigilance for any signs of failure or judgment. Perhaps most tragically, your capacity for pleasure becomes restricted, as if joy itself might threaten your vigilant stance. But this activation cannot sustain itself indefinitely. When external validation fails to materialise, your system crashes into depletion and collapse. Profound fatigue and energy crashes leave you feeling like a deflated balloon. Emotional flatness replaces the driven energy, while concentration and decision-making become nearly impossible. Your body feels physically heavy and lethargic, your digestive system sluggish and a sense of emptiness and worthlessness pervades everything.

Sophie describes this state. "My body was like a machine that couldn't turn off. Even when I achieved something, there was no real relaxation, just a momentary easing of tension before the next goal consumed me. I lived with constant knots in my shoulders and a jaw so tight my dentist warned me about grinding my teeth away. But when the validation stopped coming, I'd crash completely and be unable to get out of bed, feeling like there was no point to anything. Relaxation felt dangerous, like I would dissolve into nothingness if I ever truly let go."

The Unknown Wound State

The Unknown Wound manifests through two distinct patterns of nervous system dysregulation. Control-seeking hypervigilance keeps your system in a state of persistent scanning for any uncertainty or change. Your breathing patterns become restricted as your body braces for the unexpected. Digestive sensitivity and irritability emerge as your gut, often called the 'second brain' reflects your system's inability to process the unknown. Sleep becomes difficult as your mind cannot quiet its constant vigilance, while your startle response remains heightened even in objectively safe environments.

Muscle tension concentrates particularly around your eyes and forehead, creating the physical signature of someone constantly trying to see what is coming next. Your nervous system maintains sympathetic dominance even in environments that should feel safe, as if relaxation itself poses a threat. When this hypervigilance becomes overwhelming, your system shifts into freeze and disconnect mode. Cognitive fog descends like a thick blanket, making information processing challenging. Your body may experience physical paralysis or extreme slowness, as if moving through invisible density.

Emotional numbing and detachment replace the previous vigilance, while your breathing becomes even more shallow and restricted. Your digestive system may almost shut down entirely and extreme fatigue coupled with an overwhelming desire to withdraw takes over. Most disturbingly, you may find yourself dissociating from present moment awareness, watching your life unfold as if from outside your body.

Lori's experience reflected this survival mode. "My body was like a security system stuck on high alert. My stomach would knot at the slightest unexpected change in plans. My breath would become shallow and tight with any uncertainty. I developed migraines from the constant tension in my forehead and jaw. My system simply couldn't tolerate not knowing and it interpreted uncertainty as a survival threat. But when the unknown became too overwhelming, I'd completely shut down."

The Biological Momentum of Wound Patterns

Once established, your wound patterns develop tremendous biological momentum. Neural pathways that fire together repeatedly become myelinated; a process by which they become covered with a fatty sheath that speeds transmission and makes the pattern more automatic. Your endocrine system learns to produce specific hormonal cascades in response to wound triggers. Even your immune function becomes calibrated to your wound patterns, creating an intricate biological ecosystem organised around separation.

This biological momentum explains why willpower alone does not create lasting change. You are not merely fighting habits or perceptions; you are attempting to override deeply encoded biological programming. It is like trying to stop a freight train with your bare hands. The conscious mind, with its limited resources, simply cannot overpower the massive biological infrastructure that maintains your wound addiction. So we will be exploring in Chapter 10 the exact process to completely upgrade your nervous system.

James describes this overwhelming momentum. "When my unworthiness was triggered, it felt like being caught in a biological avalanche. My body would flood with strong sensations, my thinking would narrow, my perception would distort, all within seconds, before I could even register what was happening. By the time I became aware of the reaction, it was already in full motion and trying to stop it felt like trying to halt a tidal wave."

Now that you too may have more Consciousness around this space, I want to reassure you that it is absolutely achievable to live safely within a centred, peaceful nervous system. This is one that has a healthy response to actual physical danger and can discern when it is operating from a wound illusion and create another level of Consciousness around the response. Yet it is also important to note the deep generational connection to these patterns.

The Generational Dimension: Inherited Nervous System Patterns

The neurobiological basis of wound addiction extends beyond your personal experience to include patterns inherited from previous generations. Recent discoveries in the field of epigenetics reveal that trauma can create changes in gene expression that are passed down to subsequent generations. These inherited patterns create predispositions in your nervous system functioning that shape your susceptibility to particular wound patterns. Beyond this, there is an energetic imprint of survival and separation that is coded in the legacy of being human that we are currently all here to rewrite.

Maya discovered this dimension through her healing journey. "As I worked with my nervous system, I began recognising patterns that weren't just from my personal experience. The way my body responded to certain triggers mirrored my mother's responses exactly, the same tension patterns, the same shutdown sequence. And as I learned more about my grandmother's life, I realised she carried these same patterns. It wasn't just psychological inheritance, my body was literally continuing their biological responses."

This generational dimension does not mean you are doomed to repeat inherited patterns. Rather, it invites a deeper compassion for the biological inheritance you carry and a recognition that your healing reverberates beyond your individual life to touch past and future generations.

The Social Nervous System: Co-Regulation and Dysregulation

Your nervous system does not operate in isolation but is constantly in conversation with the nervous systems around you. This biological interconnection, what neuroscientists call co-regulation, means that your wound patterns are both reinforced and potentially healed through relationships.

When you interact with someone whose nervous system carries similar wound patterns, you experience co-dysregulation, a mutual amplification of protection responses that deepens both people's wound addiction. But interaction with someone whose nervous system maintains regulated states can create co-regulation, a biological invitation to your system to shift towards greater balance and coherence.

This social dimension explains why wound patterns often intensify in certain relationships and ease in others. Your nervous system literally entrains to the nervous systems around you, making your social environment a crucial factor in either maintaining or transforming your wound addiction.

Lisa experienced this dramatically. "When I began spending

time with people who had done deep regulation work, something strange happened. Just being in their presence would help my system settle, even without discussion of my patterns. My breathing would naturally deepen, my muscle tension would ease, my thoughts would become clearer. Their regulated systems offered my dysregulated system a template for a different way of being."
I invite you to consider:

✦ How are the relationships in your life constructed?

✦ Who is your nervous system addicted to continuing a relationship with to give it the predictable pathway of activation?

The fascinating thing is that all humans are multidimensional so the versions of your parents you get will be different to the version their friends see. Or the version of your partner that you get will be different to the version their ex experienced and so on. We can see that we pull a version of a person out of them to participate in the wound bond with us. When we realise this, it is clear to see we have tremendous capacity to shift our relationship with someone via shifting our biological or nervous system response to who we think they are and who we are in relation to them. Moving a relationship into a safe, connected space takes a great level of Consciousness and is most effective when both people are looking to achieve the same goal.

Your Wound's Hierarchy in the Brain

To understand how your wound impacts your mind, we must consider the hierarchical organisation of your brain and how patterns lodge at different levels.

✦ **Brainstem and Cerebellum:** Control basic survival functions, including breathing, heart rate and fundamental threat response. Wound patterns at this level manifest as physiological dysregulation, the automatic responses you cannot seem to control through willpower alone.

- **Limbic System:** Processes emotions, memory, attachment and social bonding. Wound patterns here create emotional reactivity and attachment distortions that feel overwhelming and automatic.
- **Neocortex:** Responsible for conscious thought, planning and meaning-making. Wound patterns at this level appear as distorted perceptions and narratives about yourself and the world.

Most healing approaches target only the neocortical level, working with conscious perceptions and thought patterns. But wound addiction exists at all three levels simultaneously, with the lower, more primitive brain regions often driving the process from beneath conscious awareness. Lasting transformation requires engagement with all three levels, particularly the brainstem and limbic systems, where the most powerful aspects of wound addiction reside.

Jenny's breakthrough came with this understanding. "For years, I tried to think my way out of my patterns, to use logic and insight to overcome my unworthiness. But the breakthrough came when I began working directly with the sensations in my body, with the primal fear responses that lived in my brainstem. The change had to start from the bottom up, not the top down."

A crucial concept for understanding your neurobiological prison is the 'window of tolerance', which is the range within which your nervous system can remain present, flexible, and engaged without resorting to protection strategies. When you are within this window, you can process information clearly, relate authentically, and access your full capacities.

Your Core Wound systematically narrows this window, creating a constricted range within which you can function before triggering protection responses. Even minor stressors can push you outside your window, activating either sympathetic hyperarousal (fight/flight) or parasympathetic hypoarousal (freeze/shutdown). This narrowed window explains why you may react disproportionately to seemingly minor triggers. It is not that you are overreacting, it is that your biological capacity to remain present and regulated has been severely constricted by your wound patterns.

How Your Nervous System Creates an Illusion of Safety

I could viscerally feel how my nervous system had become so sophisticated at creating what it perceived as 'safety' that it was keeping me trapped in a prison of limitation and confinement. I knew I was constantly scanning my environment for threats and trying to keep myself safe in the 'known', even though that known reality was painful, limiting, or soul crushing. I realised my nervous system would rather keep me in familiar misery than risk the unknown possibility of expansion.

I realised this invisible limiting force that overcame my full expression and connectivity with life was an Illusion of Safety. It kept my life experiences within a narrow bandwidth of familiarity. I was not sovereign or free but deeply stuck in a loop of false security.

And maybe you can see this too? The line you draw which you cannot cross because to leave the known confines of the Illusion of Safety would feel like dying. Your mind and nervous system working as prison wardens whispering convincing stories: *don't speak up in that meeting, remember what happened last time? Don't pursue that dream, you know you're not capable. Don't trust that person, people always leave.* These are not conscious thoughts; they are the lie that feeds the unsafety and causes you to limit, avoid, and suffer.

Lillian's experience illustrates this constriction perfectly. "My window was so narrow that even slightly uncomfortable conversations would send me spinning into anxiety or shutdown. There was almost no space where I could just be present with emotional intensity without my system going into emergency mode. It wasn't a psychological choice, my biology simply couldn't tolerate what a regulated system would take in its stride."

This manifests as a constricted life where you unconsciously avoid anything that might stretch you beyond your nervous system's comfort zone. You might find yourself automatically saying no to opportunities, feeling anxious when things go too well, or creating drama when life becomes too peaceful. Your system is literally addicted to the familiar neurochemical cocktail of your wounds, even when those wounds are causing you suffering.

Stretching Your Nervous System: The Path to True Safety

This is where you must become familiar with the process of 'stretching your nervous system'. This means that wherever in life you have felt a sense of fear, contraction or limitation, your nervous system is defining your reality. It is trying to keep you limited to your predictable, repetitive experience of the same constriction and the same outcomes; the Illusion of Safety.

Stretching your nervous system requires a conscious challenge of reality, to redefine your experience with it. You begin to stop listening to your nervous system's resistance. Like a muscle that needs to be stretched to work more effectively, the nervous system needs to be literally challenged. This means doing the exact thing your nervous system fears. It will probably be messy and chaotic as you shift from the familiar and begin to create more sovereignty over the nervous system's automation. It might look like:

+ Having that difficult or truthful conversation when you do not know the outcome.
+ Pursuing an opportunity that excites and terrifies you.
+ Allowing yourself to receive love or success without immediately creating problems.
+ Saying "No" when it is not aligned even when you fear further exclusion or missing out.

The key is to realise the nervous system is running on false threats and we want to break its grip and dominance of your reality by doing the thing that feels the most unsafe and unstable. This seems completely paradoxical, but it is here that true liberation arises. I invite you to take a few moments to consider where you feel any limitation in your life. This limitation will be constructed from an illusion of what is safe and what is not.

+ What would be one thing you could do that would pull you into the Unknown and out of the Illusion of Safety?

Creating True Internal Safety

This space of challenging the Illusion of Safety naturally leads to the creation of a true internal safety. This is when you develop an unshakeable connection to your essential self, the part of you that remains whole, intact and protected within regardless of external circumstances. It is about cultivating a visceral knowing that you can handle whatever arises because you have learned to stay connected to your energy and Consciousness even in the midst of challenge.

As you practice stretching your nervous system, you begin to discover that most of what you feared was simply your system's attempt to keep you safe. The conversations you avoided were not dangerous. The opportunities you declined were not threats. The love you pushed away was not actually going to destroy you. Your nervous system begins to learn that expansion does not equal annihilation, that growth does not mean losing yourself and that true safety comes from trusting your ability to navigate whatever life presents.

This is the profound shift from living in the Illusion of Safety to experiencing true inner safety, where you become home to yourself no matter what storms may rage around you.

This means that the external can go into what looks like a version of chaos or radical change and you know that your safety is solid and ongoing within your inner being. Inner safety is one of the most profoundly transformational feelings and it does not come from regulating your nervous system. It comes from stretching through the illusion to understand that it was simply your wound imprint that was holding reality hostage and safety is available on the other side of that.

Traditional Therapy Limitations

Understanding the neurobiological and energetic basis of wound addiction reveals why most conventional healing approaches can fall short of creating lasting transformation.

✦ Cognitive approaches primarily target conscious thought patterns while the wound operates from unconscious biological levels. You can understand your patterns intellectually, develop sophisticated insights about your childhood and even learn healthier thought patterns, yet find your body still reacting in the same old ways when triggered.

✦ Behavioural approaches attempt to modify actions without addressing the underlying neurobiological drivers. You might successfully change specific behaviours temporarily, but without rewiring the nervous system patterns that drive them, these changes typically revert when stress increases or willpower weakens.

✦ Talk therapy often happens in contexts too safe and removed from triggering situations to activate the neural pathways that fundamentally need rewiring. The insights gained in a therapist's office may not translate to the activated states where your wound patterns are most powerful.

✦ Spiritual approaches may attempt to transcend biological reality rather than transform it, creating temporary experiences of freedom that collapse when biological patterns reassert themselves.

✦ Medication may temporarily alter neurochemistry but does not create new neural pathways, leaving the fundamental patterns unchanged when medication is discontinued.

These approaches are not without value, but they remain incomplete without engaging the neurobiological foundation where wound patterns are primarily maintained. Emma's experience illustrates this limitation. "I spent years in traditional therapy, gaining incredible insights about my patterns. I could explain my childhood wounds with remarkable clarity. But when triggering situations arose, my body would still react in the same old ways. The understanding was in my head, but my nervous system hadn't gotten the memo."

Working with your relationship to reality is where you will

experience true change. Going where you fear to go and releasing yourself. The interface with reality is deeply overlooked and I believe is the bridge between the inner and outer terrain. It is a largely protected space which we are trained to avoid, yet when we work consciously and in an ongoing manner with this space, we open ourselves up for complete transformation.

Looking Ahead: Breaking Through the Prison

Understanding that we must form a new relationship with reality is one thing, but we must also acknowledge there are two powerful forces standing as guardians of your neurobiological prison; fear and pain. These are sophisticated biological mechanisms that maintain the status quo of your wound patterns. They form the final and most formidable barrier to your liberation preventing the necessary disruption for transformation.

In the next chapters, we will confront these guardians directly. First, we will explore how fear operates as the primary defence mechanism of your wound addiction, creating elaborate avoidance strategies that keep your nervous system locked in familiar patterns. You will discover how fear prevents the very experiences that could catalyse transformation and learn methods for working with fear as a gateway to pass through, not a destination to stay in.

Following this, we will dive deep into the territory most healing approaches inadvertently avoid, pain itself. You will discover how pain gates and traps your Consciousness, severely limiting the development of your nervous system. The wound addiction we have explored is, at its core, an elaborate strategy for avoiding the direct experience of pain. Yet paradoxically, it is only through a transformed relationship with pain that true liberation becomes possible.

This journey will challenge conventional wisdom about healing. Where most approaches advocate comfort, safety and gradual change, you will discover how strategic discomfort, calibrated challenge and direct engagement with fear and pain create genuine breakthroughs. When you guide nervous system development through the territories your system has most vigilantly avoided, there is no re-traumatisation or resistance, just liberation.

The path will require courage, precision and a willingness to venture beyond the familiar confines of your current identity structure. But on the other side of this territory lies a freedom your wound-driven biology could never imagine, a liberation that comes from embracing your human experience so completely that it transforms from prison to pathway.

CHAPTER SEVEN
How Fear Maintains Your Limitation

One night about a year after my awakening I woke bolt upright in bed. I knew I had to meditate. I sat on the floor against the wall and closed my eyes. The void rapidly enveloped me and plunged me into pure blackness and then all of my awareness came to my sense of smell. A past life experience was unfolding all around me. A putrid stench of sweat filled my nostrils, I slowly opened my eyes and I was not in my bedroom. I was kneeling on cold stone, my knees aching against the unforgiving marble floor. The acrid smell of unwashed bodies mixed with the cloying scent of olive oil and herbs, creating an assault on my senses that felt both foreign and strangely familiar.

My hands moved without my conscious direction, dipping a rough cloth into the bronze basin before me. The water was warm, tinged with aromatic oils, but it could not mask the reality of what I was doing. I was washing the calloused, dirt-caked feet of a man whose face I dared not look upon. My fingers, smaller and more delicate than I remembered them being, worked methodically between his toes, scraping away the grime of the dusty streets.

The weight of my situation pressed down on me like the oppressive heat of the bath house. Steam rose from multiple basins throughout the marble chamber, where other girls like me knelt in similar positions of servitude. The sound of water trickling and soft murmurs echoed off the high stone walls, punctuated by the occasional harsh command from an overseer.

I was completely powerless. My entire existence had been reduced to this, the endless cycle of bending, washing, serving. The thin linen of my simple dress clung to my skin in the humid air and I could feel my hair, bound tightly to keep it from my face, growing damp with perspiration and steam.

The man above me shifted and instinctively I lowered my gaze again, focussing on the task before me. In this body, in this time, I knew my place. I knew the consequences of overstepping, of appearing too bold or too aware. Survival meant invisibility, meant perfecting the art of disappearing into the role that had been assigned to me by circumstance and birth.

The water in the basin rippled as I wrung out the cloth and in those ripples I caught a glimpse of my own reflection. I was young, resigned, yet somewhere deep in those ancient eyes, a spark of something that refused to be extinguished remained.

Then it flashed through my vision, two pathways spread before me like diverging roads in an ancient prophecy. I could stay. In this choice, I saw my fate unfold with crystalline clarity, I saw an enraged man, drunk on wine and power, striking me with a brass pan during some future confrontation. I watched my own head split open, saw my blood pooling on the marble floor among the feet I had spent countless hours washing. Death would come swiftly and brutally, my life ending as it had been lived; in servitude, in silence, in powerlessness.

Or there was another way. I saw myself rising one night from my thin straw pallet, heart hammering against my ribs as I approached the heavy wooden door that separated the servants' quarters from the world beyond. Despite the terror coursing through every fibre of my being, I would place my trembling hand upon that door and push it open, stepping into the void of the black night where anything could happen, freedom or death, but on my own terms.

The fear was overwhelming. I felt it racing through my real physical body, cross-legged leaning against my bedroom wall. My nervous system could not distinguish between past and present as I experienced the full weight of that ancient threshold moment. This was the edge of compliance, the precipice where obedience meets rebellion, where the soul either surrenders or fights for its own liberation. I knew I had to free my soul.

With a courage that seemed to come from somewhere beyond the terrified servant girl, I stepped into the darkness. The moment my bare feet touched the earth beyond that threshold, everything shifted. I was immediately enveloped in brilliant white light, not the harsh glare of the sun, but something warm and infinite that seemed to emanate from within my very being.

Liberation. The word exploded through my Consciousness as I felt the expansion of every cell in my body, as if I had been compressed for lifetimes and was finally allowed to breathe. Energy coursed through me like electricity, breaking apart every chain that had ever bound me, dissolving every limitation I had ever accepted as permanent.

The vision faded, but the expansion remained. I opened my eyes in my bedroom, gasping, my skin alive with sensation. The next morning, my husband moved out. My timeline had changed. Like fractals of a kaleidoscope shifting, the choice I made so completely through the void somehow rippled forward through time, initiating freedom in this lifetime too. I saw that the energetic limitation of my body was not unique to now, it had been cultivated over years of survival.

If the nervous system is the prison that maintains your wound addiction, then fear is its most vigilant guard. Like any effective guardian, fear does not simply restrict your movement, it convinces you that the walls of your prison are actually protecting you from something far worse outside. In this chapter we will explore how this profound misunderstanding forms the basis of perhaps your most fundamental addiction: the addiction to avoiding pain.

The Matrix of Control

The fear that governs your life is not what you think it is. What appear as fears of rejection, failure, abandonment or uncertainty are in fact protective mechanisms designed with a single purpose: to prevent you from experiencing the pain of your Core Wound.

Think of this as a matrix, an intricate web of interconnected programs running beneath your conscious awareness. This matrix shapes your perception, constrains your choices and determines your reality with such subtle effectiveness that you rarely notice its operation. Like characters in a simulation who cannot conceive of the program controlling their reality, you remain largely unaware of how thoroughly fear has colonised your Consciousness.

When I began to witness the depth of this fear in my life, I saw it everywhere, informing everything. My choices about health, education, relationships, the information I consumed, the precautions I took; everything added up to a limited life. Simultaneously a profound new mission emerged. To liberate every aspect of my body, mind, heart and soul in this lifetime and beyond. Understanding how fear functioned and how to release it became my primary focus. Freedom on all levels was my mission.

The Single Source of All Fear

Here lies perhaps the most undeniable truth about human experience: **the only thing we truly fear is our own pain.**

Everything else, every anxiety, every avoidance, every protection strategy is simply an overlay designed to prevent us from encountering this pain.

Neuroscience confirms this understanding more deeply: fear and pain share the same neural pathways. When we experience fear, it activates the same regions in our brain that process physical and emotional pain. Your brain's threat-detection system does not differentiate between physical danger and emotional wounding, it treats both as threats to survival. Consider what you believe you fear most:

- Is it failure? Is there pain around shame or unworthiness?
- Is it rejection? Behind that lies the pain of abandonment.
- Is it public speaking? Underneath is the pain of humiliation.
- Is it commitment? Within that lives the pain of loss.
- Is it death? Here the pain of meaninglessness, non-existence or the separation from loved ones.

Each of these 'fears' is really a prediction about pain. Your nervous system is not really afraid of the situation itself, it is protecting you from the specific pain it believes that situation will trigger. You can verify this truth through direct observation. Notice your own avoidance patterns:

✦ What situations do you avoid?
✦ What excuses do you make?
✦ What patterns do you maintain?
✦ What possibilities do you reject?

Track these avoidances back to their source:

✦ What pain are you protecting against?
✦ When did you first feel this pain?
✦ How has this pain shaped your choices?

Feel the connection between your fear responses and the underlying pain, notice where you feel the fear in your body and where you feel the remembered pain. Observe how they mirror each other, how they are really one energy.

Candace's story illustrates this matrix in action. She consistently self-sabotaged opportunities for advancement believing she simply lacked confidence. But as we explored her patterns, we discovered that her fear was not really about career failure. Her nervous system had created an elaborate protection system against a specific pain: the devastating feeling of not being good enough. It was connected to an experience at age seven when her academic performance led to her father's bitter disappointment. Her brain had linked achievement with the possibility of the specific emotional pain of her father's conditional love and judgement. The fear of this pain became the invisible force directing her entire career.

"I realised I wasn't afraid of failing," Candace told me. "I was afraid of feeling something I'd spent my entire life avoiding, that crushing sense that I'm only worthy when I perform perfectly. My fear was guarding that pain like a fortress and my whole life had been organised around never having to feel it again."

The State of Fear Hypnosis

When we are in a state of fear, we surrender our authority to the nervous system, believing it tells us the truth about our experience. As we learned in the previous chapter, your nervous system does not hold any intelligence. The nervous system is outdated technology. Its evolutionary capacity has fallen far below the consciousness and lifestyle experiences we now have. You can verify this yourself when you notice that your most compelling thoughts, behaviours and emotions are fed by fear. These thoughts follow predictable patterns: *if I do or do not do this thing, something bad will happen. If I do or do not have that conversation, something bad will happen. If I do or do not respond emotionally, something bad will happen.*

These fear-based thoughts create a kind of neurological hypnosis that keeps you constantly reacting to threats that exist only in your mind's projections and are not anchored in reality. This is deeply correlated to the Wound Reality we spoke of in Chapter 1.

We unconsciously create the perfect environments to keep our nervous system activated. We believe that this keeps us safe because it is familiar, yet in reality it keeps us trapped. This is part of the holographic creation of our reality, when our nervous system is hypervigilant, reactive and focussed on perceiving threats everywhere.

Consider what you look for in your environment and interactions that imply a threat to your wounding. It might be a phone call or the absence of a phone call, a message or no message, a bill arriving or payments not arriving, an unexpected meeting or meetings that get cancelled. What is your nervous system highly attuned and responsive to?

Amanda, whose primary wound was the Unknown, demonstrated this. "I realised I was scanning every interaction for signs of unpredictability. A meeting running late, an unexpected email, even someone changing plans for dinner, my system treated each as evidence that the world is fundamentally unsafe. My fear wasn't protecting me from actual threats; it was maintaining my perception that uncertainty itself is dangerous."

The Pain Prediction Machine

This pain prediction system creates what we might call the 'pain-fear connection'. This is a direct link between your original wound and your current protective behaviours.

The implications of this understanding are profound. When you fear public speaking, your brain is not actually afraid of the presentation, it is protecting you from the pain of potential judgment or rejection. When you fear intimacy, you are not really afraid of connection, you are protecting yourself from the pain of possible abandonment. When you fear success, you simultaneously feel the weight of potential failure. The fear is always about the pain it is guarding against.

Fear is humanity's greatest mechanism of control. It drives us into set ways of being that reinforces patterns of disconnection. These patterns separate us from the truth of what is available to us because they seem to offer protection while simultaneously creating profound limitations. We convince ourselves it is safer to disengage than to connect, safer to close than to stay open, safer to fight than to find common ground. We maintain that it is safer to stay with the abuser than to leave, safer to hold onto the misaligned job than to rest, safer to get sick than truly look after ourselves.

This 'safety' becomes our most sophisticated prison and one we maintain through our own choices. The mind creates compelling rationalisations for these choices, but beneath them all lies the same driving force: the avoidance of pain.

Tanya's Unloved Wound created yet another variation of this prison. "I never allowed anyone to truly know me. I became a chameleon, adapting to what each person seemed to want, offering validation, care, and support while keeping my true self hidden. I believed this would protect me from the pain of rejection, but it created a deeper suffering and the ache of never being seen for who I really am. Even when surrounded by people, I felt profoundly alone because these connections were with a version of me I'd created, not my authentic self."

Jules, whose Unknown Wound created a persistent fear of uncertainty, described this prison. "I realised I had built my entire life around avoiding the Unknown. I had the same job for twenty years, same routines, same places, same people. I thought I was creating stability, but I was really just maintaining a trap where nothing new could enter. And the deeper tragedy? I still felt the pain of my wound, I just added the pain of limitation on top of it."

Sally, carrying the Unworthy Wound, constructed her safety prison differently. "I built an entire identity around never making mistakes. I triple-checked everything, rehearsed every conversation, and maintained exhaustive preparation rituals. I thought I was ensuring success, when instead I was suffocating my spontaneity and creativity. The most painful irony? This perfect performance never delivered the worthiness I sought. Instead, it confirmed my deepest fear: that I was only as valuable as my last achievement."

It may be helpful to understand how your biology is supporting this Consciousness. Your brain is essentially a prediction machine, constantly forecasting potential pain and creating avoidance strategies. This operates on multiple levels simultaneously. Being aware of this can also help you bring Consciousness to how this is designed, instead of accepting it as an inevitable way you perceive reality.

Neuroscientists tell us, at the physical level, your brain automatically scans your environment every second. Your alarm system, the amygdala, searches for potential threats while your internal monitoring centre, the insula, tracks what is happening inside your body. Your pain processing centre, the anterior cingulate cortex, evaluates potential harm as your brainstem prepares automatic responses, all without you consciously thinking about it. Meanwhile, at the emotional level, past pain creates future predictions as emotional memories guide avoidance behaviours. Protection patterns become so automatic that pain associations determine your behaviour without conscious awareness. The mental level adds another layer of complexity as your mind creates elaborate stories about threats. Rationalisations justify avoidance while perceptions maintain protection systems and entire meaning-making structures reinforce fear-based responses.

Yet all of these combined is nothing when it comes to the shift of Consciousness that is possible for us all when we see it and actively work to release this pain-fear connection. The brain changes, the nervous system disengages, the relationship to pain transforms completely and we find the liberated expansion of our connected self available in every moment. I will be sharing more on the exact process we need to use soon, yet more than anything I invite you to cultivate the motivation for the big work of liberating self that is coming. **You are not here to live in fear.**

The Control Matrix in Action

Perhaps the most insidious aspect of fear is how it makes us vulnerable to control at every level of existence. When we operate from fear, we become susceptible to any person, system or ideology that promises protection from our pain. This creates the foundation for all forms of coercion, domination and control. At the most profound level, fear makes us surrender our authority to anything that offers an Illusion of Safety.

In relationships, concepts around marriage, timelines for meeting partners, having families and other cultural expectations cause us to fear missing out, driving us to settle for relationships that do not truly serve us rather than risk being alone or falling behind societal milestones. This fear of abandonment leads us to accept relationships that do not serve us. We stay in situations that diminish us, believing the pain of staying is safer than the pain of leaving.

In work, fear of scarcity makes us compliant with systems that drain our life force. We accept toxic environments, unethical practices and baseline conditions because the fear of financial insecurity outweighs our inner knowing. Money accomplishes this most effectively because society has been structured to link financial means directly with survival and survival is correlated with fear. When you fear losing your basic survival needs; your home, food, healthcare, you find yourself compromising your deepest values just to maintain stability.

The scarcity programming runs so deep that you believe 'there's not enough', keeping you competing rather than collaborating. You confuse your bank balance with your personal worth, making choices based on how successful you will appear rather than what truly aligns with your authentic self. Debt becomes an invisible chain that keeps you compliant; you cannot speak up, take risks, or pursue your real purpose because the fear of financial ruin feels more threatening than a life half-lived. The threat of punishment for unpaid taxes, the threat of nowhere to live without high mortgages and rents, the threat of no electricity or water are all against the natural flow of life.

In relation to health, fear of illness makes us surrender our bodily autonomy to any authority promising answers or cures. We accept interventions that may harm us, follow protocols that do not serve us and give away our innate wisdom because the fear of death or illness overshadows our natural bodily process of creating equilibrium and health from within.

In the education system, we abandon our capacity to perceive and observe truth in our lived environments, we are told we know nothing beyond formal education and are made to fear individual thinking and concepts that disrupt the status quo. We stay silent on our perceptions or ignore our intuition as we are fed a sanitised version of our past, our geographic position in time and space and the options for our future. The fear is that we really do not know anything, leaving us open to domination, coercion and control of our minds from birth. Challenging the status quo feels like a threat to our belonging and being.

This extends to the collective level as well. Fear operates as the primary mechanism of social control. When a population is kept in fear, critical thinking diminishes as compliance increases. Creativity shuts down while community bonds weaken and Consciousness itself contracts. This makes us susceptible to manipulation through media systems that amplify fear to capture attention and shape behaviour. **We did not sign up for a system of coercion, domination and control, but we were born into one.**

So be aware. Economic systems maintain fear of scarcity to ensure participation. Educational systems use fear of failure and being ignorant to enforce conformity. Healthcare systems leverage fear of death to mandate protocols just as political systems exploit fear to maintain power structures. The list goes on...

The Protection Paradox

The ultimate irony is that our fear of pain creates more pain. This happens because our protection patterns require huge amounts of energy to maintain. Our avoidance creates distinct limitations to what is possible. Our defence perpetuates the separation pattern and causes us to keep the thing we desire unconsciously away from us and, ultimately the fear maintains the pain. We develop sophisticated strategies of 'unconscious securing', these are ways of being that seem to protect us from pain but in fact perpetuate it. These unconscious securing systems manifest as distinct programs that govern our behaviour. The achievement program drives constant striving for success to avoid the pain of inadequacy. The perfection program maintains impossible standards to avoid rejection pain. The control program manages every detail to avoid uncertainty pain, while the pleasing program adapts to others' needs to avoid abandonment pain.

Each program seems to offer protection but in reality deepens our entrapment. The woman who builds her identity around never making mistakes may achieve impressive success, but at the cost of spontaneity, creativity and authentic connection. The man who controls every detail of his environment may avoid some uncertainty, but creates a life devoid of wonder, surprise and growth. The irony is profound: in trying to avoid the pain of not belonging, we create patterns that prevent true belonging. In attempting to avoid rejection, we reject ourselves first. In seeking to escape loneliness, we isolate our authentic self. In trying to prevent failure, we never truly succeed at anything that matters. In working to avoid criticism, we become our own harshest critic. In attempting to gain love through performance, we ensure we are loved for who we pretend to be rather than who we are. We conform, adapt and suppress our authentic expression, all to maintain a sense of safety that's ultimately illusory.

This paradox explains why so many of our attempts to create safety simply cause more suffering. The person terrified of rejection builds such impenetrable walls that genuine connection becomes impossible. The one afraid of failure creates such elaborate safety nets that they never experience the exhilaration of true risk. The fear of pain does not prevent pain, it guarantees it in a different form.

Look carefully at your own life and you will find this paradox operating everywhere. The student who is so afraid of appearing ignorant never asks questions, ensuring they remain ignorant. The entrepreneur, so terrified of financial insecurity clings to a stable but dead-end job, experiencing the deeper insecurity of an unlived calling. The parent, so fearful of their child's suffering, creates overprotective environments, ultimately increasing the child's vulnerability to life's inevitable challenges.

This protection paradox operates through a neurological mechanism: what you unconsciously focus on, you project into reality to be experienced. So, as you are putting your attention on avoiding what you do not want to feel, you are creating the awareness around that and it pulls it into your experience. What you resist, you reinforce. The very programs we use to avoid pain become the source of a deeper, more persistent suffering. The programming of submission through fear creates a self-reinforcing cycle. Fear makes us seek protection, but protection requires submission. Submission increases vulnerability, which intensifies fear, completing the cycle.

Julia discovered this paradox after decades of protecting herself from the vulnerability of intimate relationships, "I thought my independence was strength, but instead it was fear wearing a convincing disguise. I built an entire personality around not needing anyone, priding myself on self-sufficiency. But the pain I was avoiding and the hurt of potential rejection did not disappear. It transmuted into a persistent loneliness that no amount of achievement could touch. My protection from hurt guaranteed a different hurt from the pain of disconnection."

To recognise this paradox in your own life, consider these essential questions:

- What am I most afraid of experiencing (rejection, failure, abandonment, criticism.)?
- What strategies have I developed to avoid this experience?
- What has this protection cost me (in terms of joy, connection, opportunity or growth)?
- What new form of pain has my protection created?
- If I were to face what I fear directly, what possibilities might open up?

What would happen if we could facilitate our own liberation through a full, conscious relationship to our own pain? Would there be anything to fear?

The Space Beyond Fear

Are you beginning to realise how this design has deeply impacted your life? The invitation now is to take a deep breath and realise how fear has inhabited the body and to begin to open more spaciousness through this simple realisation. As we keep challenging fear and maintain personal freedom at the forefront of our evolution, a radical expansion happens. We unleash the fear matrix that has held our cellular, emotional and energetic being in stasis and begin to evolve at a radical rate.

Think of how much energy it takes to maintain your fear responses, the constant vigilance, the protective patterns, the avoidance strategies. All of this requires tremendous energy, creating a state of perpetual tension in your nervous system. When this tension begins to release, this energy becomes available for creation rather than protection, for thriving rather than surviving.

This release manifests physically as deeper, more natural breathing and relaxation of chronic muscle tension. You experience increased energy and vitality alongside enhanced sensory awareness and greater physical presence. Emotionally, you develop an expanded capacity for feeling everything that arises naturally. Increased intimacy develops along with enhanced empathic ability and deeper relational presence.

Energetically, this transformation shows up as heightened creative flow and increased synchronicities as you reclaim your energetic resources. As fear diminishes your enhanced intuitive capacity emerges alongside the ability for greater manifestation and an expanded sense of possibility.

Beyond fear, there is a level of freedom that transpires across all dimensions of life. When you no longer fear, fear itself, you no longer fear death, illness, debt, abandonment. You come into a relationship with the now:

✦ Death becomes a natural part of life's cycle rather than a threat to avoid.

✦ Illness becomes information from the body rather than an enemy to fight.

✦ Financial challenges become opportunities for creativity rather than threats to survival.

✦ Relationship dynamics become opportunities for growth rather than potential sources of disconnection.

This freedom manifests as a profound shift in how you experience reality. Instead of living in anticipation of future pain or in protection from past hurt, you find yourself fully present in the now. This presence is what naturally remains when you are no longer running from your own experience.

Return to Source: The Ultimate Resolution

The deepest resolution of fear comes through reconnection with Source, the fundamental connectivity that exists prior to all fear patterns. This connection to Source manifests as a tangible shift in how we experience reality. The separate self that needed protection begins to be recognised as just one aspect of a much larger existence. From this recognition, fear naturally loses its grip and we expanded beyond the identity that fear was protecting.

Brendan describes this shift. "It's like I spent years building and maintaining walls to protect myself, only to discover that what I really am doesn't need protection. Now, life flows through me differently. Challenges still arise, but they meet something larger than my personal fears." When you create authentic internal, eternal freedom, nothing becomes as fundamentally important as maintaining that Source connection. Nothing external can remove us from that space and the work becomes a constant unhooking from an external matrix and a complete realignment into self.

True, infinite freedom must come from the Source of you. The external cannot be manipulated via money, time, people, status, impact and it cannot be measured by the physical things that you are enslaved to. It is only you in a relationship with you. This return to Source is an ongoing unfolding. Each time we meet fear with presence instead of protection, we strengthen this connection. Each moment of staying with discomfort instead of avoiding it becomes an opportunity to deepen this remembrance of our true nature.

The next chapter reveals how pain itself becomes the pathway to liberation. There, I will guide you through the process of working with pain transformatively and show you how to release your identity from the unconscious patterns that govern your life.

CHAPTER EIGHT
Pain is the Path to Freedom

We have explored the inherent truth that your fear exists solely to protect you from pain, creating elaborate programs of protection that ultimately perpetuate the very suffering they were designed to prevent. Now, we must turn towards what you may have spent a lifetime avoiding: the pure experience of pain itself.

While your entire existence may have been organised around escaping this encounter, I invite you to consider the most radical possibility of all: the very pain you have been running from is your greatest teacher, your deepest healer and the doorway to the freedom you have been seeking through every addiction, every protective pattern, every unconscious program you have ever created. The truth of pain is something that must be experienced and embodied. My own understanding of pain's transformative power came through such a moment, one that merged the physical and metaphysical realms in ways that still fills me with wonder.

Let us go back to a year after my experience on the beach. I was still very much anchored more into energy and Consciousness than lived reality and was wondering how I would ever ground myself back into life. By a profound synchronicity I connected with an interdimensional freedom fighter from Kansas. Ann was a powerful guide to investigate the very design of reality itself. I would eagerly wait for her late-night call and we would sit together in darkness, witnessing as the space between us revealed truths about the nature of existence.

Even though we were on opposite sides of the world, we would work together as if sitting next to each other looking at the same screen of dimensional experience. We moved through dimensional layers, examining their constructs and patterns, we looked deeply at the construct of reality, not as a fixed experience but layers of light, frequency and information. We mapped how the liberating paths of humanity were blocked and how the confining experiences are reinforced. I would stretch out through Consciousness in all directions, exploring and expanding. Ann would provide the guide rails, support and deeper dimensional access.

But it was one seemingly ordinary day that would crystallise everything we were learning into visceral understanding. One hot, bright Australian summer morning I had taken the kids to the beach to cool off. While in the ocean with my two small daughters a king wave with a tremendous amount of water rolled over us. I had my daughters' hands in mine and I lost my footing and we were engulfed by the wave. We were submerged in the water for longer than our breaths could hold, I felt the fire in my lungs burning as the oxygen ran out. I felt my arms being pulled as I gripped for dear life onto my precious girls. Eventually the wave subsided and we popped up. With all my energy I dragged the girls back to shore, every cell activated in a survival mode. I collapsed on the beach holding them so close and released such a deep visceral pain. My body shaking and releasing, I felt myself connecting to my life and my children's lives in a new profound way that I had not felt before that pain.

We returned home and I set about making lunch. I was moving back and forth between the bench and the fridge over the clean wooden floor. Suddenly, I doubled over in excruciating pain. A shard of glass over a centimetre long had somehow embedded itself into my heel, not at an angle, but perfectly perpendicular to my foot's sole, like a needle piercing through skin and nerves.

As blood pooled on the floor, I examined the glass with equal parts pain and fascination. The positioning defied normal physics, yet there it was embedded vertically in my heel. In that moment of searing pain, I felt a multidimensional portal opening, revealing an essential truth: **Pain is a Portal and our greatest liberator.**

Later that night, before I could share what had happened,

Ann called with an extraordinary revelation. Her son had broken a glass in their Kansas kitchen and several large pieces had literally vanished before she could clean them up. I knew that one shard had somehow rematerialised through space and time ending up in my kitchen in Australia.

That night I slept deeply and experienced an astral operation, my lungs that were only acclimatised to breathing through fear and limitation were replaced with an expanded cellular design. I started to breathe the energy of freedom, sovereignty and true internal power. The awakening to using what I call the 'Pain Portal' beyond fear had begun. What I share with you now is wisdom gained through direct experience and years of witnessing pain's power to liberate both myself and others.

The Single Source of All Pain

Imagine for a moment a spiral expanding outward from a single point. From a distance, each loop appears separate, distinct from all others. Yet, follow any loop back to its source and you find they all emerge from the same centre. Your pain operates in exactly this way. What appears as many different hurts: the betrayal in a relationship, the wound of rejection, the ache of loneliness, is one core pain expressing itself through various circumstances, relationships and experiences.

When you look deeply into any moment of pain and really allow yourself to feel it without the story your mind creates about it, you will discover something remarkable: the raw sensation of pain remains consistent across all experiences. The story changes, the circumstances differ, but the essential quality of the pain itself is unchanged.

This understanding revolutionises how we approach our pain. Instead of trying to heal multiple wounds, we can recognise that we are working with one fundamental pain expressing itself through time. This is why attempting to fix external circumstances often fails to bring lasting relief as we are treating the symptoms while leaving the source untouched.

A client came to me in despair after another failed relationship. Each one ending with the same feeling of being unseen and unvalued. "What's wrong with me?" she asked. "Why do I keep choosing the same man in different bodies?" As we explored her experiences, something remarkable emerged. The pain she felt in her marriages was identical to the pain she experienced as a child when her overwhelmed mother could not truly see her. Once she recognised this core pain, she stopped trying to fix her relationships and began meeting the original wound directly.

Like a hologram where each fragment contains the entire image, each instance of pain contains the totality of your Core Wound. When you fully meet any moment of pain, allowing yourself to experience it completely without resistance or story, you are not just healing that specific instance, you are accessing the Core Wound itself.

I witnessed this principle in action with Hilary, a client who had carried deep wounds of betrayal throughout her life. During one session, she allowed herself to fully feel the pain of a seemingly minor betrayal at work when a colleague took credit for her idea. As she stayed present with the raw sensation of this pain, without getting lost in the story about her colleague, something extraordinary happened. All her past betrayal wounds began spontaneously surfacing and releasing. The current pain had opened a portal to the Core Wound itself, allowing a healing that rippled across time.

This is why you do not need to process every painful experience you have ever had. You do not need to dig through years of memories or relive past traumas. What you need is to fully meet the pain that is arising in your experience right now. This present moment contains everything needed for complete transformation.

The Reality Beyond Physical Sensation

What you experience as physical pain is a stored energetic pattern manifesting through your body. It is about deeply understanding how you relate to pain. Energetic patterns become physical sensations in your body. So, when you sink into what causes you the most emotional pain, your body will respond with pain.

Your body is not betraying you when it presents you with pain. It actually serves as the most loyal messenger, revealing exactly where your Consciousness needs to expand. Every sensation of pain is like a flag marking the spot where transformation is possible. But this transformation cannot happen if you remain at war with the messenger.

However, there is a crucial understanding you need to have: pain and suffering are not the same thing. Pain is the raw sensation arising in the present moment. Suffering is the story you tell about that sensation. Pain is natural, temporary and will ultimately reconnect you to yourself. Suffering is created, perpetuated by the mind, fuelled by emotions and separates you from your experience and yourself.

Think of pain as a pure signal and suffering as static interference. When you clear away the static of your stories, judgments and resistance, you can work directly with the signal itself. This is where real transformation becomes possible.

I have seen this distinction change lives. Michael came to me carrying the weight of a life of suffering. As we explored his experience together, something became clear: much of his anguish came not from the sensation itself, but from his story about it. His mind kept arguing: *this shouldn't be happening. This will never end. This means I'm broken.* When he learned to separate the pure sensation from these thoughts, his experience transformed. The pain might still be present, but the suffering began to dissolve. **The pain is real, the story you tell about the pain is the illusion.**

When you relate to pain directly, without the overlay of mental commentary, several things change:

✦ The intensity often diminishes naturally.
✦ The pain becomes workable rather than overwhelming.
✦ The sensation reveals its message more clearly.
✦ The energy and Consciousness bound in resistance becomes available for healing.
✦ The suffering component dissolves, even if the sensation remains.

Consider Lucy, who struggled with chronic anxiety. For years, she battled the physical sensations: racing heart, constricted breathing, knots in her stomach. But the turning point came when she stopped calling it 'anxiety' and simply experienced it as a raw sensation. "The moment I dropped the label and the story, something shifted," she told me. "These sensations weren't my enemy anymore, they were just energy moving through my body. I could be with them without being controlled by them."

The Architecture of Avoidance

If pain holds such transformative power, why do we go to such lengths to avoid it? The answer lies deeper than you might imagine. We think we fear rejection, abandonment, failure or loss. But these are just stories about what we fear. What we actually fear is the raw, somatic experience of pain itself. Everything else is just a narrative about what might cause that pain.

This fear creates an intricate architecture of avoidance in your life. Our relationship to our pain is deeply affected by the fear instilled in us by caregivers. When we did not feel safe when we had an emotional experience, we were taught to avoid this space by blocking out or acting out the pain. The direct connection with it was distorted and undermined.

The great irony is that these protective patterns become your prison. The person who fears abandonment becomes clingy, often creating the very abandonment they fear. Those afraid of failure avoid risks, ensuring they never discover their true capabilities. People terrified of rejection maintain walls that prevent genuine connection. In trying to avoid pain, you create a life that is pain-free but also joy-free, love-free, growth-free.

I invite you to take a few moments to reflect on the reactions you received to your pain as a child.

- ✦ Were you heard and honoured and given space to meet yourself?
- ✦ Were you suppressed?

- Were you avoided?
- Were you met with an angry shut down?

This awareness is an important step to unfold the unconscious relationship to why you will fear going into your pain.

Beyond the Mind's Solutions

Most approaches to pain focus on making sense of it. Traditional therapy often seeks to understand pain, to make it logical, to find its historical causes. While insight has value, it can create a deeper loop if it is not expanded to completion within your wider consciousness and emotional experience. Your mind desperately wants to make pain meaningful, to create a story that explains it, to find a solution that fixes it.

This is where traditional therapy, despite its good intentions, can sometimes lead us astray. When you sit in a therapist's office talking about your pain, you are often solidifying the very program you are trying to dissolve. Each retelling of your story, each analysis of your past, each rational explanation can often take you further from the raw truth of your pain. Think about it: how many times have you explained your pain to others? How many times have you analysed its origins, understood its causes, mapped its patterns? Has all this understanding fundamentally changed your relationship with pain? Or has it simply created a more detailed story about why you hurt?

Your mind wants to make pain 'make sense'. It wants to find the perfect explanation, the ultimate reason, the complete understanding that will finally set you free. But pain does not need to make sense, it needs to be felt. It does not need to be understood, it needs to be experienced. It does not need to be analysed, it needs to be allowed. Jules discovered this truth after years of traditional therapy. "I could explain my trauma perfectly. I knew all the psychological terms, all the patterns, all the connections between my childhood and my current struggles. But I was still suffering. It wasn't until I let go of needing to understand my pain and simply allowed myself to feel it directly that something finally shifted. The healing wasn't in the insight, it was in the direct experience."

The Gated Consciousness: Trapped in Time

To truly understand the persistence of pain in your life, we must explore a crucial phenomenon: the gating of pain within your nervous system and how it simultaneously gates your consciousness. This concept is foundational to understanding why pain from decades ago can still feel so immediately present and why certain aspects of your development seem frozen in time.

Pain is fundamentally a sensation; energy moving through your system. When this sensation first arrives, especially during formative periods of development, your nervous system makes a critical assessment: *Can I process this?* If the intensity exceeds your capacity or if you lack the support needed to move through it naturally, something remarkable happens. Your system gates the pain, walling it off, compartmentalising it, preventing its full integration. When pain gets gated, so does the Consciousness that was present at that moment. Part of you literally remains trapped in that unprocessed experience, frozen at that developmental stage, unable to evolve beyond that point.

This explains the strange time-collapse that occurs around our deepest wounds. The adult who still responds with a child's terror when facing authority figures. The accomplished professional who becomes a helpless five year old when criticised. The otherwise confident person who dissolves into preverbal panic when facing abandonment. These are not metaphorical regressions, instead they are actual expressions of Consciousness that remained gated within unprocessed pain.

Samantha's experience illustrates this phenomenon with striking clarity. Despite her intellectual brilliance and professional success, she found herself completely shut down in intimate relationships. "It was as if the adult me disappeared and I became this terrified child with no language, no resources, no capacity to respond appropriately," she explained. "For years, I thought these were flashbacks to childhood trauma, but I came to realise it was more profound: a part of me had never left that traumatic moment. My consciousness around intimacy had remained gated alongside the pain of my earliest abandonment."

The implications of this understanding are profound. It means that many of our most persistent patterns are not simply habits or psychological conditioning, they are expressions of Consciousness that have remained developmentally frozen in unfelt pain. So, it is crucial to go beyond addressing the adult Consciousness and instead focus on the pattern that exists outside normal time perception and is driven by a gated, immature Consciousness.

This gating process creates what I call 'Consciousness enclaves', pockets of awareness that remain isolated from your overall development, operating according to the reality perceptions that were present when the pain was first experienced. These enclaves do not evolve naturally with time and experience, as the rest of your Consciousness does. They remain fixed, responding to current triggers with outdated protection strategies that once made sense but now create suffering.

Samantha's breakthrough came through understanding this phenomenon. "I realised I wasn't dealing with anxiety as my therapist had labelled it. I was experiencing the actual terror of my three-year-old self, who couldn't process the overwhelming loss of my mother's presence. That part of me never grew up, never developed new resources, never learned that I could survive separation. It remained frozen alongside the unprocessed grief, emerging whenever current circumstances triggered similar feelings."

The most profound aspect of this understanding is that Consciousness itself, your capacity for awareness, for presence, for mature response, remains partially trapped at these points of unprocessed pain. This explains why, despite years of growth in many areas of life, you may find yourself strangely incapable, regressed or reactive in specific circumstances. This regression reflects Consciousness that has been gated in pain, unable to benefit from your subsequent growth and development. It is not a character flaw or lack of effort.

The path to liberation, therefore, is not just about processing pain, it is about using the Pain Portal to free trapped Consciousness. This requires a fundamentally different approach than most conventional therapies offer. You do not need to develop better coping strategies or to gain more insight into patterns. It is about creating the conditions where previously intolerable sensations can finally be processed, allowing the gated Consciousness to integrate into your mature awareness.

Alex describes this process. "When I finally met the terror I'd been running from my entire life, something unexpected happened. It wasn't just emotional release, though that was part of it. It opened my ability to remain present with intense emotion without shutting down and this expanded my capacity to feel and be present with life."

The Timeless Nature of Pain

Before we explore how to be with the pain, you must understand something crucial about its nature: the pain you feel now is exactly the same pain you felt as an infant, child and teenager... Pain exists outside of time, unchanging in its essential quality. The only thing that changes is the stories we wrap around it.

This timeless quality of pain is a direct result of the gated Consciousness we explored earlier. When pain becomes overwhelming and gets compartmentalised in your system, it does not age or evolve. The Consciousness trapped with it remains frozen at that developmental stage, creating pockets of experience that exist outside your normal timeline. This explains why a minor trigger in the present can suddenly catapult you into feeling exactly as you did decades ago, the pain has not aged because the Consciousness experiencing it has not aged.

Think back to your earliest memories of pain. Perhaps you were very young, facing a situation where your nervous system was not developed enough to process. In that moment, you needed support to fully feel and move through the pain. But what happened instead? Like most children, you probably encountered a society profoundly uncomfortable with pain's raw expression. Reflect now on what you experienced as a child:

- ✦ When you cried out in pain, were you shushed?
- ✦ When you expressed anger, were you scolded?
- ✦ When your body shook with emotion, were you told to calm down?
- ✦ When you tried to speak your truth, were you dismissed or humiliated?

Each of these moments taught you that pain was unsafe, that your natural response to it was somehow wrong.

This societal conditioning runs deep. It is why you might still find it difficult to cry in public, take a day off just to feel, let your body shake with emotion, voice your pain without apologising or allow pain to move through you naturally. These learned restrictions on our emotional expression create additional layers of disconnection from our authentic experience, forcing us to carry pain privately and process it alone rather than allowing it to flow naturally through our system. You are carrying your own conditioning, but also generations of collective trauma around pain. This is why creating a new relationship with pain is both personal healing and a revolutionary act.

The Guards of Pain: Depression and Anxiety

Before we can meet pain directly, we must understand what can block it. Depression and anxiety are intelligent, protective responses to unprocessed pain. They stand guard at the door of your deepest feelings, each serving a specific purpose.

Depression is a shutting down, a moving away, a desperate attempt to not feel. It numbs not just the pain but all of life, creating a grey world where both agony and ecstasy are kept at bay. If you are experiencing depression, honour it as your system's response to overwhelming pain. It has been protecting you, keeping you functioning when everything seems impossible.

Anxiety, on the other hand, is pain in its vigilant form, constantly scanning for threats, trying to prevent the next wound. It creates a state of perpetual alertness, watching for any sign of impending pain. Your anxiety is no longer your enemy; it has been trying to keep you safe in the only way it knows how.

Consider Christine's story, which illustrates how these patterns work across generations. Raised in a strict Catholic family, she endured sexual abuse from her brother. The abuse came wrapped in a devastating message: that she was evil and deserved her pain. This perception became a self-fulfilling prophecy, leading her into an abusive marriage where the pattern continued.

The breakthrough came when Christine realised she had completely suppressed her natural emotional responses to submit to what she saw as deserved punishment. As we worked together, she began to reclaim her right to feel. For each memory that surfaced, she reimagined it; screaming for help, calling her mother, alerting the police. She was not just processing old pain; she was reclaiming her fundamental right to respond to pain naturally.

The Sacred Art of Being With Pain

What I am about to share with you might seem radical, even dangerous to your conditioned mind: **instead of trying to create safety from pain, we must learn to create safety *for* pain.** This subtle distinction changes everything.

Think of how you currently relate to pain. When it arises, your immediate impulse is likely to fix it, escape it or at least understand it. This is what you have been taught. This is what your entire culture supports. But what if pain itself has an intelligence that your solutions are interrupting? What if your very attempts to handle pain are preventing its profound medicine from working for you?

I witnessed this truth unfold dramatically with Mark, a successful executive who had built his entire life around never showing weakness. His fear of experiencing vulnerability had created an impressive but imprisoning structure: a controlling leadership style, distant personal relationships, chronic anxiety and a complete inability to receive support. It was only when a health crisis forced him into vulnerability that he discovered something astonishing. The pain he had spent his life avoiding opened a gateway to the deep connection and authentic power he truly sought.

Becoming Pain's Disciple

Here is where *The Consciousness Method*™ asks us to become radical. Instead of trying to master pain, we must apprentice ourselves to it. We begin to surrender to the wisdom of our pain. This surrender is not passive; it is the most active stance you can take.

When pain arises, your first task is to drop all agendas about it. Stop trying to fix it. Stop trying to understand it. Stop trying to make it meaningful. Simply be with it, completely present, utterly willing to feel whatever is asking to be felt on a visceral level.

This requires a profound shift in orientation. Rather than asking yourself: *How can I make this pain go away?* begin asking: *What is this pain trying to show me?* Instead of seeking relief, seek revelation. Rather than viewing pain as an obstacle to your peace, recognise it as a portal of reconnection to you.

During a recent retreat, I watched this transformation unfold in Rachel, who had struggled with severe anxiety for decades. Instead of trying to calm or understand her anxiety, she brought pure attention to the raw sensation of it. For forty-seven minutes, she stayed present with the intense energy moving through her body. Suddenly, something shifted; the energy transformed into a deep peace she had never known. The anxiety pattern had dissolved through pure presence, not management.

The Technology of Transformation

Let me share with you the technology of this transformation. This is a relationship to be developed and wisdom to be received. The steps below may not happen sequentially but instead are phases of awakening to the pain that need to be kept in mind.

1. You must create sacred space for meeting pain. You need to become available to meet your pain, to bring a quality of presence to the moments when pain naturally arises. When you feel that familiar contraction, that tension, that discomfort, stop. Turn towards it with your full attention.
2. Be very aware, any level of fear is simply the front row bodyguard of that pain. It is safe to feel this pain fully. Witness the fear as trying to keep you in an Illusion of Safety.
3. Drop into your body. Pain always lives in the body first, even when it seems to be mental or emotional. Find where the sensation is strongest. Move your awareness there as if you are sitting down with a dear friend who has something important to tell you.
4. Now comes the crucial part, drop all stories about the pain. Every interpretation, every explanation, every meaning you have given it, let them all fall away. What remains when you are not telling any stories about your pain? What is the pure experience beneath all your thoughts about it?
5. Allow whatever movements or sounds that want to come. Pain often carries frozen energy that needs to move. Your body knows how to release it if you let it. Trust the intelligence of this process. It knows its own way.

What happens in these moments of presence is far more profound than merely feeling sensation. You are creating the conditions for previously gated Consciousness to be liberated. As you stay present with the raw energy of pain without resistance or story, the Consciousness that has remained frozen alongside that pain begins to thaw, to move, to integrate with your mature awareness.

Jennifer's experience illustrates this profound process. For years, she experienced inexplicable panic whenever she needed to speak in public. Despite extensive therapy and coaching, the terror remained overwhelming. During our work together, she followed this sensation to its origin, a moment at age seven when she was humiliated while reading aloud in class. As she stayed present with the raw energy of this experience, allowing it to move through her body without resistance, something remarkable happened.

"It wasn't just that the fear lessened," she explained. "It was as if a part of me that had been stuck at seven years old suddenly had permission to grow up. I could literally feel my Consciousness expanding, integrating aspects of myself that had been frozen in time. The next time I gave a presentation, I was experiencing public speaking from an entirely different Consciousness, one that included capabilities that had previously been inaccessible to me."

The Generational Web of Pain

Your pain does not exist in isolation. It is part of a vast web of human experience, stretching back through generations. The way your grandmother learned to suppress her grief, the way your father learned to hide his vulnerability, the way your mother learned to silence her anger, all of these patterns live in you, too.

Consider Thomas's story. He came to me struggling with an inexplicable rage that would surface in his relationships. As we explored this anger together, a remarkable pattern emerged. His father had been a quiet, contained man who never raised his voice. His grandfather, however, had been known for explosive outbursts that terrorised the family. Thomas's father had sworn never to be like his own father, creating a new pattern of rigid, emotional control. Now, Thomas found himself swinging between these two inherited patterns of explosive rage and complete suppression.

The healing came through understanding these patterns and allowing himself to feel the raw energy beneath the rage and control. As he learned to be with this energy directly, without either expressing or suppressing it, both patterns began to dissolve. When we do this work we are releasing a suppressed, limited and dense Consciousness and as everything is connected, this work has a direct impact on the energetic patterning of all your ancestors. We are not just healing our own pain; we are transforming a generational legacy.

The Case of Alexandra: Gated Consciousness in Action

Alexandra, a businesswoman in her forties, came to me with what she described as 'inexplicable abandonment issues'. Despite her professional confidence and generally fulfilling life, romantic relationships followed a predictable pattern: initial connection, growing intimacy, then overwhelming anxiety and eventual sabotage when her partner showed any signs of independence.

"I become someone I don't recognise," she explained. "My logical adult mind knows he's just busy with work or needs time with friends, but another part of me takes over completely, desperate, clingy, convinced I'm being abandoned. I've ruined multiple relationships this way and I don't understand why I can't control it."

As we began exploring her experience, I invited Alexandra to notice where she felt the abandonment fear in her body. She immediately placed her hand on her solar plexus, describing a 'black hole of panic' that emerged whenever a partner was not immediately available. As she stayed with this sensation without trying to analyse or fix it, memories began to surface, not just mental images, but full-body, multisensory experiences.

At age four, Alexandra's mother had been hospitalised for several months with a serious illness. No one had explained to her what was happening or when her mother would return. Her father, overwhelmed with work and hospital visits, had left her with a succession of relatives and neighbours. Every morning, she would wake up not knowing where she was or who would be caring for her that day.

As Alexandra stayed present with the sensations in her solar plexus, something remarkable happened. Her posture changed, her voice shifted to a higher pitch, and she began speaking from the perspective of her four year old self. "No one is coming back. No one tells me anything. I don't know where I am. I don't know where my mummy is."

What we were witnessing was not merely a memory or emotional release. It was the direct expression of Consciousness that had remained, gated alongside unprocessed pain for nearly four decades. This part of Alexandra had not grown, had not developed new resources, had not integrated the subsequent experiences that could have brought healing and perspective. It remained frozen at age four, perceiving current situations through the lens of that original abandonment.

Over the next several sessions, Alexandra developed a profound relationship with this aspect of her Consciousness. Rather than trying to 'fix' her abandonment issues, she learned to create internal safety for the experience itself. She stayed present with the sensations, allowed the movements and sounds that wanted to emerge, and listened deeply to what this part of herself had been trying to tell her for decades.

The critical breakthrough came when Alexandra realised she was not just healing a wound or processing emotion, she was liberating Consciousness that had been trapped in time. As she provided the presence, safety, and attunement that had been missing during the original experience, the gated aspects of her awareness began to integrate with her adult Consciousness.

"It feels like a missing piece of myself is coming home," she explained. "When I realised I don't have to manage my triggers or constantly understand why I feel abandoned, I can really focus on the part of me that stopped developing at age four and support her to finally grow up. Finally learning that I have resources now, that I can tolerate separation, that connection doesn't have to mean fusion."

Alexandra's transformation did not happen through insight or behaviour modification. It happened through direct engagement with previously gated Consciousness. As this integration continued, her relationships changed dramatically. The panic around separation gradually dissolved because the part of her that experienced normal separation as life-threatening abandonment had finally received what it needed to mature.

The Trap of Processing Pain

When you use methods that bypass conscious participation; whether it is plant medicine, hypnosis or other approaches, you are literally excluding yourself from the experience of conscious transformation. While these modalities can offer powerful experiences, they often leave you dependent on external intervention for change. The question to ask yourself is: *Am I conscious in my exploration of myself or am I relying on something external to me?*

This is where many modern approaches to pain miss something crucial. They focus on processing pain, managing pain or releasing pain, all approaches that subtly reinforce the idea that pain is something we need to unconsciously get rid of. Instead, we want to change the relationship to pain from something to be processed, to a portal that must be actively entered.

I watched this understanding transform Sandra's healing journey. After years of various therapeutic modalities, she had become what she called a 'professional patient', skilled at processing trauma but somehow never quite free of it. The breakthrough came when she stopped trying to process her pain and simply began to be with it. The very pain she had been trying to heal became her greatest teacher.

The Revolutionary Approach to Freedom

As you develop this relationship with pain, something extraordinary begins to happen. You discover your true invulnerability, because you no longer fear the pain. This changes everything about how you move through life.

Cristian's story illustrates this revolutionary freedom. After decades of avoiding emotional pain through achievement and control, he committed to a different approach of meeting his pain directly, without resistance or story. "The strangest thing happened", he told me. "As I stopped running from pain, I stopped needing to control my life so tightly. I became more spontaneous, more creative, more connected. The very situations that would have devastated me before became opportunities for growth. It wasn't that painful things stopped happening, it was that pain itself changed its meaning in my life. It became a guide rather than an enemy.'

External circumstances lose their power to determine your peace. As you learn to be with pain consciously you are pioneering new territory for human Consciousness. This transformation manifests in specific ways:

✦ **Authentic Presence:** When you are no longer organising your life around pain avoidance, you become fully available to what is happening now. This presence emerges naturally when you stop running from it.

✦ **Relational Freedom:** As pain loses its threatening quality, relationships transform. You no longer need others to behave in specific ways to protect you from pain. This creates connections based on choice rather than need.

✦ **Creative Flow:** Much of creative blocking comes from fear of the pain of rejection, criticism or failure. When pain cracks open, creative energy flows naturally, unimpeded by protection strategies.

✦ **Embodied Wisdom:** The body, once seen as a source of threatening sensations to be controlled, becomes a profound source of wisdom. You develop a collaborative relationship with your physical experience.

✦ **Expanded Consciousness:** When pain no longer requires constant vigilance and management, Consciousness naturally expands. You have access to states of awareness that were previously unavailable.

The Death of the Limited Self: The Ultimate Liberation

We have explored how meeting pain directly leads to transformation. But a deeper truth emerges when this work reaches its natural completion. There is a profound inner death process that transcends our conventional understanding of healing.

This death is the actual dissolution of the limited self that has been constructed around pain and fear. When you have thoroughly met your pain, followed it to its source and allowed it to reveal its deepest teaching, something extraordinary happens: the entire reality structure organised around pain begins to collapse.

This collapse can feel like a dissolve of self because it is. The identity that you have carefully constructed, which is the self that has been designed to navigate a reality perceived as threatening, begins to dissolve. The predictable patterns of perception, emotion and meaning-making that have defined your existence start to fall away.

What in fact happens in this inner death process is the final integration of all the fragments of gated Consciousness that have remained frozen in time. As each pocket of trapped awareness is liberated through your direct relationship with pain, a profound re-organisation occurs. Your Consciousness is no longer compartmentalised around unprocessed experience and it becomes whole, unfragmented, fully available in the present moment, and this creates the foundation for an increase in your relationship with Source.

Tara described this experience with haunting precision. "It wasn't like having an insight or even a spiritual awakening. It was a complete system failure. Everything I thought I was, everything I believed about reality, every structure I'd built to make sense of my experience, it all began to unravel. I wasn't just facing my fear or feeling my pain; I was dying to the entire construct of who I thought I was."

This inner death process reveals something astonishing: what you have perceived as 'reality' has been largely a pain-generated construct. The world you have been navigating is not objective reality but a projection created by your wound patterns and maintained by your gated Consciousness. Your Core Wound has not just influenced your experience, it has literally generated the reality you perceive.

When this construct dissolves through the integration of previously gated Consciousness, what emerges is an entirely different order of experience, one that exists beyond the fundamental duality of pain and pleasure, safety and threat, self and other.

Sandra's experience illuminates this radical transformation. "After years of working with my pain, something unexpected happened. I realised I wasn't actually healing my pain. I was dying to the entire self that experienced pain. What emerged wasn't a healthier version of my old self, but something that feels like it exists prior to the old version of self. From this place, pain still arises, but no one needs to be protected from it. It moves like weather through the sky, leaving no trace."

This is a radical embracing of life so complete that it burns through the very structures that have maintained separation, not bypassing or escaping your embodied experience. The death of the pain-based, limited self reveals what has always been true beneath your protection strategies: you have an intrinsic safety that does not depend on external conditions.

Sandra describes this intrinsic safety. "What I discovered beneath all my fear and pain wasn't an absence of threat but a presence so fundamental that it makes the concept of threat meaningless. It's not that bad things don't happen, they do. But they happen within a field of such profound okayness that my nervous system no longer needs to organise around protection. There is safety here that can't be threatened because it exists prior to the very concept of danger."

This inner death process cannot be forced or manufactured. It emerges naturally as the culmination of fully meeting your pain. As you develop the capacity to be present with what you have been avoiding, as you allow completion of interrupted response cycles and as you bring Consciousness to unconscious patterns, the entire structure begins to reveal its provisional nature.

You do not need to seek this death, that would be another strategy of the pain-based, limited self. The invitation is simply to be utterly honest about your experience, to follow pain to its source with unwavering presence, to question every assumption about what you are and what reality is. The death is through the natural dissolution of what was never true to begin with.

What awaits on the other side of this death is a fundamental shift in the nature of experience itself, from a reality organised around protection to one organised around creation. From a self defined by its wounds to a presence that includes, yet transcends all definitions...This is the ultimate resolution of pain.

It is the complete integration of the pain into a Consciousness spacious enough to recognise that what you truly are has never been damaged, never been separate, never been anything less than the entirety of existence itself, appearing as this particular human experience.

The path through pain does not just lead home. It reveals that you have always been home and that the very pain you feared would destroy you was the very doorway to this recognition. You can follow the process below and listen to the masterclass on the pain portal in the resource section.

Deepening your relationship to Pain Practice

As your pain is embedded in your cellular, energetic body, it is important to identify where in the body it is and the attached thought forms or perceptions that support that pain.

Ultimately, pain is the portal to more inner connection and Wholeness, so we need to apply more Consciousness and awareness to the space within where pain is trapped.

1. Get comfortable and drop your awareness deep into your body and scan for any discomfort, tension or sensation.
2. When you identify it, begin to dialogue directly to that part of you and ask: *What is so painful?* and *What do you fear?*
3. Simply listen and apply more and more awareness.

4. Do not try to make things better or suppress any emotions that arise.
5. Simply keep inquiring and going deeper and deeper into the pain.
6. The intention is twofold; to understand the suppressed Consciousness your pain is holding and then to make the pain feel completely safe.
7. As you go deeper, you sense that you are moving through a portal to a deeper level of connection and self knowing.
8. Remember, your pain is real, the story you tell about your pain is the illusion. Feel the pain and release the story.

As we conclude our exploration of the Pain Portal, you may feel a mixture of emotions, perhaps a sense of possibility alongside lingering hesitation. This is perfectly natural. Be gentle with the process. The pain may need to trust you to reveal itself completely. Opening to pain rather than avoiding it represents a profound shift in how we relate to our human experience, one that already sets you apart from conventional approaches to healing. Yet what awaits you in the next chapter goes even deeper.

The journey through pain leads to a threshold that few healing modalities dare to cross, the revolutionary process of what I call, 'Dying to the Limited Self'. Here, we move beyond merely accepting our wounds or managing our pain. We enter the sacred territory where transformation moves beyond simply creating a better version of you and instead dissolves everything you have believed yourself to be.

If you have felt the limitations of traditional healing approaches, if you have experienced temporary relief only to find yourself continually caught in the same patterns, what follows offers a different path entirely. It is about discovering what exists on the other side of your carefully constructed identity, where genuine freedom awaits.

Take a deep breath as you turn the page. The journey ahead asks for courage, but it promises something beyond improvement or healing. It offers the possibility of rebirth into your truest nature.

Part III

CHAPTER NINE
Dying to the Limited Self

In the previous chapter, we explored how pain serves as a portal to freedom and how meeting it directly, without resistance, can transform our relationship with life itself. Now, we must journey even deeper; we must confront what lies beyond the acceptance of pain: the revolutionary process of Dying to the Limited Self. I invite you to take a moment and to feel into your body and sense what weight the word 'dying' carries in your body. In our culture it is wrapped in fear and finality and I want to offer a rewriting in the words to come. In saying this, if you feel any sense of instability around actually wanting to live I invite you to seek immediate and thorough support.

The 'dying' I am speaking of here is not physical. It is energetic, emotional and spiritual and it is the mechanism for liberation that creates the most profound transformation possible. This path recognises a radical truth: true freedom comes from realising you are already Whole and allowing the limitations that shroud your Wholeness to release completely.

The expansive space that became my home during my spontaneous out-of-body experience was not a destination I could simply visit once and claim as conquered territory. When I returned to my body on that beach all those years ago, I carried within me what I can only describe as a transmission, a cellular knowing of what lay beyond the limitations of identity, beyond the prison of addiction, beyond the familiar walls of who I thought I had to be to survive. But knowing and living are two different territories entirely. What I discovered in the months and years that followed was that accessing this profound state of Consciousness, this potent space between death and rebirth, required something far more demanding than I had initially understood. It required me to transform my entire life into a laboratory of Consciousness.

The Daily Practice of Dying to the Limited Self

What emerged was a stark realisation: if I wanted to maintain access to that Consciousness, I had to be willing to die to myself on a daily basis. This is the actual practice of releasing my attachment to the limited, wounded identity that kept me separate from that Divine, expanded connection, from Source.

I began to notice that every time I clung to a familiar pattern: seeking validation to avoid feeling unworthy, staying in situations that felt safe but limiting, numbing myself through various addictions, abandoning myself to receive love, I was choosing the prison of the known over the freedom of the void. The very behaviours that had once helped me survive were now the barriers between me and the truth I had tasted.

This practice required tremendous courage. It demanded that I meet my pain head-on, that I traverse the very territories I had spent a lifetime avoiding. Instead of seeking reassurance or distraction, I learned to breathe into the sensation and ask:
What part of me needs to die here?
What identity am I clinging to that is keeping me from the truth?

When I was clear on the pattern I set to work. Firstly, it was necessary to remove myself from the space where my addiction got fed and to restrain myself from continuing in it. This might be a relationship, behaviour pattern, work aspect, family dynamic or unhealthy habit. The removal was important so I could no longer feed off the false, external energy.

It felt like putting myself in a high level, spiritual rehab. The motivation to hold myself firmly relied on a deep understanding of what I was doing and how I was liberating myself and my reality. As my limited identity was literally being starved of the energy it craved, the Pain Portal would surge and I would get pulled deep into the void of inner sensation and stretch my nervous system to hold myself through the release of the density. When you do this completely, it feels like you are 'dying'.

This death is energetic, visceral and cathartic. It relies on you being the overarching Consciousness to hold yourself through the process. Conscious that no matter how painful it gets, it is simply the human attachment to pattern, sensation and the known. As you begin to feel the release, a void emerges, a pure completion zone. There is nothing to do, just rest into the Unknown and allow the Source of self to begin to flow.

It may start as a trickle and becomes a surge of infinite energy, generating and moving within every cell. The quotient of light activates and evolves every aspect of you, within you and all around you. All the energy that had been seeking external control and survival becomes available for the authentic self to create from Source. You have shifted your current and created energetic self-sufficiency and complete liberation from the pattern. You become the conduit of Source and the expression of it all around you. A life force rises within and you begin to truly remember who you are and why you are here.

I believe this is one of the greatest evolutionary pathways for humanity and the offering is for you to explore it fully for yourself. So let us become aware of the steps that we will take to facilitate this profound transformation.

The Phases of Dying to Self

Raising Consciousness of Where you are Trapped

You will feel a sense of uneasiness in your life, as if there is something just below the surface that is affecting you but you may not be able to discern what it is. From here you begin to observe yourself deeply, your thoughts, feelings and behaviours. You begin to ask yourself: *How am I showing up in this space?* From this questioning you start to see and feel the compulsions and drives to do repetitive things to create an Illusion of Safety around you. You become aware of the addiction and start to feel the fear pulsing beneath this space.

Stopping the Engagement with the Addictive Patterns

This is when you become clear that you are engaging in looping thought forms and behaviours and consciously restrain yourself from the predictable action that gives you some form of relief from your pain and fear. This denying the predictable path starts to create a sense of agitation, overwhelm and unease within. This will begin to build and the feeling that: *if I don't do that thing, I will die,* begins to arise.

Increasing the Pain Portal

This is where you become aware there is deep pain within your body and mind. Instead of turning away you step closer and closer. You activate and increase the sensations and stay with the feelings that arise, knowing the pain is real and the story you have told about it is an illusion. The presence of this pain takes you to another level, a huge cathartic wave of emotion can roll through the body and might begin to feel like you cannot function under its weight. So you surrender to it fully, knowing there is nowhere to go, nothing to do, but allow this limited version of yourself to be released.

Experiencing the Catharsis

Being in a safe physical place where you can go through this journey is so important and ultimately having someone who knows the experience you are going through and is there to let you know it is safe to allow the limited self to release can be very reassuring. This process is incredibly potent and conscious. The ways people release emotion can be varied, for some it is an immense stillness and collapse, for others it feels like a panic attack and complete overwhelm, for others it involves a purging of the body. The most important thing is that we are creating space for releasing the stored emotional density.

The In-Between and Beyond

When the pain has been released, a pervasive calm enters the system. Some describe it like a 'rebirth' where your authentic self emerges, liberated from the pain and limitation. A new level of trust in self arises and an alignment to truth beyond the illusions becomes apparent. More freedom, more awareness and a lightness enters. At the same time the self is no longer operating in a limited loop, so there is no clear path and you enter into the Unknown. Resting here in the In-Between and not feeling pushed out into the world is important while the internal reorientation takes place. You will begin to realise that this space is where true creation can take place.

Learning to Distinguish Death from Dissolution

One of the most crucial skills I had to develop was learning to recognise the difference between true identity release and psychological dissolution. In those early years, there were moments when the dissolution of identity felt terrifying rather than liberating. I had to learn the difference between the limited identity death that leads to greater Wholeness and the type of dissolution that leads to fragmentation.

True Dying to the Limited Self always led me back to the connected space of infinite Wholeness and unconditional love and ultimately a greater relationship with life. It was accompanied by a sense of coming home, even when it was painful. Psychological dissolution, on the other hand, felt like falling apart without a foundation, like losing myself without accessing something greater. The key was learning to die with Consciousness rather than simply falling apart. This meant developing the capacity to witness my own process, to remain present as an observer even as the observed identity crumbled. It meant cultivating what I came to understand as internal safety that allowed for the release of the limited version of myself while simultaneously expanding my connection to the Divine.

The Resistance of the Psyche

My psyche did not surrender gracefully to this process. There were months when every cell in my body seemed to resist the ongoing practice of dying to what felt familiar and safe. The part of me that had learned to survive through control, through maintaining a certain image, through avoiding pain at all costs, fought fiercely against this dissolution. I encountered many faces of resistance: the voice that told me I was being self-indulgent, that I needed to be stable and consistent, that this spiritual pursuit was taking me away from my responsibilities. That if I stopped important aspects of my life, I would fail, miss out, lose everything. There was the fear that if I kept dying to myself, there would be nothing left and that I would lose my capacity to function in the world.

What I learned through years of meeting this resistance was that it contained huge amounts of Consciousness. Each layer of resistance pointed to another attachment, another identity structure that was keeping me from greater freedom. The resistance became something to explore with curiosity and compassion rather than overcome.

I have practiced Dying to the Limited Self across every area of my life. My relationships with family and partners, my connection to money, my understanding of purpose, my living circumstances and health. Each time, I have had to relinquish the control that came from seeking something external to make me feel safe. I have had to stop perceiving reality through the lens of my wounds, which only confirmed the very limitations I was trying to escape.

Instead, something beautiful began to emerge. I started to feel a deep connectivity to the creative, expanded aspect of myself. This felt different from manifestation or trying to make things happen. This part of me was simply aligned to the frequency of freedom itself. From there everything began formulating around me in ways that showed me everything was fluid and everything was possible. I understand the thought of 'letting go' in order to grow feels paradoxical, right? Our conditioned minds tell us we should hold tighter, control more, ensure outcomes. But this Dying to the Limited

Self reveals the deeper truth of surrender. In that surrender, you discover that what you thought was keeping you safe was in fact keeping you small and disconnected. What felt like protection was reinforcing imprisonment. Instead, the dying reveals the living. The active letting go reveals the receiving. The surrender reveals the true creative power that has been waiting within you all along and then the experience of truly living begins.

It became increasingly clear that my core motivation was to experience energetic, emotional and physical sovereignty here. **To live as a free being.** To realise myself as a Divine human in a physical body. It was then that I realised I am the ultimate creator of everything in my experience. The more connected to the light, information and Consciousness I became, the easier I could bend reality to align with my highest timeline. It was as if every death created an uplevelling and receiving of the next level of life.

The Gradual Building of Capacity

What surprised me most about this journey was how gradual the building of capacity had to be. I could not simply leap from my initial experience into a state of constant Consciousness. Like any skill, the ability to consciously die and rebirth requires practice, patience and progressive development. I began to recognise that there were different levels of dying available to me. Some days, I could only manage to die to a small addiction of having to overgive to others. Other days, I felt capable of releasing entire aspects of my identity: my role as the one who had to hold everything together, my perception that I needed to earn love through performance.

The practice became one of meeting myself where I was, rather than demanding that I access the deepest levels of Consciousness every time. I learned to honour the small deaths as much as the profound ones, understanding that each release was building my capacity for the next level of surrender.

As my practice deepened, I began to recognise that life was constantly offering me portals for conscious dying. Conflict in relationships became opportunities to die to my need to be loved.

Financial challenges became invitations to release my attachment to security as identity. My children's resistance to my expectations became chances to die to my need to control outcomes. What had initially felt like problems to solve revealed themselves as perfectly designed opportunities for evolution. The pain I had spent so much energy avoiding became the gateway to greater Consciousness. The fear that arose when things felt uncertain was showing me exactly where my identity was still attached to the familiar, predictable, known.

This recognition transformed everything. Instead of trying to manage my external circumstances to feel safe, I began to use every challenge as information about where I was still clinging to limitations. The portal of dying to limited self was constantly available in the moment-to-moment experience of being human and it gifted me the most beautiful relationship to life. **Dying to the Limited Self is when you begin to truly live.**

The Trap of Protective Modalities

Something that I have noticed protects us from the liberation of Dying to the Limited Self is our eagerness to heal. We often reach for techniques and modalities that promise quick relief: EMDR, NLP, positive affirmations, manifestation practices, and countless other approaches. While these modalities can serve a purpose, they frequently become another form of psychological bypassing, creating a 'protective coating' over our core pain.

This coating might help us function and feel better temporarily, but in fact it prolongs our true healing journey. Think of it like applying layers of beautiful wallpaper over crumbling walls. The surface looks better; we might feel more functional, but underneath the structure continues to deteriorate. Each new technique, each positive affirmation, each round of energy clearing adds another layer of protection between us and the pain we must eventually face. We become invested in maintaining these protective layers, mistaking them for healing itself.

Consider Jo, who had spent over $200,000 on various healing

modalities over fifteen years. She had tried everything from reiki to psychology to energy healing. Each approach provided temporary relief and insights, yet she found herself caught in the same core patterns, particularly in her intimate relationships. "I became what you might call a professional seeker," she told me. "I could speak the language of every modality, explain my wounds with perfect psychological clarity, and even facilitate certain practices for others. But underneath all this knowledge and technique, I still operated from the same wounded core. Each new modality just gave me a more sophisticated way to manage my pain rather than truly transform it."

Instead of adding more techniques to our transformational toolkit, we must develop the courage to be naked before our own pain. This means facing our wounds without the buffer of positive thinking, without the comfort of techniques, without the protection of spiritual concepts.

The Conscious Death

Unlike the esoteric, spontaneous spiritual awakening that comes from a near-death experience or an intense psychedelic journey, this Dying to the Limited Self is conscious. It happens via Consciousness. You build up the internal essence and grace of knowing that the wounded illusion is no longer serving you and you commit yourself to the death of the illusion of you.

This act takes bravery. Your nervous system tells you that the design of your external reality, even your sense of survival, depends on the perpetuation of your fear patterns. Yet when you take that pattern, witness it completely, and actively assert that you will no longer feed that pattern in a predictable way, your whole self steps into a realm of the Unknown. The self that has been organised around fear is dissolving. The identity constructed to avoid pain is falling away. The strategies that seemed essential for safety are being surrendered. This feels like death because it is: the death of an old way of being to make room for something new to emerge.

June described this inner death process vividly. "Facing my

fear of unworthiness felt like dying. Everything in me screamed to run back to the familiar protection strategies of achievement, control, perfectionism. But I stayed with the raw feeling, the exposure, the vulnerability. There was a moment when I felt completely undone, as if my very self was dissolving. And then, on the other side of that surrender, I found something I never expected: a sense of worth that didn't depend on anything external, a freedom I hadn't known was possible. I found myself."

The Mechanics of Dying to the Limited Self

True transformation requires a complete relinquishment of everything you have been doing to maintain your Wound Reality. This is because your wound lives primarily in your nervous system, creating a complex web of thoughts, emotions and behaviours that perpetually recreate the same limited reality. Every reaction, every coping mechanism, every strategy for control feeds this wounded program. Think of it like a machine that keeps running as long as you supply it with energy; your energy. When you commit to Dying to the Limited Self, you:

- Stop participating in every aspect of your wounded programming
- Break the addiction to familiar thought, emotional and behavioural patterns
- Transverse the Pain Portal
- Allow yourself to enter the void state
- Rest in the space between your old reality and what is emerging

This is an intensive process: moving from your Wound Reality to the In-Between Space will feel like 'dying' because, energetically, that is exactly what is happening. Your entire system has been emanating the same reality from the fracture of your wound for your whole existence. When you withdraw from these patterns, it creates an intense withdrawal period, much like entering rehabilitation.

Here is what I have discovered: the limited aspect of yourself, the part that clings to control, that seeks external confirmation in all forms, that operates from wound patterns, keeps you attached to a limited version of your life. Every time you challenge this reality and release your grip on these patterns, you experience an upgrade of your external circumstances that feels so aligned and surprising, it surpasses anything your limited mind could have designed.

Ren's story illustrates this process with striking clarity. A successful therapist herself, she had built an identity around being the 'healed healer', someone who had done her own work and could now guide others. Yet beneath this carefully constructed professional identity lay a deep wound of feeling Unloved that sabotaged her personal relationships and creative expression.

During our work together, Ren realised that her very commitment to 'being healed' protected her against feeling the core pain of her lack of true connection. Even with her therapeutic skills, including her ability to name patterns, regulate emotions, and maintain perspective, they had become barriers to the raw experience her system needed to process.

"I realised I was using my therapeutic knowledge to maintain control," she told me. "Every time the pain of being alone would start to surface, I would immediately analyse it, understand it, contextualise it, anything to avoid actually feeling it directly. My expertise has become my greatest obstacle."

Ren's breakthrough came when she committed to what felt like professional and personal absence. She stopped using every therapeutic tool she had mastered. She allowed herself to enter the terrifying territory of not knowing, not managing, not maintaining control. For the first time in decades, she let herself experience the raw, unfiltered pain of feeling Unloved without trying to heal it, understand it, or transform it. "The dying to self was surrendering to layers buried so deep I had no idea they were there. When you let go, there's pain like you've never felt before but you have to trust the process and stay with it. When that pain I'd been holding onto for so long finally released, there was this rebirth. I wasn't the person I created just to survive anymore. All the pretenses, the fakeness, it all dissolved. There's this getting to know the real me for the first time. When old patterns would surface, I had this awareness: 'This isn't who I am anymore.' There's peace within now, and freedom to just be myself. It's like the rose-colored glasses I'd always worn were suddenly gone. I could see everything with clear vision. The pain was real, the release hurt as I was literally dying to who I was and becoming what I was always meant to be. Just like a butterfly emerging from its chrysalis."

The Connection to Everything

At the heart of this process lies what I call 'quantum projection'. We are continuously creating our reality from our internal design patterns, but most of us remain completely unconscious of this process. Every thought pattern, every emotional charge, every perception system we carry acts as a frequency that we broadcast into the quantum field. This field responds by organising experiences that match our internal state.

When our design patterns operate unconsciously and carry our wounds, we project a limited reality back to ourselves. If you carry a deep Unworthy Wound, for example, you will unconsciously seek out and create experiences that confirm this perception. You might find yourself in relationships where you are undervalued, careers where you are overlooked, or situations where you consistently feel like you are not enough. This is quantum projection in action.

The fascinating part is that we often fight against these very experiences we are creating, which only reinforces the pattern. We become trapped in a loop where our wounded Consciousness creates circumstances that wound us further, confirming our original programming.

But when we become conscious of these limitations through seeing everything around us as a mirror to our internal being and choose to die to our grip on them, something profound happens at a quantum level. We release into a deep inner connection with Source Consciousness. Our frequency shifts from wound to Wholeness, from limitation to infinite possibility. That connection then projects a reality of expansiveness and flow. This creates an entirely new level of truth and meaning in our lived experience.

The quantum field responds to this shift by reorganising around our new frequency. Opportunities appear that align with our expanded Consciousness. Relationships transform or new ones emerge that reflect our inner Wholeness. Resources flow in ways that support our authentic expression. It is as if reality itself conspires to match our internal state of freedom.

The Critical Void Space

Yet this new creation does not always appear instantaneously and that is not because you are doing it wrong. True change also needs the participation of the alchemy of time. Once the energetic dying occurs, a new space of 'nothingness' emerges. This nothingness is not what it seems, it is a potent space of birthing potential. Instead of a fixed design projecting from you, you are in an open, infinite, space.

The capacity to rest in nothing is the greatest challenge. Not rushing to fill the space, not grasping for new understanding, not trying to 'figure it out'. When you rest in the 'void space' of nowhere to go, nothing to do, no one to be, nothing to grasp onto, the real transformation happens. This void is your connection to Source, it is everything and nothing simultaneously, you cannot grasp a fixed reality from this state.

It is crucial to understand that this void emerges when you stop feeding the addiction externally with your wounded patterns. Most of us spend our entire lives running from this void using relationships, work, substances, spiritual seeking or countless other strategies to avoid feeling the emptiness. When you consciously choose to stop these external fillers, you enter a space of profound nothingness: nowhere to go, nothing to do, no one to become. This is the void where the deepest transformation occurs.

Think of this process as going cold turkey from a profound energetic addiction. Just as a physical addiction creates biochemical dependencies that cause withdrawal symptoms when the substance is removed, we develop deep, energetic addictions to external sources of validation, distraction and identity. The difference is that this energetic addiction runs far deeper than any physical dependency, it is woven into the very fabric of how we have constructed our reality. Breaking this external energetic flow is everything. For your entire life, you have been investing your life force outward into relationships, achievements, possessions, perceptions, anything really to avoid coming home to the Source within.

The initial stage of this practice requires you to sever that outward flow completely, redirecting your energy inward. But before the inward flow can establish itself, you must endure the emptiness that emerges when the outward flow stops. The void space is the quantum field of pure potential that exists before new patterns emerge. When you rest here:

+ It will feel uncomfortable and foreign
+ You will be exploring 'being' rather than 'doing' at the deepest level
+ Your wound's addictive patterns will flare up intensely
+ You must stay until all compulsions subside
+ You will be creating safety

This process can take weeks, months or even up to a year. You are consistently peeling back layers of the wound, processing them and resting back into the quantum void space of nothing. Each layer brings its own challenges:

+ The initial intensity of withdrawal from familiar patterns
+ Waves of deeply stored emotional and somatic release
+ Periods of disorientatiown as your reality restructures
+ The temptation to fall back into old ways of being

For Simon, a builder who had built his life around achievement and control, the void space initially felt like an unbearable torture. "My whole existence was structured around doing, fixing, accomplishing," he explained. "The void was like kryptonite to everything I thought I was. My system interpreted it as death, not metaphorical death, but actual biological extinction."

In the early stages of his process, Simon would move into the void for short periods before being overwhelmed by survival mechanisms and urgent impulses to check email, make calls, create plans, anything to escape the nothingness. Each time, I would guide him back, extending his capacity to remain in the space of non-doing.

"What I discovered in that void was beyond anything I could have imagined," he shared. "At first, it was just emptiness and terror. But as I developed the capacity to stay, something changed. The void wasn't empty at all, it was filled with a presence so vast and so intimate that it made all my striving seem like a desperate distraction. I realised I'd been running from this presence my entire life, building an identity specifically designed to avoid it."

As for Georgina, a single mother and artist, she had structured her entire life around maintaining security for herself and her child. Every decision, from her choice of career to her daily routines, was filtered through the lens of ensuring stability. This pattern had roots in her childhood experience of poverty and unpredictability, creating a wound of insecurity that dominated her nervous system. The invitation to release her security structures felt impossible at first. "You're asking me to let go of what keeps my child safe," she protested. But as we explored deeper, she realised that her security patterns had literally created a life of limitation and fear, one that she was unconsciously passing to her daughter. Her constant worry about security generated the very insecurity she was trying to protect against.

Georgina's breakthrough came during a weekend retreat where she committed to completely releasing her security programming. For forty-eight hours, she allowed herself to experience the raw overwhelm that emerged when she stopped participating in familiar patterns of control, planning, and protection. "It was the most intense experience of my life," she recalled. "I felt waves of pure biological panic moving through my body, heart racing, breath restricted, muscles contracting. But instead of going into my usual management, I just let it move through me completely. At one point, I found myself curled on the floor, shaking and crying like a child. The depth of the pain and sadness was almost unbearable. But instead of trying to stop it, I just kept saying 'Yes' to whatever was arising."

By the second day, something remarkable had shifted. After a particularly intense wave of sensation had moved through her system, Georgina experienced what she described as 'complete energetic surrender'. She explained to me, "It's not like my fears disappeared, it is more that I completely stopped fighting against what I was feeling. In that surrender, I discovered a safety in my pain that was so profound that it made all my protective structures seem primitive and unnecessary. I realised that what I'd been calling 'security' was instead a complex prison that required constant maintenance. When I fully released it, I discovered that reality itself could hold me in a way that my control mechanisms never could."

When she returned to her life, her trust in everything had shifted exponentially. Georgina continued to create, but from a new pure energy of her inner Source. She discovered herself in a flow of natural abundance and inner safety that radically transformed her whole life.

Identifying Where You Need to Die

The most powerful places where you are asked to experience Dying to the Limited Self are often the ones you are most afraid to examine. Your system will resist looking here because these are the core structures of your survival programming. But this resistance itself is your compass, pointing directly to where transformation is possible Ask yourself:

✦ What would be 'the death of me' if I lost it?
✦ Where am I most afraid to look or go in my life?
✦ What am I desperately trying to maintain or control?
✦ What feels completely non-negotiable to my survival?

Paradoxically, the places where you feel most safe are often where you are most deeply ensnared. The relationships, perceptions, identities and patterns that you think are protecting you may in truth be the bars of your prison. You are being asked to honestly examine where you have built walls instead of wings. Signs it is time to die to self:

1. You have reached an evolutionary impasse and are looping in limitation
2. You are caught in repetitive patterns despite understanding them
3. There is a gap between your current reality and your deeper knowing
4. You feel energetically dead or stagnant in certain areas
5. Your commitments and identities feel like heavy obligations rather than choices

Anna, a spiritual teacher with a devoted following, came to me when she recognised she had reached such an impasse. On the surface, her life appeared successful. She had written books, led retreats, and helped thousands of people. But privately, she felt an increasing sense of constriction and inauthenticity. "I've become trapped in my own teaching," she confessed. "What started as genuine insight has hardened into a structure I have to maintain. I find myself saying things I'm no longer sure are true, performing a version of spirituality that feels increasingly hollow. But I don't know how to stop as people depend on me and honestly, this identity is all I have."

Anna discovered that her spiritual identity, the very thing that had once liberated her, had become her energetic siphon. Her fear of examining this identity was why it needed to die. The evolutionary threshold she faced was not about becoming a better teacher or developing more refined techniques; it was about letting the entire structure of 'spiritual teacher Anna' collapse completely.

The process was not about abandoning her community or responsibilities. It was about allowing the identity that had crystallised around her role to dissolve, creating space for something more authentic to emerge. This required her to face her deepest fear: that without this spiritual identity, she might be nothing at all. "I had to confront the possibility that everything I'd built was a protection mechanism," she shared. "That underneath all my teaching about surrender and presence, I was actually terrified of truly surrendering into the Unknown. My spiritual identity had become the ultimate shield against the very vulnerability I was teaching others to embrace."

The Blind Spots

What makes this work challenging is that our most limiting patterns often hide in blind spots. In the areas so normalised in our experience that they become invisible. These patterns are usually:

✦ Heavily guarded by routines and commitments
✦ Justified by rational-sounding explanations
✦ Supported by social and cultural norms
✦ Deeply embedded in your identity structure

This is why Dying to the Limited Self requires radical honesty. You must be willing to question everything, especially the parts of your life that seem 'fine' or 'normal'. The constructs and identities you have built around your work, relationships, parenting, health, spirituality, really any area, can become a fortress of limitation if it is protecting a Core Wound.

Rebecca, a dedicated mother of three, came to me when she realised that her identity as the 'perfect mother' had become a trap, not just for her but for her children as well. "I've built my entire life around being an exceptional parent," she explained. "I've read every book, attended every workshop, structured my entire career around being available for my kids. Yet something feels increasingly off. The more perfect I try to be as a mother, the more I feel like I'm suffocating both myself and my children."

What made this pattern particularly difficult to identify was its social approval. Everyone celebrated Rebecca's dedication to motherhood. Her sacrifice was seen as noble, her commitment as admirable. Yet beneath this socially sanctioned identity lay an Unworthy Wound that she was unconsciously playing out through her parenting. "I realised that my 'perfect mothering' wasn't about what my children needed, it was about proving my own worth," she shared. "Every time I sacrificed my needs for theirs, every time I exhausted myself meeting their every desire, I was actually trying to heal my own childhood wound of feeling fundamentally Unworthy of care and attention."

Rebecca's breakthrough came when she allowed herself to question this identity completely. This was not about becoming a 'bad mother' but about letting the entire construct of perfect motherhood die so something more authentic could emerge. As she stopped participating in this identity, intense waves of shame, grief, and terror moved through her system. "I felt like I was committing a kind of sacrilege," she explained. "Like I was betraying not just my children but some fundamental law of what a good woman should be. The guilt was overwhelming at times. But beneath that guilt, I discovered a raw truth: my children never needed a perfect mother. They needed a real one. Someone who could model authentic humanity rather than perpetual sacrifice."

As Rebecca allowed the identity of 'perfect mother' to die, something remarkable emerged in her relationship with her children. "By dying to who I thought I needed to be for them, I finally became who they actually needed," she reflected. "Not a perfect mother, but a real human being in an authentic relationship with other real human beings. The irony is that this is what I thought I was giving them all along, but my wound had distorted everything, turning love into control and care into limitation." Without the pressure of perfection, genuine connection flourished. Her children began sharing more honestly, no longer feeling the subtle burden of her sacrifice. Most importantly, they began developing the very self-reliance and inner authority that had been inadvertently suppressed by Rebecca's over-functioning.

Preparing for the Death Journey

As you identify where you need to die to self, it is essential to prepare consciously for this journey. This preparation involves:

+ **Stopping Addiction:** No longer committing yourself to the predictable emotional, behavioural or thought addictions.

+ **Creating Sacred Space**: Designate time and physical space where you can be completely uninterrupted during the intense phases of this process. This might mean taking retreat time, re-arranging your schedule or setting clear boundaries with others.

+ **Releasing External Obligations:** Wherever possible, temporarily reduce responsibilities that require your wounded patterns to function. This is about creating space where you can stop performing your habitual roles.

+ **Finding Attuned Support**: While this journey is ultimately yours alone, having witnesses who understand this process can be invaluable. No-one can 'fix' you, but someone trained in supporting deep processing can hold space without trying to rescue you from the necessary dissolution.

+ **Surrendering Outcome:** Release all expectations about what should happen or how you should feel. The dying process follows its own intelligence and timeline, which rarely conforms to your mind's ideas about transformation.

+ **Committing to Completion:** Make a clear commitment to seeing this process through, even when your system creates urgent impulses to escape the intensity. This commitment becomes your anchor when the death feels unbearable.

The one thing that will keep you from taking this journey is the illusion of having to survive: *What will happen if I am not working, not showing up online or for others, not doing all the things I feel I need to do to make life happen?* You will realise that this is where your identity has been trapped in a survival identity, in a space of limitation. That space will have a set energetic pattern with very defined boundaries, reflective of the ones you are running within. It does not matter what your situation is, taking time out of the rampage of modern life is essential for this work. Some can find an afternoon, a Sunday, a week, some can find a larger chunk of time. It does not matter as it is the intention of the release of the grip, to liberate yourself more completely.

Sometimes it is not about clearing the space but instead receiving it when it arrives. This means being aware that when it calls, you answer. And a warning, you may not plan or prepare at all. There are no perfect conditions. Your only job is to make a clear, conscious choice to stop participating in your wounded patterns, creating enough space for the void to emerge and work its transformative magic. The more deliberately you enter this process, the more fully you can surrender to it, allowing each death to reveal the freedom that lies beyond identity.

In the next chapter, we will explore how to navigate the intense thresholds that arise as you fully commit to Dying to the Limited Self, traversing the Pain Portal to discover what exists beyond your wounded identity. We will examine specific death thresholds and the remarkable transformation that occurs when you allow yourself to die completely to what you thought you were, revealing the true self that has been waiting all along.

Consciousness is on the move.

CHAPTER TEN
The New Inner Orientation

My commitment to Dying to the Limited Self has been so profound and ongoing that I now feel a constant flow of reinvention and infinite energy in my being and creations. Breaking my energetic addiction to external patterns has created a profound void space where true transformation becomes possible. At the heart of my motivation is liberation and the gift of living as a sovereign being, free from wounding, addiction and false limitations.

However, this passage through the Pain Portal is not for the faint of heart. It requires courage and commitment, rare in our comfort-seeking culture. But those willing to face these thresholds will also discover something remarkable: what lies on the other side of your greatest fear is your most authentic expression, your deepest freedom and a way of being that transcends the limitations of your wounded identity.

Nicky expressed this beautifully when she said, "I can feel how I push my energy out in front of me like a bow wave to meet reality. It also creates an energetic safety zone around me. The problem is it takes the most colossal amount of energy to keep this force shield up and keeps me separate from life. I'm afraid of being engulfed by reality if I don't hold it at bay." This is the fear we are dying into, the fear of life itself, so we can finally live.

The Visceral Nature of Dying to the Limited Self

While many spiritual traditions speak of ego death, what I am describing goes far beyond a conceptual understanding of releasing the self. It is a profound physical process that your nervous system must navigate, quite literally feeling like death to every cell of your being.

When people speak of ego death, they often imagine it as releasing an intangible part of themselves such as their thoughts, perceptions or identification patterns. But true Dying to the Limited Self is intensely visceral. Your nervous system, which has spent years or even lifetimes building survival mechanisms, must step through what feels like actual death. This is why positive thinking or intellectual understanding alone can never create the profound transformation available through this practice.

Imagine your nervous system as a tightly wound coil of survival patterns. Each pattern represents a way you have learned to stay safe, to cope, to maintain some sense of control. When you begin Dying to the Limited Self you are asking this coil to completely unwind, to release its death grip on known reality. This can create intense physical sensations, waves of fear, trembling, dissociation, even feelings of suffocation or dissolution. Your body literally believes it is dying because, energetically, that is exactly what is happening.

This is where most people turn back. The intensity of physical sensation becomes too much and they retreat to the safety of their familiar patterns or seek refuge in spiritual concepts. But the true threshold of transformation lies just beyond this point of maximum discomfort. Your nervous system must learn to stay present with sensations it has spent lifetimes avoiding, to traverse the very experiences it believes will destroy it.

When you can stay present through this intense threshold, something remarkable happens. Your nervous system discovers that what it thought was death was ironically a doorway to greater life. The very pain it was protecting you from becomes the portal to liberation. This experience develops capacity within your system to move through these 'death' thresholds again and again, each time releasing into greater freedom and authenticity.

This is why true transformation cannot be rushed or bypassed. Your nervous system must be allowed to unwind at its own pace, to process each layer of stored pain and protection as it arises, trusting that each death leads to greater life. Amanda, a trauma survivor who had spent decades in various therapeutic modalities, described this visceral process with striking clarity. "Nothing in my previous healing work prepared me for the intensity of this inner death process. This wasn't about understanding my trauma or releasing emotion or changing perceptions. It was about my entire organism going through what felt like actual biological death."

In the early stages of her process, Amanda would experience waves of sensation. "It wasn't like a panic attack or emotional release," she explained. "It was as if every cell in my body was reorganising itself, letting go of patterns so fundamental that they felt wired into my DNA. There were moments when I couldn't breathe, when my heart felt like it was stopping, when I was certain I was actually dying." What made Amanda's journey possible was developing a relationship with Consciousness that could hold these extreme states without trying to change or escape them. "I had to learn to let my body go through what felt impossible, to trust something beyond my physical survival mechanisms. The key was recognising that what my body perceived as death wasn't actually threatening my existence, it was threatening my limited identity, my familiar reality, my sense of who I thought I was."

Consciousness as Your Anchor

When facing these death thresholds, it is crucial to understand that we are not trying to soothe or regulate the nervous system, as that would only create another form of protection. Instead, we are strengthening the Consciousness that knows the absolute safety and necessity of this process. This Consciousness exists beyond your survival mechanisms, beyond your pain, beyond even your current understanding of who you are.

This expanded Consciousness recognises that what feels like death to your nervous system is really a profound evolutionary opening. It understands that these overwhelming thresholds that feel like they might destroy you, are where your greatest liberation awaits. You will develop an unshakeable knowing that you are safe even in the complete dissolution of everything you think you are.

When your body is shaking, when your system is screaming that this is too much, this is where Consciousness must hold the deeper truth. These sensations are not signs that something is wrong; they are evidence that you are finally allowing the profound reorganisation your system has been waiting for. Your Consciousness becomes the unwavering witness that can hold space for this intensity without trying to change or escape it. In other expressions of the process it may feel like release into nothingness, a fundamental mental shift that breaks down barriers or a profound dropping of the weight of density.

However the moment arrives, think of it like this: your limited self experiences these thresholds as death because that is exactly what they are. The death of everything that has been holding you in limitation. Your Consciousness knows this death as a doorway to greater life. It recognises that each threshold you move through releases old pain and evolves your entire being into greater alignment with truth. This Consciousness does not need your nervous system to feel safe in order to proceed. In fact, it knows that the very feeling of safety your system seeks has been keeping you bound to old patterns. Instead, it holds the paradox that the most profound safety comes through being willing to feel completely unsafe, to let everything you have used to feel secure be stripped away.

When you anchor in this level of Consciousness, you develop an entirely different relationship with these death thresholds. Instead of seeing them as something to survive or manage, you recognise them as sacred portals of evolution. Your Consciousness becomes the steady flame that lights the way through each threshold, knowing with absolute certainty that what lies on the other side is worth every moment of commitment to this process. This is true spiritual maturity, not the capacity to avoid pain or maintain comfort, but the willingness to let Consciousness hold you as everything you think you are dies into greater truth. Each threshold becomes an opportunity to deepen this trust, to strengthen the knowing that you are safe even in complete dissolution, that every death is serving your highest evolution.

Navigating the Death Thresholds

The most challenging thresholds often arise in areas where your survival programming runs deepest. Understanding these specific gateways helps Consciousness recognise and welcome them as evolutionary catalysts rather than threats to be avoided.

The Identity Death Threshold

This threshold emerges when you face the dissolution of who you think you are. It might arise when your career, relationships, or core perceptions are dismantled. Your system will create intense sensations of groundlessness, as if you are falling through space with nothing to hold onto. Consciousness knows this falling is exactly what is needed as it is the release of every false identity you have constructed to feel safe. Instead of trying to find new ground, consciousness allows the complete release into the Unknown.

Michelle encountered this threshold when her entire professional identity began to unravel. After twenty years of defining herself through academic and career success, she found herself experiencing inexplicable panic attacks during work meetings. These attacks intensified until she could not function in the role she had spent her life mastering. "I felt like I was having a complete psychological breakdown," she told me. "Everything I'd used to define myself was suddenly inaccessible. I couldn't think clearly, couldn't perform, couldn't maintain the confident persona I'd built over decades. It was as if my mind itself was dissolving."

Rather than trying to fix this dissolution through medication, therapy, or pushing through, Michelle courageously chose to follow it all the way down. She took a leave of absence and committed to the inner dying process. What she discovered shocked her: the panic attacks were not symptoms of breakdown but powerful evolutionary catalysts trying to dismantle an identity that had become too limiting for her soul's expression.

"As I allowed myself to completely fall apart, to stop being 'Michelle the success story' and just be the raw, unfiltered awareness watching everything dissolve, something extraordinary happened. I discovered a sense of self so much vaster than the identity I'd been maintaining. The uncertainty I'd been fighting against turned out to be the very freedom I'd always longed for."

The Biological Death Threshold

The biological death threshold is perhaps the most intense gateway, where your body actually feels like it is dying. You might experience sensations that feel like not being able to breathe, your heart might ache, you might shake or become very hot or cold. Your nervous system interprets these sensations as literal death because energetically, that is what is happening: you are dying to an entire layer of biological patterning. Consciousness holds you steady here, knowing that this biological restructuring is essential for evolution.

Nicole, who had survived severe childhood trauma, encountered this threshold during a retreat. As she allowed herself to fully feel sensations she had been running from for decades, her body began to physically reveal where it was holding the pain. "My breathing became shallow and irregular, my limbs went completely cold, and I experienced a wave of overwhelm," she recounted. "Something deeper in me knew that this wasn't a medical emergency but a necessary passage through the density that had been stored and was now releasing."

As Nicole stayed with these intense sensations, allowing her biological systems to move through what felt like death, something profound happened. Her body began to release holding patterns that had been locked in her tissues since childhood, patterns so deep they were affecting her organ functioning, immune response, and endocrine system.

"It wasn't pleasant, but it was necessary," she explained. "My body had to experience the release of survival mechanisms that had been running unconsciously my entire life. As I moved through this threshold, I could literally feel my nervous system rewiring itself, creating new pathways that weren't organised around trauma and protection."

The Relational Death Threshold

When you start dying to old patterns, your relationships will be profoundly affected. You will feel the death of familiar dynamics, the dissolution of old agreements and ways of connecting. Your system might panic, trying to preserve these relationships exactly as they are. Yet, Consciousness recognises that true connection can only emerge through the death of these limiting patterns and the true connection to the Source of you.

Jennifer faced this threshold when she began the deep work of dying to her people-pleasing patterns. As a lifelong 'good girl', who had built her entire social world around being helpful, supportive, and never causing conflict, she was terrified to discover that authentic expression meant allowing some relationships to fundamentally change or even end.

"I realised that many of my closest relationships were actually based on my willingness to abandon myself," she shared. "When I stopped participating in these dynamics, when I began speaking truth instead of what others wanted to hear, setting boundaries instead of always accommodating, and expressing needs instead of just meeting everyone else's, it was like dropping a bomb in my social world."

Several friendships that Jennifer had considered essential to her survival simply could not survive her authenticity. Family relationships that had seemed loving were revealed to be complex webs of obligation and control. Her marriage entered a crisis that required complete reorganisation.

"It felt like social death," she explained. "Every time I chose authenticity over my habitual patterns, I was choosing to lose connections I thought I needed to survive. My nervous system created intense sensations of abandonment and isolation, screaming that I would end up completely alone if I continued on this path."

By staying present through this relational death threshold, Jennifer discovered something remarkable: the very relationships that could evolve with her became deeper and more authentic than she had ever imagined possible. New connections emerged that resonated with her authentic expression. And most surprisingly, she discovered a capacity for solitude that revealed inner resources she never knew she possessed.

"The relationships I have now aren't perfect, but they're real," she told me. "They're based on who I actually am, not who I pretend to be. And I've discovered that the connection I was really longing for all along wasn't with other people, it was with myself, with life, with a presence that can only be felt when I'm not abandoning myself to please others."

The Reality Death Threshold

The reality death threshold occurs when your entire construction of reality begins to dissolve. Everything you thought you knew, every way you have made sense of the world, starts falling apart. Your system might create intense fear or confusion as your familiar reality construct crumbles. Consciousness welcomes this dissolution, knowing it makes space for a more expanded reality to emerge.

Alex, a rational scientist who had built his worldview on materialist principles, encountered this threshold during a period of spontaneous spiritual awakening. What began as curious anomalies in his experience, synchronicities, intuitive knowings, non-ordinary states of Consciousness, eventually accelerated into a complete dismantling of his reality structure.

"It was the most terrifying experience of my life," he recounted. "Everything I'd used to make sense of the world started breaking down. The solid, predictable, material universe I'd built my career studying began to reveal itself as something far more mysterious and multidimensional. My mind couldn't integrate what was happening."

For several months, Alex moved through what traditional psychiatry might label as psychosis but what many wisdom traditions recognise as a spiritual emergency, a radical reorganisation of Consciousness and perception. His nervous system created intense fear as familiar reference points dissolved. Linear time became fluid, solid objects revealed themselves as energy, and the boundary between self and world became increasingly porous.

"I was losing my mind, but not in the way people think of madness," he explained. "I was losing a particular mind, a specific way of organising reality that I'd been taught was the only valid one. What I discovered beyond that limited perspective was both terrifying and more beautiful than anything I could have imagined."

By allowing himself to move through this reality death threshold without rushing to re-establish familiar meaning structures, Alex discovered a way of knowing that transcended yet included his scientific training. His Consciousness expanded to hold multiple dimensions of reality simultaneously, connecting him to a universe far richer and more alive than the one he had previously inhabited.

"I didn't abandon reason," he clarified. "I found its proper place within a much larger ecology of knowing. My scientific mind became a tool rather than my master, allowing me to move between different ways of perceiving and making meaning. What looked like the death of reality was in fact an invitation into a far more complex and beautiful one."

The Control Death Threshold

This gateway appears when you face the complete relinquishment of control. Not just external control but also the deeper patterns of managing your internal experience. Your system might create sensations of extreme vulnerability or exposure. Consciousness knows that true power emerges only when you fully release the illusion of control, allowing life to move through you without resistance and moving you into the vast Unknown.

Sophia, a business owner and self-described 'control freak', encountered this threshold when a series of health challenges left her completely dependent on others for basic needs. What began as temporary assistance became a prolonged journey into what she experienced as a terrifying surrender of autonomy.

"I had built my entire identity around being capable, independent, and in control of every aspect of my life," she explained.

"Suddenly, I couldn't find the drive to do anything, my system went into complete panic. Not just about the practical challenges but about the existential terror of not being in control."

As Sophia's condition persisted, she faced a profound choice: continue fighting against her circumstances, creating additional suffering through resistance, or surrender to the death of her control patterns. With guidance, she chose the latter, allowing herself to experience the raw vulnerability of complete release without trying to manage or transcend it.

"It felt like I was being turned inside out," she shared. "Every cell in my body was screaming about the danger of letting go of control. I had to face my deepest fear: that without my strategies for managing life, I would be completely annihilated."

What Sophia discovered through this threshold was a paradoxical truth: her strategies for maintaining control had been limiting her access to a much deeper power. As she allowed the death of these control patterns, something unexpected emerged. She discovered a capacity to be with life exactly as it was unfolding, to receive support without manipulation, to flow with circumstances rather than constantly fighting against them.

"I had to die to everything I thought made me powerful," she reflected. "What I found beyond that death was a power so much greater than control: the power of complete surrender to life itself. I discovered that true strength comes from having the courage to remain open no matter what arises."

A Reminder about Intensity

It is important to be aware that the various layers of release may come with physical symptoms and cathartic expression, ranging from intense to what can feel extreme. It may be allowing deep sadness and grief you have been avoiding or unaware of to well up and be freely expressed. Maybe it is facing and acknowledging an aspect of yourself that you wish did not exist. Whatever way the shift happens for you, is no less evolutionary. As the light of your awareness gradually reveals your addictions, the compulsion to old ways of being, reacting and feeling, simply ceases.

You may look around and see that on the surface nothing has changed but deep within, you realise it is all different now. You have fundamentally shifted from the inside out and your relationship to the previous addictions and patterns has been inexorably re-written by traversing through your own fear and pain. There is a knowing that the change has happened at the deepest level not just a surface intellectual one. An inner knowing emerges that this process can be repeated for every pattern and fear point you encounter in your daily life.

Your way of meeting these unique thresholds, will undeniably be yours. There is no right or wrong, there are infinite paths to your own personal evolution. All you must be aware of is no longer energising your limited identity and allowing the full release of the core wounding patterns back to the Source of you.

The Art of Non-Protection

There is a profound difference between consciously choosing to be unprotected and simply being vulnerable. When Consciousness commits to non-protection, it is making a radical choice to meet reality without any buffers or barriers. You do not need to become defenceless, instead simply recognise that your protections themselves are what keep you bound to limited patterns. Through the inner death process, Consciousness maintains unwavering clarity that every:

+ Impulse to protect is your system trying to preserve old patterns
+ Attempt to understand or make meaning creates a new layer of protection
+ Desire for comfort or relief is resistance to the inner death process
+ Spiritual concept can become a shield against direct experience

Raw and Unfiltered Reality

Consciousness knows that true liberation requires a willingness to meet your experience completely raw and unfiltered. This means when:

- ✦ Waves of terror arise, you do not try to calm them
- ✦ Confusion floods your system, you do not seek clarity
- ✦ Physical sensations become overwhelming, you do not try to regulate
- ✦ Reality starts dissolving, you do not grasp for solid ground

This level of non-protection feels impossible to your system because it goes against every survival mechanism you have developed. Your body will create intense sensations, your mind will generate emergency signals and your emotions will flood with overwhelm. But Consciousness holds steady in knowing that these very sensations, when met without protection, are the doorway to freedom.

Robert, a meditation teacher who had spent decades practicing equanimity and non-reactivity, faced this invitation to non-protection when primal rage began spontaneously emerging during his meditation sessions. Despite his extensive spiritual training, these waves of anger terrified him.

"I had built my spiritual identity around being peaceful, compassionate, and non-reactive," he explained. "When this volcanic rage started erupting, my immediate impulse was to calm it, understand it, or transform it using the very techniques I taught others. But something deeper in me recognised that all these approaches were sophisticated forms of protection, ways of avoiding the direct, raw experience of this energy."

With guidance, Robert learned to stay present with his rage without any attempt to modify or transcend it. This meant allowing the full intensity of sensation without labelling it as 'anger'; feeling the raw energy without creating a story about its origin or meaning and letting his body move and express in ways that defied his image of spiritual maturity. "It was humbling and terrifying," he admitted. "I had to face the fact that beneath my spiritual persona lived energies I had deemed unacceptable. More importantly, I had to recognise that my entire spiritual practice had become a sophisticated form of protection, a way of managing and controlling my experience rather than meeting it directly."

As Robert developed the capacity for non-protection, allowing himself to experience these primal energies without modification, the very rage he had feared became a powerful catalyst for awakening. It revealed aspects of his authentic nature that had been suppressed beneath layers of spiritual conditioning. "I discovered that what I had labelled as 'negative' emotions weren't obstacles to freedom but essential aspects of my Wholeness," he shared. "By meeting them without protection, and without trying to calm, understand, or transcend them, I accessed a freedom far beyond what my controlled spiritual practice had ever provided."

The Ultimate Safety

What makes this possible is the conscious recognition that true safety is found in the complete willingness to be unprotected. That there is nothing to protect from. This is not a concept or perception. It is a direct knowing that emerges when you stop running from your experience and meet it fully. **It is an embodiment of deep inner safety.**

Consciousness understands that our protection is what keeps you separate from life, that identity defences are what maintain your pain and safety comes from completely merging with what is. Ultimately, true power emerges when you stop trying to control your experience and begin to receive it consciously.

Grace described this paradoxical safety perfectly. "For decades, I tried to feel safe with hypervigilance, control mechanisms, emotional walls and perfectionism. But no matter how sturdy these defences became, the core feeling of safety always eluded me. It was like trying to fill a bottomless pit." The transformation came when she realised what she truly longed for was not better protection but liberation from the very need to protect. This meant facing her deepest fear: that without her defences, she would be completely destroyed by the intensity of her experience.

"I had to let myself feel completely unsafe," she explained. "Not as a technique to eventually feel safer, but as a complete surrender of the goal of safety itself. I had to let go of every strategy I'd developed to manage my experience and simply allow myself to be completely exposed to life. It's from here I realised reality was safe, as my true safety came from within." What Grace discovered through this radical non-protection was a safety so fundamental that it made her previous pursuit of security seem like a tragic diversion. "Real safety doesn't need me to build stronger walls," she reflected. "It's about discovering that what you truly are can't be harmed in the first place. But you can only discover this by being willing to feel completely vulnerable, to let all your protections dissolve completely."

When Fear Becomes Your Ally

Fear serves as a compass, pointing directly to where pain is stored in your body. Your physical form becomes the portal for transformation, with each layer of fear leading to deeper layers of stored Consciousness. The very pain you have been avoiding holds the key to your liberation. By following fear's guidance rather than running from it, you begin a profound journey into the depths of your being. Every fear that arises in your experience is literally pointing to where freedom is possible. Consider these core fears that most humans experience:

✦ Fear of abandonment
✦ Fear of failure
✦ Fear of rejection
✦ Fear of death
✦ Fear of loss of control
✦ Fear of unworthiness

✦ Fear of being alone
✦ Fear of being misunderstood
✦ Fear of being stuck
✦ Fear of lack

Each of these fears is like an arrow pointing directly to where you need to experience Dying to the Limited Self. The very experiences your system is designed to avoid are the ones that hold the potential for your greatest transformation.

Claire, who had struggled with debilitating performance anxiety throughout her career as a musician, discovered this paradoxical relationship with fear during a crucial audition. After years of trying to manage, reduce, and overcome her fear, she made a radical decision to follow it instead. "I have tried everything to get rid of my performance anxiety: medication, therapy, visualisation and hypnosis. Some approaches helped temporarily, but the fear always returned, sometimes stronger than before," she explained. "The pivotal moment came when I decided to stop fighting my fear and instead allow it to show me exactly what needed to be seen."

Before her audition, instead of engaging her usual anxiety management techniques, Claire made a conscious choice to follow her fear all the way down. As she sat in the waiting room, she allowed the sensations of terror to intensify rather than trying to calm or suppress them. She followed these sensations directly into her body, discovering they led to a Core Wound around visibility and judgment that had shaped her entire life. "What I found beneath my performance anxiety was a much deeper fear: that being seen fully for who I am would lead to annihilation. This wasn't a rational fear; it was a primal, bodily knowing that had been driving my behaviour since childhood. By following my fear rather than fighting it, I was led directly to this Core Wound and the pain it had been protecting," she shared.

As Claire allowed herself to feel this pain directly without trying to heal, transform, or transcend it, something remarkable happened: she stretched to experience the truth of reality and herself. The very fear that had tormented her became a passage to a freedom she had never known was possible. "I walked into that audition in a completely different state. Not because I had conquered my fear, but because I had followed it to its source and died to the structures it was protecting," she explained. "I was full of the energy that had previously manifested as fear but was now flowing freely as aliveness, presence and creative power."

Claire's performance that day was not just technically excellent; it had a quality of authenticity and vulnerability that moved the judges to tears. She was offered the position on the spot. But the real transformation was not in the external outcome but in her internal relationship with fear itself. "Fear is no longer my enemy," she reflected. "It's my most trusted ally, constantly showing me exactly where I need to go next in my evolution. When fear arises now, I don't try to manage or overcome it. I say 'Thank you' and follow it directly to what needs to be seen, felt and ultimately released."

The Void Space of Truth

My own spontaneous out-of-body experience on the beach years ago revealed what happens when you fully surrender to the release of your limited self. You touch what I call the 'void space of truth'. A state of pure, infinite awareness beyond identity and form. In this space, your Consciousness merges with the All, revealing the true freedom and unconditional love that exists beyond our limited constructs.

The void space of truth cannot be something you create or achieve. It is what remains when everything you thought you were has been stripped away. It is the natural state of Consciousness when it is not contracting around protection and identity. This void is not empty in the conventional sense. It is empty of limitation but full of potential. It is not nothing; it is everything before it takes specific form. When Consciousness enters this space, several qualities become apparent:

- **Boundlessness:** The rigid boundaries between self and other dissolve
- **Timelessness:** Linear time gives way to an eternal now
- **Formlessness:** Identity is recognised as fluid rather than fixed
- **Infinite potential:** All possibilities exist simultaneously
- **Unconditional love:** As the fundamental nature of reality

Emily, who had built her life around achievement and control, encountered this void space during a profound crisis that dismantled everything she thought she was. After losing her high-powered job, going through a divorce, and facing a serious health scare all within six months, she found herself in what she described as 'complete existential freefall'. "Every structure I had used to define myself was stripped away," she recounted. "My career, my marriage, my health, my financial security, everything I thought made me 'me' was suddenly gone. I had nothing left to hold onto, nowhere to hide, no identity left to protect."

In this complete dissolution, Emily experienced what initially felt like a terrifying void: the absence of everything familiar and secure. But as she allowed herself to fully surrender into this space rather than frantically trying to rebuild her identity, something extraordinary happened. "What I initially experienced as emptiness revealed itself as a fullness beyond anything I could have imagined," she shared. "It wasn't that I had lost everything; it was that I had been liberated from the limited construct of who I thought I was. What remained wasn't nothing, it was everything."

In this void space, Emily discovered a sense of self so vast and inclusive that it could not be contained within any identity or role. This was not a temporary spiritual experience that faded when Emily rebuilt her life. It fundamentally transformed how she related to every aspect of existence. When she eventually returned to the corporate world, it was not to reconstruct her old identity but to express something much vaster through the specific form of her work and relationships. "I no longer derive my sense of self from what I do or have," she explained. "I move through life with the knowledge that everything can be taken away again at any moment, and that this loss would not diminish who I truly am. It's the most profound freedom I could imagine: the freedom to fully engage with life without needing it to be any particular way."

Evidence in Absence

The effectiveness of this practice reveals itself through what I call 'evidence in absence'. When you experience Dying to your Limited Self, you will notice people, situations and problems naturally falling away. Your reality becomes more holographic in nature, with the void facilitating space for new creation. You become the Unknown creation, no longer bound by predetermined patterns and limitations. The absence then becomes pregnant with potential. This evidence in absence manifests in several ways:

- ✦ Relationships restructure or dissolve: Connections based on old patterns naturally transform or fall away without drama or effort.

- ✦ Chronic problems disappear: Issues you have struggled with for years suddenly resolve themselves without direct intervention.

- ✦ New possibilities emerge: Opportunities that seemed impossible within your old reality structure spontaneously appear.

- ✦ Synchronicity increases: Reality begins responding to your Consciousness rather than your history, creating meaningful coincidences and connections.

- ✦ Effort decreases, flow increases: Life unfolds with greater ease, requiring less forcing and management.

George, a writer who had struggled with creative blocks for years, experienced this evidence in absence after committing to the Dying to the Limited Self process. "I had tried everything to overcome my writer's block: writing exercises, inspiration practices, therapy focussed on creative wounds, even hypnosis. Nothing created lasting change," he explained.

The breakthrough came when George recognised that his writer's block was not a problem to solve but a construct to die to. Instead of trying to become more creative, he allowed the entire identity of 'blocked writer' to dissolve. This meant stopping all efforts to write, all practices to enhance creativity, all stories about why he was blocked, and all visions of who he should be as a writer.

"I completely stopped participating in the entire drama of being a blocked writer," he shared. "I didn't replace it with a new identity as a flowing writer. I simply let the whole construct collapse and rested in the void that remained."

For several months, George did nothing related to writing. He did not try to create, did not talk about being blocked, did not imagine future success. He allowed himself to exist in the absence of any writing identity whatsoever, a complete relinquishment of the entire structure.

What emerged from this void surprised him. "I woke up one morning with words flowing through me so powerfully that I barely made it to my computer in time to capture them," he recounted. "For four hours, I wrote in a state I can only describe as being written through. The words weren't coming from my familiar sense of self or creative process. They were emerging from the void itself."

This spontaneous creative flow was not a one-time occurrence. It continued daily, requiring no effort or management on George's part. "I'm not writing in the way I used to understand writing," he explained. "There's no 'me' crafting sentences or developing ideas. There's just this open space where words emerge naturally in response to what wants to be expressed."

Most striking to George was that he had not solved his writer's block through any direct intervention. "The problem didn't get fixed; it ceased to exist because the entire reality structure that contained it dissolved. What emerged wasn't an improved version of my old creative process but something entirely new, something that couldn't have existed within my previous understanding of myself as a writer."

The Love-Fear Relationship

What makes this practice truly revolutionary is how it transforms your fundamental relationship with both love and fear. Through this work, you discover that your greatest fear transforms into your deepest love. Your pain becomes the gateway to awakening and what you perceived as death reveals itself as rebirth. Your energetics, the very life force you have been using to maintain limited patterns, become your greatest commodity, free to flow in new directions.

This transformation reveals a raw truth: what you fear most turns out to be what you love most. The experiences, emotions and aspects of yourself that you have been most afraid to face are the ones that hold your deepest liberation and most authentic expression. Through this process, you discover that fear of abandonment transforms into love of true connection, fear of failure becomes love of authentic expression and fear of powerlessness reveals itself as love of surrender. The terror of judgment dissolves into love of truth, while even the ultimate fear of death transforms into the deepest love of life itself. These are not separate processes but expressions of the same fundamental energy; what manifests as fear when contracted around protection, flows as love when allowed to move freely through your being.

Lucy, who had structured her entire life around avoiding vulnerability, discovered this paradoxical relationship when she finally allowed herself to face her deepest fear: being truly seen by others. From childhood, she had developed sophisticated strategies to maintain a perfect façade, ensuring that no one could ever witness her flaws, struggles, or raw humanity. "My greatest terror was that if people saw who I really was, with all my mess, confusion, and imperfection, they would reject me completely," she explained. "I maintained exhausting levels of performance in every area of my life, constantly managing others' perceptions and hiding any hint of vulnerability."

This protection strategy had created a successful but profoundly isolated life. Despite her achievements and social connections, Lucy felt fundamentally Unknown. "I had created the very isolation I was trying to avoid," she realised. "By protecting against rejection, I had made genuine connection impossible."

Her breakthrough came through the Dying to the Limited Self process, where she committed to exposing exactly what she had been hiding. This was not about strategic vulnerability or carefully managed authenticity. It was about allowing herself to be completely seen, without controlling how others would respond. "I began expressing thoughts and feelings I'd always hidden, showing up without the perfect façade, allowing people to see my struggles and limitations," she shared. "Every time I did this, my system would create intense fear, waves of shame, and terror. But instead of retreating into protection, I stayed present with these sensations, allowing them to move through me completely."

What Lucy discovered through this process stunned her: her greatest fear of being truly seen, transformed into her deepest love. "As I allowed myself to be vulnerable without protection, I discovered that what I had been running from was actually what my soul most longed for, an authentic connection where I could be fully known and accepted."

This was a complete energetic transformation. "It's the same energy," Lucy explained. "When I'm trying to protect against being seen, it manifests as fear. When I allow myself to be fully visible, that same energy flows as love and connection." This transformation extended beyond Lucy's relationships into every area of her life. The energy that had been bound in maintaining protection became available for creative expression, professional innovation, and spiritual expansion. "I realised how much life force I had been using just to maintain my façade," she reflected. "When that energy was liberated, it became available for living rather than just surviving."

The Relief of Release

The liberation that comes through Dying to the Limited Self transcends anything your limited identity could imagine. It represents a return to non-dualism and Source Consciousness, freeing you from the endless pursuit of fixing or improving yourself. When you release the addiction to who you think you should be, you experience the sweetest, most potent gift you could give yourself – the gift of true freedom.

This freedom comes with a deep authenticity: you stop trying to be someone in particular and allow yourself to be exactly as you are. This release creates a lightness of being that no amount of self-improvement could ever produce.

The qualities of this liberation emerge naturally as layers of seeking and becoming fall away. You discover freedom from the exhausting pursuit of becoming someone better, different or more evolved. There is a profound release from the constant evaluation of experience as good or bad, spiritual or mundane. You find yourself liberated from the endless project of fixing yourself, no longer carrying the burden that something fundamental about you needs to be corrected or improved. Relief comes from no longer needing to maintain a particular identity or image, allowing the exhausting performance of being someone specific to dissolve completely. Perhaps most significantly, you experience freedom from the suffering of resistance to what is, no longer fighting against reality but flowing with whatever arises in each moment.

Once you have experienced genuine Dying to the Limited Self, your relationship with reality fundamentally shifts. Death and rebirth become familiar companions on your evolutionary journey. Your energy, no longer bound by limiting patterns, flows freely in new directions. Perhaps most importantly, you develop the capacity to rest in the Unknown with complete trust.

This process does not end with one profound dissolution. It becomes an ongoing dance with existence, where you continually die to what no longer serves and allow new expressions to emerge naturally. This creates a life driven by constant evolution rather than clinging to false stability, fluid identity rather than attaching to a fixed self-concept and trust in the Unknown rather than attachment to the familiar known

Maya, a therapist who had worked through multiple layers

of Dying to the Limited Self, described this evolutionary flow, "I used to think transformation meant reaching some final healed state where I would be forever free from patterns and limitations. What I've discovered instead is the continuous process of death and rebirth, which keeps revealing new dimensions of both limitation and freedom."

This understanding transformed how Maya related to emerging patterns in her life. Rather than seeing them as evidence of incomplete healing or spiritual failure, she recognised them as the next invitation to die to self. "When a limitation appears now, I don't try to fix or transcend it" she explained, "I recognise it as showing me exactly where I need to die next, what aspect of identity is ready to dissolve."

This approach created a remarkable lightness in Maya's evolutionary process. Instead of the heavy, serious work of healing and transformation, she experiences life as a continuous unfolding, with each death leading naturally to new birth. "There's a playfulness to it now" she shared, "I'm not trying to arrive anywhere or achieve some final state. I'm dancing with existence, allowing each death to reveal what wants to emerge next."

The New Creation

The Dying to the Limited Self process supports you to achieve personal liberation but something greater also emerges. You download a Consciousness that causes you to participate in evolution in entirely new ways. As you free yourself from the limitations of your wounded identity, you become available as a vessel for new possibilities to manifest – not just in your personal life but in the collective field. This new level of creation has several distinct qualities, it:

- **Emerges rather than being forced:** Instead of creating from your limited identity with its agenda and vision, you allow creation to emerge through you from the field of pure potential.

- **Serves evolution rather than ego:** The creations that flow through you naturally contribute to the evolution of Consciousness rather than reinforcing existing structures or seeking personal gain.

- **Bridges dimensions:** You become capable of bringing through innovations, insights and expressions that connect multiple levels of reality, translating higher dimensional awareness into forms accessible in this dimension.

- **Is holographic rather than linear:** Your creations contain the Wholeness of Consciousness within them, operating as fractal expressions of the greater field rather than fragmented pieces.

Remember that your identity, no matter how precious it seems, is ultimately open to evolution and change. The true release comes when you are willing to traverse the pain you have been avoiding through your addictions. When you become truthful with where that pain meets your life, you arrive fully in the present moment, no longer dragging the past or projecting it into the future. In this space, you are renewed, with more energy and essence available for your relationships, purpose and the pure joy of being.

This is the path of true transformation and it is available to anyone brave enough to walk it. The invitation stands. The doorway is open. And Consciousness is waiting to show you what becomes possible when you finally stop running from death and allow yourself to truly live, now. The coming chapter explores how this is possible for all of us.

CHAPTER ELEVEN
The Energetic Liberation

The depth of this work had revealed layers I never anticipated. After applying the processes we have explored, by moving through the Pain Portal and experiencing the dissolution of my limited identity, I found myself in a state I can only describe as intensely raw, yet profoundly alive.

One cold morning, as I walked along the lake near my house, something shifted in my awareness. In what felt like a sudden inner vision, I perceived what appeared to be my own energy, like a misty, spiralling pattern, flowing outward and away from my body into the vast, infinite sky above. This was not something I saw with my physical eyes, but rather a vivid inner knowing that suddenly made sense of something I had been feeling but could not name.

As I tuned into this visualisation, I experienced what can only be described as an intense internal depletion. Then the understanding came with startling clarity: *I must reclaim my energy. I must complete the energetic cycle within myself rather than continuously sending it outward. I must create energetic sovereignty and freedom.*

This moment illuminated something crucial about our human experience. The wounds, the pain, the unconscious programs we have explored throughout this book, they all create energetic leaks. We walk through life unconsciously feeding our precious life force into everything beyond us and in doing so, we separate from ourselves in the most profound way. This is why we struggle to find lasting closure, relief, or transcendence because we automatically keep sending our most valuable resource outside ourselves in an attempt to survive.

What if I told you something we are never taught; this energy is ours to maintain and use internally. That it is designed to help us access our own inner source of fulfillment and power our authentic sovereignty? This recognition became the foundation for everything that follows.

The Living Field: Understanding Our Deeper Reality

This realisation about energy led me to explore what lies beneath everything we see, touch and experience. What I began to sense, and what mystics throughout history have described, is something extraordinary: an infinite field of pure potential, a living, intelligent foundation from which all existence appears to emerge.

Think of this field like an ocean, but not the water itself, rather the space that allows water to exist and move. While this is a metaphor rather than a scientific claim, it helps us understand something profound about the nature of reality. What appears as solid, separate objects; your body, this room, these words, are temporary expressions of this one underlying field, like waves arising from and returning to an ocean.

Modern physics explores similar concepts through what is called Quantum Field Theory, where particles are understood as excitations in underlying fields. While I am not making scientific claims about Consciousness and quantum mechanics as this remains highly debated among physicists, these scientific discoveries offer helpful metaphors for understanding spiritual experiences of interconnectedness.

Your existence appears to spring from this field through what we might call your unique energetic signature. This creates an intriguing paradox: you are simultaneously part of a unified Whole and a distinct individual expression. This apparent duality, or splitting of parts, is a gift because it makes experience possible. Without this sense of being a separate self, you could not experience life at all. There would be no 'you' to witness a sunset, feel love or contemplate these words.

We exist as both creators of our experience and as beings navigating the human condition. This dual nature allows us to be both connected to something greater and wonderfully, messily human. Understanding this opens a profound journey of learning to navigate existence while honouring both our unity with life and our unique expression within it.

Simone, who worked with these concepts over many months, described her shift this way: "It's like I had been looking at the world through a tiny keyhole my entire life, seeing only separate objects and isolated events. When I finally let go of my familiar patterns of feeling Unworthy and Unloved, it was as if the entire wall dissolved. I could see that everything I had been perceiving was interconnected, nothing was separate, it just appeared that way because of how I had been conditioned to observe reality."

The Dance of Consciousness and Experience

What makes this deeper reality extraordinary is its intimate relationship with Consciousness. In our everyday experience, things appear separate and solid. But in deeper states of awareness, we may sense that nothing exists as fixed until it is observed or experienced. Our Consciousness itself seems to play a role in bringing potential into actuality.

This understanding transforms everything about how we perceive our relationship with reality. We are not separate observers of an external world that exists independently of us. We are participants in a continuous dance of creation, where our Consciousness is constantly interacting with the field of possibility to manifest specific experiences.

When we first arrive in this human experience, we begin as expressions of pure energy in material form. Energy sustains us as our life force; the fuel of our expression. Yet we are not taught to understand its nature or how to work with it consciously. We begin to unconsciously seek the fulfillment and safety from energy outside ourselves, in the external world. This is where we begin the pattern of energetic separation that sits at the heart of all the Core Wounds we have explored.

Colin, a physician who experienced this understanding directly, described his shift, "I used to think of myself as existing 'in' reality, like a separate entity navigating through an external world. Through this work, I recognised that my Consciousness is not 'in' reality, it is an integral aspect of how reality unfolds. I'm not just observing the world; I'm participating in its continuous creation through my attention and choices."

Energy Mastery: The Path to Sovereignty

Your energy is your most precious resource. It is the currency through which you create your reality, the sacred fuel that drives every aspect of your existence. Where you invest this energy literally determines where you are creating your experience of life. Yet most of us have never learned to work with our energy directly. Instead, we struggle with material manifestations by fighting symptoms of reality patterns we feel we did not choose, rather than recognising ourselves as the energetic source.

Understanding and mastering your relationship with energy forms the foundation of authentic freedom and personal power. When you recognise yourself as an energetic being rather than merely a physical form, everything shifts. You begin to understand that your thoughts, emotions, circumstances and relationships are all expressions of energetic patterns. This recognition allows you to work at the causal level rather than being trapped in effects.

The challenge is that we have continuously fed our energy into maintaining relationships with external achievements, people or possessions, trying to complete our inner emptiness. Yet this fundamental void comes from being disconnected from your own energetic essence. Your energy is sacred because it is the only thing that will truly complete you.

For too long, we have been playing a game that keeps us disconnected from our true power. This separation operates on multiple levels:

Separation from our True State: We have forgotten that we are Consciousness itself, temporarily focussed through a human experience.

Separation from our Natural Existence: We have been conditioned to believe that struggle, scarcity and suffering are natural rather than recognising our inherent capacity for ease and flow.

Separation from our Wholeness: We have been taught to seek completion outside ourselves, fragmenting our energy across countless external pursuits.

Separation from our Sovereignty: We have given away our power to external authorities, systems and structures that profit from our disconnection.

Understanding these separations is the first step towards reclaiming what has always been yours. In the sections that follow, we will explore how to practically work with your energy, how to identify where it is being drained and most importantly, how to call it back home to yourself.

Energetic Reclamation: Understanding the Flow

The most concerning aspect of our energetic separation is how unconsciously we allow our life force to flow outward. We experience depletion through:

- ✦ Unconscious emotional reactions that drain us
- ✦ Mental loops that consume our attention without resolution
- ✦ Relationships that extract more than they nourish
- ✦ Systems and structures designed to capture our energetic resources
- ✦ Habits and patterns that keep us operating from limitation

This energetic flow operates through two interconnected levels:

Internal Programming: The perceptions, conditioning and patterns we carry that cause us to unconsciously direct our power outward. These are the stories we tell ourselves about limitation, unworthiness and separation.

External Programming: The structures, systems and cultural conditioning in our environment that are designed to capture our attention and energy. These systems function most effectively when we remain unconscious of our sovereign nature.

From birth, we learn to navigate our external world for survival. This happens largely unconsciously, with little awareness of our internal energetic relationship. Eventually, the external focus becomes primary, perceived as essential for our very existence. All our attention moves to managing external circumstances, all our mental programs organise around this management and our sacred energy gets invested in maintaining these external relationships.

But here is a profound realisation: your energetic investment shapes your experience of reality. When you watch, listen, engage and give attention to everything around you, you are feeding it with your precious life force. The wound patterns we explored earlier create the foundation for this outward investment.

How the Core Wounds Direct Energy Flow

Let us revisit how the Core Wounds create distinct energetic patterns:

The Unloved Wound generates energy depletion through compulsive giving. You become an energy source for others, flooding them with your attention and care. The energetic flow is so intense that you consistently overinvest in others, driven by the fear that if you do not fill the space with love, no one will return it. This pattern maintains feelings of abandonment, loneliness and never receiving enough love.

The Unworthy Wound creates depletion through seeking external validation. It manifests as a constant search for external energy to fill an internal void. Imagine having a container with a hole in the bottom where no amount of validation ever feels sufficient. You become focussed on accumulating external markers of success or 'enoughness' because they temporarily reflect back that you are acceptable.

The Unknown Wound disperses energy through searching for connection and certainty. This wound feels like being perpetually lost in translation. Your energy moves halfway out to meet the world and waits there, deeply yearning to be met. There is a profound longing for reality to recognise you and provide safety.

The Practice of Energetic Sovereignty

Most of us have never experienced what it feels like to have our energy contained within our own being. You might wonder: *If our energy is infinite, shouldn't it be everywhere?* While this may be true on one level, we must acknowledge that we inhabit physical bodies and are having human experiences. This requires us to honour both our infinite nature and our embodied reality.

Bringing our sacred energy back into alignment with our physical form is how we access ourselves as conscious creators. From this place, we can meet external reality through a completely different internal operating system. This new relationship recognises that everything appears separate yet is fundamentally connected. However, we cannot arrive at this understanding from a place of energetic depletion and external seeking.

To work with this energetic movement, remember that energy is the foundation of every molecule. While our senses perceive us as material, if we zoom into every cell, we discover we are predominantly energetic beings. The miracle of our existence is that we direct energy. We move it through space and time through our attention and intention. When we look at something or someone, our energy moves towards that focus. We invest in it and this investment shapes our experience.

The wound patterns support this unconscious, external investment in the environment. The compulsion to manage the experience around us draws us out of our centre into the world at large. This is how we have been conditioned to live and while it may be difficult to recognise, this represents a form of self-abandonment and self-depletion.

The Energetic Gateway Practice

It became important for me to feel into how we reclaim this energy actively and thoroughly. I discovered a profound energy point at the centre of the sternum. This is not tied to the traditional chakra systems but represents a significant point of awareness. It is the space where your internal Wholeness meets the external world of duality. Within you exists a creative space of potential; outside exists the realm of apparent separation.

Try placing your fingertips gently on the sternum where there is a small depression. *How does it feel? Can you feel a sensitivity or tenderness?* Just take a few moments to feel into this space and become curious about its importance. When you place your awareness on this area, you can begin to sensitise yourself to where your energy is focussed. During times of high external overcommitment, you may feel the over-extension beyond yourself; your sternum area may register a sense of longing, lack or exhaustion. This is the felt sense of energetic separation.

Conversely, the only way to truly understand external energetic investment is to experience the power of conscious reclamation. This occurs as a mindful drawing back of your energy through the sternum point. Using your inner vision to sense the parts of external reality you engage with through thoughts, emotions and actions, allows you to see the construct of these relationships. Then you can witness how your precious energy and essence are involved in maintaining these structures.

This is the design of separation: something external that requires your energy to maintain its hold on your attention. The desire to feed your energy outward often comes from projecting an Illusion of Safety onto the external space. The pull that you must create safety by ongoing outward investment can feel compelling and relentless. Actively reclaiming and calling back this energy represents a critical movement home to yourself, back to your Wholeness. This practice can be engaged at any moment and shifts your energetic relationship with reality. External investment from separation comes from wounding; internal energetic sovereignty represents completion.

From this place, you become able to engage in a new energetic relationship with life. You become sovereign and your priorities in engagement change. No longer are you looking to see how reality can save you. You are now prepared to contribute to reality and Consciousness from your most authentic state.

The visceral experience of internal Wholeness initiates a new way of being, one that supports your evolution. This Wholeness creates harmony between your spiritual and human qualities. It manifests as deep alignment in purpose and relationships, abundance in resources and support and sustainable energy from our integrated physical being. It is about engaging from fullness rather than emptiness, from choice rather than compulsion, from sovereignty rather than dependency. When we operate from this internal completion, our external relationships become expressions of our Wholeness rather than attempts to achieve it.

Practical Steps to Energetic Sovereignty

Energetic sovereignty is when you come to know your energy as primary and powerful. The Consciousness then shifts radically and nothing outside of you holds any power, as you understand that to give it your power is to be in your wounded state. Your energy will keep spiralling out of you to oblivion.

This reclamation of Sovereignty is what you are here to do in your evolutionary experience; to remember yourself as the powerful creator that you are, one who creates from intention alone. Not bound to anything beyond you, you have the opportunity to create from the truth of you. Ultimately, this will be inclusive, loving, creative and committed to creating a reality around you that reflects that.

This process is not so you live in a cave alone on the side of a mountain hoarding your precious energy. It is so that you know the felt experience of energetic sovereignty. When all the building blocks of reality are dissolved into energy and you reclaim yours to sit in your own energetic self-sufficiency, then you create from a very powerful place.

Once you have breathed yourself energetically back home; expand your Consciousness and allow your awareness to expand from this centred place, to dissolve attachment to a fixed reality and release you into the Unknown possibility and potential.

Your Consciousness expands and understands that often what you perceive as a threat, is an illusion, it is simply a threat to your wounding. When you begin to recognise this, you can stretch your reality so that instead of being in a reactive state, you are in a witness state, allowing reality to move around you and reveal its truth. The foundation for this practice includes:

1. Morning Connection: Begin each day by sensing the energetic field beyond physical boundaries:

- ✦ Before planning or checking devices, pause to feel your energetic nature.
- ✦ Place your awareness at your sternum, the gateway between internal Wholeness and external duality.
- ✦ Visualise any energy that has been dispersed outside yourself returning to you.
- ✦ Feel the gathering of your energy back within the borders of your skin.
- ✦ Set an intention to maintain energetic self-sufficiency throughout the day.

2. Energy Tracking: Throughout the day, track your energy levels and where your energy is being invested:

✦ Notice when you feel depleted versus energised.

✦ Pay attention to which activities, thoughts or interactions consistently drain your energy.

✦ Observe when you are overgiving (Unloved Wound), seeking validation (Unworthy Wound) or trying to create certainty (Unknown Wound).

✦ Practice consciously bringing your energy back to yourself in these moments.

3. The In-Between Space: Create the In-Between Space; a moment of Consciousness between stimulus and response:

✦ When you feel the compulsion to seek external validation or certainty, pause.

✦ Use the technique of drawing your energy back into your body.

✦ Allow the space between the compulsion and the action to widen.

✦ In this gap, acknowledge any fear, anxiety, tension or discomfort that arises.

✦ This void space is where you can take a break from your Wound Reality and simply learn to be energetically self-sufficient.

4. Energetic Reclamation: Practice actively reclaiming your energy from external investments and addictions:

✦ Identify specific external structures where you have been investing your energy (relationships, work, social media, perception systems).

✦ Identify addictive patterns of pain avoidance and the thoughts, feelings and behaviours attached.

- ✦ Visualise the energetic connections between yourself and these structures.
- ✦ Consciously call your energy back, seeing it return to the centre of your being through your sternum point.
- ✦ Feel the sensation of becoming more energetically full and complete within yourself.

Grace, who practiced these techniques consistently for six months, described her experience, "The first few weeks were incredibly challenging. I felt like I was going through withdrawal, my system was so accustomed to seeking energy outside myself that turning inward felt alien and uncomfortable. But gradually, I began to experience moments of what I can only describe as energetic completion. I'd feel this sensation of fullness in my chest, a sense of being enough just as I was. These moments gradually expanded until they became my baseline state. Now, I still engage with the world, I have relationships, work and social activities, but I'm no longer energetically dependent on them. I'm creating from a place of Wholeness rather than lack. Participation rather than control, fear and separation."

The Movement of Energy

To understand how this energetic pattern works, it helps to recognise that when we invest energy outside of ourselves without conscious awareness, there can be an endless pull outward. There is no natural completion point in these loops because external sources cannot fill unconscious internal voids.

Translating this to our Core Wounds; we keep investing our energy into external experiences and people, hoping that at some point we will receive exactly what we desire and feel complete. We believe we will finally know that we are enough, loved and known through external validation. But this creates a fundamental dependence that keeps us seeking rather than discovering our own capacity for self-acceptance and inner fulfillment. While meaningful connections with others are essential for human wellbeing, relying exclusively on external sources for our sense of worth creates an unstable foundation.

Here is what many of us do not realise; the qualities you seek from outside: validation, acknowledgment, love, attention, understanding, security and safety, can really only be cultivated within yourself first and from there experienced in the external reality. This does not mean rejecting genuine connection with others, but rather developing the capacity to offer yourself what you have been seeking externally.

Your sense of completion and Wholeness can develop through reclaiming a conscious relationship with your own energy and worth. The connection you are craving is the recognition of your own inherent value, your capacity for self-acknowledgement, self-love, self-understanding and internal security. When you feel depleted from constantly reaching outward for what you need, this is a valid signal that your energy is dispersed rather than integrated. This recognition represents an awareness of truth: your energy and attention are precious resources. Your conscious relationship with them internally means you can create more sustainable patterns within your own being while still maintaining healthy connections with others.

Julian described how this understanding complemented his approach to health challenges, "Rather than focussing exclusively on external solutions, I began paying attention to the energy patterns underlying my experiences. This didn't mean rejecting appropriate medical care but rather bringing more awareness to how my internal state influenced my wellbeing. I noticed that my persistent health concerns were connected to my pattern of constantly searching outside myself for safety and certainty. When I began to develop a more caring relationship with myself, while continuing to work with my healthcare team, I experienced improvements that surprised me. The combination of internal awareness and appropriate external support created conditions for healing I hadn't experienced with either approach alone."

A New Way of Engaging

This understanding can transform various aspects of your life, from personal challenges to relationships to creative endeavours. It represents a shift from seeing ourselves as separate entities struggling in an external world to recognising ourselves as conscious participants in our own experience.

In your personal experience I invite you to move from feeling fixed in patterns to sensing more possibility; from isolation to connection, from limitation to growth. In relationships, we can shift from desperate need to genuine choice, from constant effort to natural flow, from fear-based attachment to trust-based connection. In creative expression, we can move from forcing outcomes to allowing emergence, from rigid planning to responsive adaptation.

Rather than seeing yourself as a solid entity trying to influence an external world, you can recognise yourself as an aware being capable of conscious response to life's experiences. This understanding can transform how you create, heal, live and evolve. The field of infinite potential represents the space of possibility that becomes available when you are no longer organising your life around avoiding pain or desperately seeking external completion. Having traversed the Pain Portal, released identification with your limited self-concept and reclaimed your energy, you now have access to more conscious choice in how you engage with life.

In our next exploration, we will examine how to maintain this awareness while navigating real-world systems and structures. We will explore how to engage with everything from professional environments to family dynamics to financial systems while maintaining your sense of Wholeness and energetic sovereignty. You will learn to bring more awareness and intentionality to how you meet life's complexities, while participating fully in the human experience of relationship, contribution and growth.

Part IV

CHAPTER TWELVE
Conscious Engagement with Reality

What if your deepest sense of powerlessness stems from not understanding how to consciously engage with reality itself? As I continued exploring this inner work, traversing the Pain Portal and dissolving my limited-self, I realised there was a crucial piece missing. I could see the loop of endlessly working on myself while failing to see true shifts in my external experience.

That is when it dawned on me. *What if the problem was not that I needed to become a better person or heal more deeply? What if I simply did not understand how reality operates?*

I felt like I had been thrown into the ocean of life, desperately fighting against every wave, exhausting myself trying to swim against a powerful current. I was convinced the water was my enemy, that every wave was a personal attack, every challenge a sign of my inadequacy. All my inner work had been building stronger muscles and better breathing techniques, which were certainly valuable skills. But I was still trying to fight the ocean instead of learning how to surf.

This realisation changed everything. I was not broken or inadequate. I just did not understand the ocean's design, its currents, patterns and rhythms. I needed to learn how to read the waves, feel where the power was building and discover how to work with reality's immense force rather than against it.

Without taking conscious responsibility for how you respond to reality, external forces will shape your experience through conditioned programs you never chose. Your family's perceptions about money will determine your relationship with abundance. Your culture's stories about relationships will script your partnerships. Your society's definitions of success will drive your choices. When you operate unconsciously, these inherited programs become your default responses to life's challenges.

Understanding the Design

When you truly understand how conditioning operates, something profound shifts. You no longer feel at the mercy of automatic reactions. Instead, you begin to feel capable of conscious choice because you have become familiar with the patterns, triggers and mechanisms that previously controlled you.

This work operates at the interface between your inner awareness and the external world, between unconscious programming and conscious choice, between the stories you have inherited and the truth you discover through direct experience. It transforms your relationship with discomfort and uncertainty from limiting factors into gateways of genuine freedom.

The Hidden Pattern of Unconscious Response

Underlying much of our human experience lies a subtle yet pervasive pattern of unconscious response. We react to circumstances based on old programming rather than present awareness. While countless approaches promise to help us escape this pattern, transformation begins with recognising how thoroughly these automatic responses have shaped our reality.

This unconscious pattern manifests as feeling controlled by circumstances beyond your influence. External reality seems to take you on a journey you cannot direct. Your sense of personal agency feels stolen, leaving you paralysed. You experience the gnawing fear that things are not working in your favour and there is nothing you can do about it, the deep doubt about your ability to navigate life successfully.

The result? We second-guess ourselves and surrender to external systems, thinking: *What would I know?* We stay in marriages, jobs, medical treatments, educational paths, or financial situations because we fear the Unknown. These patterns make us feel powerless while simultaneously providing an Illusion of Safety through predictability.

This unconscious response pattern lives deep within our bodies. Your shoulders tense, your breathing becomes shallow, your vision narrows. You literally experience the physiological state of being trapped, despite having no actual physical constraints. This bodily experience reinforces the mental story of powerlessness, creating a feedback loop that feels impossible to escape.

The Interface Problem: Where Programming Really Lives

What is crucial to understand is that this sense of powerlessness goes beyond personal inadequacy. It is an 'interface problem' between you and external reality. You are trying to fit yourself into systems designed without regard for your authentic needs, your intuitive knowing, or your individual path to fulfillment.

This interface problem manifests in countless daily scenarios. Consider how we typically engage with:

Healthcare systems: Your intuitive understanding of your body must be translated into acceptable medical language to be taken seriously. Your symptoms get categorised and treated according to standardised protocols that may miss your unique needs and healing capacity.

Educational institutions: Learning gets structured according to arbitrary timelines and standardised metrics that often fail to recognise diverse intelligences and learning styles. Your natural curiosity and passion may be stifled rather than nurtured.

Workplace environments: Productivity gets measured by hours logged or outputs produced rather than meaningful contribution or creative expression. Your unique gifts may be undervalued while conformity gets rewarded.

Financial systems: Your worth gets quantified by credit scores and income brackets, with access to resources determined by past performance rather than present potential. Your capacity for abundance may be constrained by artificial scarcity programming.

Relationship systems: You feel bound by legal contracts and social expectations that may no longer serve the actual people involved. You might stay in relationships that have lost their vitality because of external pressures or inherited perceptions about commitment.

In each scenario, when we approach these systems from unconscious response patterns, we surrender our power and accept their limitations as absolute reality. When we recognise the interface problem, we can begin to engage differently, maintaining our conscious awareness while working within or around these structures.

The Body as Intelligence: Working with Embodied Patterns

Our bodies serve as sophisticated guidance systems in this journey. They act as early warning systems, letting us know when we are slipping into unconscious response patterns before our minds even register what is happening. The body holds memories of past experiences and reacts to present situations based on previous associations.

Unconscious response patterns live in our cells. The body holds patterns of contraction, bracing and disconnection that reflect and reinforce our sense of powerlessness. Working directly with these embodied patterns creates transformation that mental understanding alone cannot achieve.

Try this practice to recognise unconscious response patterns. Stand with your feet hip-width apart, knees slightly bent, notice areas of tension or contraction in your body. As you exhale, exaggerate this contraction: hunch your shoulders, tighten your jaw, clench your fists, whatever your body naturally does when feeling overwhelmed or controlled. Feel the full sensation of this contracted state.

Then, with a deep inhale, begin to open your body. Let your arms extend outward, lift your chest, soften your face and ground through your feet. Feel the expansion and spaciousness this creates. Move back and forth between contraction and expansion several times, noticing how each state affects your awareness. This practice makes visible the physical component of unconscious response patterns and trains your system to recognise and shift them.

Working with the body as intelligence means honouring its wisdom rather than trying to override it. Your physical sensations offer guidance about when you are caught in old patterns and when you are aligned with conscious choice. Learning to decode these signals creates an internal guidance system more reliable than any external authority.

Breaking Free from Unconscious Programming: Jessica's Health Journey

Jessica's experience with her daughter's health challenges illustrates how we can begin to work with these patterns consciously. When her daughter required multiple hospital visits for recurring infections, Jessica found herself caught in familiar patterns of giving away her decision-making power to external authorities. With every round of antibiotics, every IV insertion, every conflicting doctor's opinion, her anxiety would spike. Yet this time, she could observe the pattern playing out.

Through deeper exploration, Jessica discovered how her childhood experience with her physician father had created unconscious associations between illness and receiving attention. This pattern now influenced how she engaged with her daughter's health challenges. She was trapped in the programmed perception that medical intervention was the only path to healing, while simultaneously feeling disconnected from her own intuitive understanding of what her daughter needed.

What made this realisation transformative was taking concrete steps to reclaim her conscious participation in the healing process while still working with medical professionals. She began researching treatment options herself, asking doctors detailed questions about their recommendations and trusting her intuition about her daughter's needs. When one specialist dismissed her questions, she found another who respected her input.

Jessica also addressed the emotional component of her daughter's illness, creating space for her to express fears and frustrations rather than just treating physical symptoms. She incorporated gentle supportive practices alongside conventional treatment, noticing how her daughter's body responded to different approaches. Most importantly, she recognised when her own anxiety was driving decisions versus clear discernment.

This balanced approach led to a remarkable shift. Her daughter's healing process became smoother and sustainable and their stress levels decreased dramatically. What had changed was not the medical treatment alone but Jessica's relationship with the entire situation. She was no longer an unconscious participant in the medical system but a conscious advocate working with it as a resource, while maintaining her own discernment and agency.

The Web of Unconscious Judgment

Embedded deeply in unconscious response patterns lies a constant mental categorisation of our experience. We project arbitrary assessments onto everything around us, creating a perpetual state of mental separation that feels like safety yet serves to deepen our sense of inadequacy.

Watch how this operates in daily life: we assess our physical appearance, income, social media following, living situation and immediately categorise it as either acceptable or unacceptable. We look at strangers, colleagues, even our closest relationships and unconsciously sort them into categories of worthy or unworthy. We evaluate our partners, children and friends across time, constantly measuring them against external standards.

This constant categorisation becomes our way of trying to create security, making moment-to-moment adjustments to improve our standing in various hierarchies. But it is a game that cannot be won. No amount of adjusting can stop the judgment or truly create lasting satisfaction. The judgment itself becomes an addictive pattern, masquerading as a safety mechanism while instead creating an energetic commitment to external validation.

Breaking free from this pattern requires compassionate self-observation. Notice how often your mind automatically judges your experience as good or bad, right or wrong, enough or not enough. These judgments are not objective truths but habitual thought patterns that perpetuate separation from your authentic experience.

When caught in judgment, try this practice: breathe deeply, name the judgment without attaching to it, instead observe: *I notice I'm judging my body as not good enough* and consciously feel into what lies beneath the judgment. Often you will find fear, pain, or a genuine need that the judgment is trying to protect.

With practice, you begin to recognise the gap between your direct experience and your judgment of it. This gap is where freedom lives, the space of pure awareness before the mind sorts reality into limiting categories. As this gap expands, you discover that you can experience life directly, without the constant overlay of judgment that has constrained your reality.

Anxiety as Intelligence:
The Signal of Misalignment

Anxiety often serves as valuable intelligence that you are not engaging with reality in alignment with your authentic needs and values. These core values, like Core Wounds, for the most part operate unconsciously and embed themselves in our system. However, unlike wounds that arise from fracture, core values emerge from Wholeness. They provide guidance for returning to alignment and offer the orientation needed to experience genuine connection with life.

Rather than treating anxiety as something to eliminate, we can approach it as useful information about our relationship with reality. When anxiety arises, ask yourself:

✦ What value am I not honouring right now?
✦ What aspect of myself am I abandoning?
✦ What inner boundary needs to be established?
✦ What truth am I not acknowledging?

Anxiety often emerges when we are operating from unconscious response patterns, when we have given our decision-making power away to external circumstances, people, or systems. It signals that we are engaging with reality in a way that violates our integrity. By recognising this signal and responding to it with conscious choice rather than automatic reaction, we transform anxiety from an enemy into an ally on our path to conscious living.

The Prison of Inherited Shame: Emma's Story

Emma's experience illustrates how unconscious programming can create internal prisons that persist long after external circumstances change. Growing up in a controlling family environment, her mother would consistently demand compliance, declaring her wrong and problematic if she did not conform or dared to express herself freely. The criticism was relentless and daily, alternating between intense judgment and emotional volatility to silent treatment and avoidance. Called a liar and used to fuel her parents' arguments, Emma learned early that authentic expression felt dangerous.

Later, working in a professional environment, she found herself crippled by anxiety about speaking up. Attempting to manage her conditioning through hypervigilance, she would analyse everything she said, fearing she was wrong or too much. She had developed an internal critical voice so powerful she no longer needed her parents to maintain this pattern. She carried her own mechanism of internal judgment with her in every moment.

What made Emma's situation particularly challenging was how this shame-based programming had become normalised. In meetings, she would deliberately under-contribute, afraid to take up space. When she did speak, she would immediately analyse and criticise her own input. Her colleagues noticed only her competence, unaware of the internal battle raging within her.

This shame-based internal dialogue affected every aspect of her life. In relationships, she would constantly apologise for her needs, her desires, even her existence. She would accommodate others to such an extent that she lost connection with what she really wanted. Her friends saw her as selfless and giving, not realising this behaviour stemmed from a deep programming that her authentic needs did not matter.

Even her body reflected this internalised oppression. Her shoulders curved inward as if to make herself smaller, her voice often dropped to a near whisper and she developed chronic digestive issues from the constant stress of self-monitoring. The physical manifestations of shame had become so ingrained that even when she intellectually challenged her limiting perceptions, her body continued to express them.

The turning point came when Emma began working with her shame as information about her conditioning rather than truth about her worth. She started noticing the exact moments when shame flooded her system and learned to be present with the sensation without believing the accompanying story. She discovered that when fully felt without resistance, shame would reveal the authentic need or value that had been suppressed.

Emma began practicing small acts of authentic expression, starting with low-risk situations and gradually building her capacity to honour her truth even when it might be unwelcome. Each time she spoke authentically and the world did not collapse, her nervous system learned that self-expression could be safe. Over time, her internal programming shifted from 'hide to survive' to 'express to thrive'.

The Journey from Unconscious Response to Conscious Choice

The pathway out of unconscious response patterns requires willingness to examine everything you have accepted as normal. We absorb programs like sponges, using them as meaning-making mechanisms to navigate complex social realities. But where do these programs really reside? They are embedded in a wider matrix of family conditioning, cultural expectations and inherited patterns of limitation and fear.

Your role involves understanding these patterns so completely that they transform from invisible constraints into conscious choices. Every moment of unconscious response becomes an invitation to awareness. Every experience of anxiety becomes information about misalignment. Every pattern of judgment becomes a doorway to direct experience.

This journey from unconscious response to conscious choice involves several key shifts:

From External Authority to Inner Wisdom: Rather than seeking validation and direction from outside yourself, you learn to trust and act from your own deep knowing, while still gathering relevant information from others.

From Reactive to Creative: Instead of reacting to circumstances from habitual patterns, you consciously choose your response and explore new possibilities within the constraints of reality.

From Separation to Connection: Where you once perceived isolation and alienation, you begin to experience profound interconnectedness with life while maintaining healthy boundaries.

From Fixed Identity to Fluid Responsiveness: You release rigid self-concepts that limit your expression and discover the freedom of responding authentically to each situation.

From Fear-Based Contraction to Curiosity: Rather than contracting around fear to feel safe, you expand through curiosity to explore what is truly possible.

These shifts do not happen permanently and not all at once. The journey involves continual practice, moment-by-moment choices to align with conscious response rather than defaulting to unconscious programming. With each choice, you strengthen new neural pathways and behavioural patterns that gradually become more natural.

Practical Liberation: Working with Systems Consciously

You can undertake this process of conscious engagement in any area of life. Examine any perception that keeps you unconsciously accepting systems that do not serve your authentic development. Question your automatic responses to relationship dynamics, financial pressures, educational expectations, health challenges, or social norms. Remember, you are here to engage consciously with reality, not to be unconsciously controlled by inherited programming. Begin with these practices:

System Inventory: Identify one system in your life where you feel most unconscious or reactive (healthcare, education, finances, relationships, work, family dynamics). Write down the automatic responses this system triggers in you and the specific perceptions that keep you engaged unconsciously.

Truth Excavation: For each limiting perception, ask yourself:

- ✦ Is this absolutely true?
- ✦ What would be possible if I didn't automatically believe this?
- ✦ What do I know from my own experience to be true instead?
- ✦ What values am I dishonouring through this pattern?

Conscious Action: Choose one small action that honours your conscious awareness within this system. This might be asking different questions, researching alternatives, expressing your authentic needs, or setting appropriate boundaries.

Embodied Practice: Create a physical gesture or posture that represents your shift from unconscious reaction to conscious response in this area. Practice embodying this stance whenever you engage with challenging systems or situations.

Rather than automatically relinquishing your power within systems, explore where your inherited programming has created unconscious responses. Question these patterns within yourself. Simply examining these spaces reveals the automatic nature of your responses. From there, you can liberate yourself from unconscious participation, discovering genuine empowerment through conscious choice.

Interface Architecture: The Art of Conscious Engagement

While inner awareness and healing work provide essential foundations, they fall short to generate lasting tangible life transformations. We become more aware, conscious and present, yet find ourselves cycling through similar external patterns and relationships. Instead of just working inwardly we need to work in the space where our internal world meets the experience around us, the interface.

'Interface architecture' represents the deliberate reconstruction of how we engage with the external structures of reality. It is the practice of bringing conscious awareness to the boundary where your inner experience meets external systems, relationships and challenges.

Think of it this way: if Consciousness work helps us see the water we are swimming in, interface architecture teaches us to swim differently, navigate currents more skillfully and eventually find new bodies of water altogether. This involves active conscious participation with reality rather than passive awareness of it.

Interface architecture operates at the boundary where your awareness meets external systems. Understanding your patterns internally is not enough; you must reconfigure how you interact with all the systems and programs of reality around you: healthcare systems, financial institutions, relationship dynamics, work environments and social structures. This reconfiguration happens through:

Boundary Intelligence: Developing sophisticated boundaries that are not rigid walls but intelligent responses, allowing certain influences while redirecting others based on your values and needs rather than fear or conditioning.

System Translation: Learning to communicate your inner knowing in languages that various systems can understand without losing your authentic voice in the process. This means developing confidence in voicing your needs and expressing your truth clearly.

Pattern Interruption: Consciously disrupting habitual interactions with external reality that reinforce unconscious response patterns. This involves being an active participant in life, questioning assumptions, reframing situations and refusing to accept limiting programming as unchangeable truth.

Energy Reclamation: Withdrawing your investment from systems that perpetuate unconscious responses while redirecting that energy towards creating conscious interfaces. This means recognising when you are giving your power away and choosing to engage differently.

Reality Testing: Regularly checking whether your inner shifts are creating meaningful changes in your external experience. This means using your current life circumstances as feedback about the effectiveness of your Consciousness work.

The person who develops self-worth through inner work but continues accepting underpayment has not completed the transformation cycle. Another who understands his relationship patterns intellectually but remains in dysfunctional dynamics has not bridged the gap between awareness and change. In both cases, the interface between inner knowing and external reality remains unconscious.

True liberation emerges when we recognise that Consciousness work prepares us for the real transformation that happens at the interface. As you move beyond awareness into active interface redesign, your healing finally manifests as tangible reality shifts rather than temporary internal insights.

The Ongoing Practice of Conscious Living

Conscious engagement with reality does not mean achieving a perfect state where unconscious patterns never arise or triggers never activate. It means developing a new relationship with your human experience. You learn to recognise when you have slipped into unconscious response patterns and develop the skills to return to conscious choice.

The patterns we have discussed: seeking external completion, addiction to familiar responses, and unconscious participation in limiting systems, may still arise. But now you can see them for what they are: invitations to awareness, opportunities to choose differently and to practice conscious engagement.

The freedom you seek is not found in escaping these patterns but in understanding them so completely that they become doorways to greater Consciousness. Every moment of unconscious response becomes information about your conditioning. Every experience of anxiety becomes guidance about alignment. Every encounter with limiting systems becomes an opportunity to practice conscious interface.

You stand at the threshold of a new way of engaging with life. The understanding you now hold can transform every aspect of your experience if you choose to live from it. You have the opportunity to participate in the human experience more consciously, more creatively, more authentically.

Remember, you are not powerless against reality. You are a conscious participant in it. The same awareness that can recognise unconscious programming can now consciously create patterns of authentic engagement. The journey from unconscious response to conscious choice represents the evolutionary edge of human Consciousness itself.

Step through this threshold. Your conscious engagement with reality awaits and through it, a life of genuine agency, authentic expression and meaningful contribution to the world around you.

CHAPTER THIRTEEN
Your Limitless Potential

When you make a commitment to work with the design of reality, the boundaries between inner and outer worlds begin to dissolve. You discover that what you thought were separate domains of experience can now be experienced as facets of one unified field of Consciousness.

Having learned to work with reality's design, you are ready for the next revelation: the patterns themselves of feeling Unloved, Unworthy and Unknown. They are invitations to remember who you are beyond all patterns.

This chapter guides you beyond conceptual understanding into direct embodiment of the unified field in daily life. You have the capacity to align with the intelligence of the field itself, allowing it to guide your evolution in ways your individual mind could never conceive.

The game is changing. You have learned to play it masterfully. Now you are ready to discover that you are the one making the rules.

From Understanding to Living

There is a profound difference between intellectually understanding field principles and embodying them as lived reality. Many spiritual and philosophical traditions speak of non-duality, unity and the illusory nature of separation, but these remain conceptual frameworks until they are directly experienced through your own being.

As Nicki, a long-time spiritual seeker, discovered, "I had been studying non-dual philosophy for twenty years and could eloquently explain the illusion of separation. But I was still living as a separate self, trying to understand unity. The breakthrough came not through more understanding but through directly experiencing reality beyond my conceptual frameworks. This was not about adding new spiritual concepts but about allowing my direct experience to transform how I perceived and participated in life." The journey from concept to embodiment requires a fundamental shift in how you relate to your experience; moving from thinking about reality to perceiving and participating in it directly.

We must understand the true nature of patterns. What we experience as fixed emotional wounds of feeling Unloved, Unworthy or Unknown can be understood more as high probability waves in the field. These configurations of energy and Consciousness feel impenetrable only because of how we have learned to observe them from our deepest survival fears.

Think of your most persistent Core Wound patterns, perhaps a chronic sense of being Unloved in relationships, feeling Unworthy despite external success or the perpetual experience of being Unknown and misunderstood. These do not exist as fixed aspects of your being, though they certainly feel that way. They are more like habits of observation, ways your Consciousness has learned to collapse the infinite possibilities of the field into familiar experiences that match your expectations and perceptions.

Helen, who struggled with a deep sense of abandonment for decades, describes her realisation. "I always thought my Unloved Wound was an actual thing inside me, a real injury that needed to be healed. Understanding field dynamics showed me that what I called my 'wound' was actually a pattern of observation that kept collapsing infinite possibilities into experiences of abandonment. The pattern felt completely real and solid but only existed because I kept observing reality through that particular lens." When we are caught in Wound Reality we become like an observer in a physics experiment who has learned to look for only certain possibilities. This creates a looping of repetitive experiences. Our Consciousness has become entangled with limited ways of observing and therefore creating reality.

Developing Field Perception

Understanding how to work directly with energy and Consciousness fields transforms our entire approach to life. Rather than trying to fix problems at the level of form, we learn to work with the field where all possibilities exist; from here you develop a powerful relationship with the intelligent field that underlies all reality.

The first step in this work is developing field perception, the ability to sense and interact with energy patterns directly. This is not as esoteric as it might sound. We are already constantly perceiving energy fields, we simply have not learned to process this information consciously. Think about times you have walked into a room and immediately felt the 'atmosphere' or met someone and sensed their energy before they even spoke. These moments of intuitive knowing are not a mysterious sixth sense, they are natural field perception that occurs before your analytical mind processes the information.

Developing body-centred awareness forms the foundation of field perception. Begin by feeling the energy field of your own body beyond physical sensation, the subtle sense of aliveness that permeates and extends beyond your physical form. Notice the vibrations, currents or qualities of energy that move through different areas of your body. With practice, you will sense how this field extends beyond your skin's boundary, creating an energetic envelope that interacts with your environment. Gradually, you will develop sensitivity to different qualities of energy, the density and lightness, expansion and contraction, flow and stagnation, that provide direct information about your state of being.

As your perception develops, expand into relational field sensing. Notice the shared field that forms between yourself and others and how it has a distinct quality, different from your individual field. Pay attention to how different people affect your energy field, creating expansion or contraction, activation or calming, clarity or confusion. In group environments, sense the collective field that forms, how a room of people generates a palpable atmosphere beyond individual interactions. With practice, you will develop awareness of field entanglement in relationships, recognising how your patterns of feeling Unloved, Unworthy or Unknown interact with others' patterns, creating mutual reinforcement of Core Wound realities.

Pattern recognition becomes possible as your field perception refines. You will notice how the different Core Wounds create distinct energy configurations that can be sensed directly rather than just intellectually understood. As you develop sensitivity to shifts and changes in these familiar patterns, you will recognise when they begin reorganising at the field level before showing visible evidence in your experience. Perhaps most importantly, you will learn to recognise field distortions created by protection and resistance, allowing you to work directly with these patterns at their energetic source rather than just addressing their external manifestations.

As Lisa describes, "At first, I could only feel energy in obvious ways, tension, emotion, basic sensations. But as my perception developed, I began to sense the actual patterns in the field. I could feel how my sense of unworthiness created a particular configuration, how it attracted certain experiences and repelled others. This wasn't just emotional insight, it was direct perception of the field patterns underlying my experience."

Working with Field Intelligence

When you work with energy fields you do not need to force, change or manipulate patterns. Instead, it is about developing a partnership with the intelligent field itself or 'field intelligence'. When we learn to sense and interact with these patterns while maintaining field awareness, we allow natural intelligence to guide the evolutionary process.

Working with field intelligence involves several key aspects that transform our relationship with energy patterns. Field dialogue becomes possible as you develop two-way communication with the intelligence of the field itself. You can ask questions and sense responses through subtle feelings, intuitive knowing and direct perception. You gradually learn the language of energy, how the field communicates through sensations, images, emotions and direct knowing that bypasses conceptual thinking. As this dialogue deepens, you learn to follow guidance that emerges naturally from field awareness, trusting the subtle directional pulls and expansions that indicate alignment with greater intelligence.

Equally important is developing pattern recognition without identification, this is simply observing energy patterns without becoming entangled in them. You learn to recognise configurations in your field without judgment or resistance, sensing them as temporary energy organisations rather than fixed aspects of identity. Even difficult or painful patterns reveal their underlying purpose and intelligence when approached with curious awareness rather than rejection. By allowing patterns to reveal their nature and purpose without immediately trying to change them, you discover the evolutionary intention behind even the most challenging aspects of your experience.

Supporting natural evolution becomes possible through this non-interfering relationship with the field. You develop sensitivity to what 'wants' to emerge or transform at any given moment, following rather than forcing evolutionary movement. Instead of imposing agenda-driven change, you provide conditions for natural reorganisation through your aligned presence and attention. Throughout this process, you deepen trust in field intelligence to guide the process in ways your limited mind could never conceive, in ways that allow the greater field of Consciousness to express itself through you.

Chris shares how this transformed his approach to a persistent health challenge, "Instead of seeing my condition as something to fight or fix, I began relating to it as an energy pattern with its own intelligence. I would sit quietly each day, sensing the configuration without trying to change it and asking what it was trying to communicate. Over time, I began to feel subtle shifts and new possibilities emerging. The healing that followed wasn't what I had imagined or planned, it was far more comprehensive and integrated than anything my limited mind could have conceived."

Finding Spaces Where Patterns Do Not Exist

One of the most powerful approaches to transcending limitations is learning to find spaces where these Core Wound patterns do not exist or do not operate in their usual way. Instead of trying to fix or overcome a pattern directly, we learn to shift our awareness to areas of our experience where this pattern is absent.

This understanding completely transforms our approach to personal evolution. Instead of focusing solely on trying to fix or heal what we perceive as wounds or a sense that something is missing, we learn to shift our observation point to where these patterns do not exist, where the wound is untrue. I call this the 'alternate space'. A space free of wounding but one that we may have repeatedly missed or ignored.

My own experience of this alternate space arose after a failing relationship showed me how all my energy was funnelled into that person loving me and caring about me. When I broadened my attention and focus to all the loving relationships in my life, I was overwhelmed at how limited my vision and experience had been. I realised the wound creates a tunnel vision for you to survive that one experience and negates others that are contrary to its limited pattern. Others I have worked with have been so absorbed in surviving their Unworthy Wound in stressful work environments that they forget all their other life achievements and the value they bring to all spaces in their life. I have seen those with the Unknown Wound lament that no one ever hears them at home but they arrive at work and lead board meetings with ease.

By acknowledging and exploring those experiences that directly contradict our wound stories, we can begin to see how to meet our unmet needs elsewhere. Over time this allows for new possibilities in relation to the wounded spaces and the people in them. It is like broadening the lens of perception from limited, constricted and repetitive to expanded, open and full of potential. This is a shift of Consciousness. I invite you to take a few moments to consider where you could expand the limitation of your 'wound lens' into more truth. The more challenging you find this, the more ingrained the wound pattern is for you. Simply witness this and allow a greater awareness to grow in this space over time and with more experience.

Rachel's journey illustrates this principle, "I had what I thought was an unshakeable pattern of the Unworthy Wound in my professional life. No matter how much success I achieved, the sense of unworthiness remained constant. Understanding field dynamics helped me see that what felt like a solid pattern wasn't present in every moment or situation. I began noticing spaces, sometimes brief moments, sometimes entire days, where the unworthiness simply wasn't there. Instead of focusing on fixing the unworthiness, I learned to expand these pattern-free spaces, giving my attention to where Wholeness already existed."

This approach completely inverts conventional transformation work. Instead of identifying problems and working to solve them, we learn to identify spaces of Wholeness and allow them to expand naturally. It is about recognising that no pattern exists everywhere or all the time and deliberately shifting our observation to spaces where different possibilities are already present is very empowering.

The practice begins with Wholeness identification, which is a conscious attention to moments or situations where limiting Core Wound patterns are naturally absent. These might be brief experiences during certain activities, with particular people or in specific environments where you naturally function beyond your familiar limitations of feeling Unloved, Unworthy or Unknown. Give your full attention to these pattern-free experiences, feeling their quality without immediately analysing or trying to understand them. Notice the distinct signature of Consciousness in these spaces, how awareness feels when not contracted around your Core Wounds. Allow these experiences to expand naturally through continued attention, not by forcing their growth but by letting your awareness linger in their quality.

Another practice is to develop skills in pattern interruption by recognising when familiar Core Wounds are beginning to activate. When the Unloved, Unworthy or Unknown patterns emerge, practice shifting your observation to spaces where these patterns do not exist. When you stop fighting against what is arising and instead expand your field of awareness to include both the emerging pattern and the spaces of freedom that coexist with it, you can break habitual loops of thought and feeling by introducing different possibilities into your field of awareness. As these loops are interrupted, new possibilities naturally emerge without having to be deliberately created.

Field amplification happens naturally as you give attention to spaces of Wholeness within your experience. By consciously feeling the quality of these spaces throughout your being, allowing them to naturally strengthen and expand. This pattern-free awareness begins to inform similar situations where limitations previously dominated, creating new ways of responding without deliberate effort. Throughout this process, trust the natural expansion of Wholeness that occurs when given attention, and space. Trust that Consciousness naturally evolves towards greater freedom, unless impeded by habitual patterns of observation tied to Core Wounds.

Navigating Pattern Dissolution

When a pattern begins to dissolve, it can feel like losing something essential to your identity. Your system might resist this dissolution, trying to maintain familiar configurations even when they limit you. This resistance is a natural part of your safety mechanism trying to keep you in the known. The key is learning to stay present with both the dissolution and the resistance without trying to manage either. So, when a trigger arises we avoid habitual responses and reactivity to witness the internal process and the deeper pattern that is shown through the trigger.

Steps of Pattern Dissolution

When navigating pattern dissolution, the first step is recognition; developing a sensitivity to when patterns are naturally ready to evolve. Ironically this will also be the patterns you find most painful, create the most fear and the ones you want to avoid. Yet there is a deeper inherent impulse towards Wholeness that exists within every pattern, even those that seem problematic. You will notice a certain quality of readiness, a subtle shift in how a familiar pattern feels or operates. Along with this recognition comes the ability to sense resistance without fighting against it, acknowledging that resistance is a natural part of the process rather than an obstacle to overcome.

As dissolution progresses, skilled navigation becomes essential. This means staying fully present through what can sometimes be intense transitions as your Consciousness reorganises itself. Rather than trying to control or direct this reorganisation, you are called to trust the inherent intelligence guiding this evolutionary process. Your role becomes one of witnessing and supporting what is emerging rather than trying to determine what it should be. Do not get pulled back into being committed to the pattern because it creates the 'known' and an Illusion of Safety.

Thomas describes his experience, "When my perfectionism pattern began dissolving, it was terrifying. This pattern had defined me for decades, it really was how I achieved success and created safety. As it started reorganising, I felt like I was losing my core identity. The key was learning to stay present with both the dissolution and my terror about it, without trying to control either. I had to trust that what was emerging would be more aligned with Wholeness than what was dissolving, even though I couldn't yet see or understand it."

Relationship Fields and Consciousness Evolution

When we understand relationships through field principles, we recognise them as dynamic fields of evolving Consciousness rather than interactions between separate entities. This transforms how we approach connection, intimacy and apparent conflict. You do not need to merge identities or lose boundaries, instead it is about recognising how our individual expressions of Consciousness participate in a larger field of possibility.

Sienna shares her discovery, "I used to see my relationship patterns as problems to solve between two separate people. Now I understand them as Consciousness fields evolving together. When my partner and I learned to sense these fields, we stopped trying to fix our dynamic and started allowing it to evolve naturally. We discovered that our apparent conflicts were simply Consciousness trying to expand beyond old patterns."

In field-based relationships, several key aspects transform how we connect with others. First is the practice of shared field sensing, feeling the relationship as a unified field rather than a series of interactions between separate individuals. This involves noticing how your individual patterns and those of others create distinct configurations in your shared field. With practice, you begin to sense the relationship itself as a third entity with its own intelligence and purpose. This awareness extends to recognise the even larger field that contains both individuals, providing context and resources beyond your personal perspectives.

As this awareness deepens, you will notice how patterns naturally evolve within relationships. Individual patterns do not exist in isolation, they interact, sometimes amplifying each other, sometimes creating friction that signals the need for transformation. Allowing space for this natural evolution without forcing specific outcomes invites the intelligence of shared Consciousness to guide your connection into greater alignment and harmony.

Communication itself transforms through field awareness. You begin sharing perceptions of the relationship field rather than just exchanging information or opinions. When speaking, you come from field awareness rather than pattern identification, expressing from a place of Wholeness rather than fragmentation. Listening becomes a practice of attunement to field intelligence beyond individual perspectives, hearing not just the words but the field speaking through them. Together, you create from shared Consciousness, allowing something greater than your individual ideas to emerge through your connection.

David and Lori's experience illustrates this approach, "We

had been stuck in the same conflict pattern for years. I would withdraw when feeling criticised and Lori would pursue more intensely, feeling abandoned. Individual therapy helped us understand these patterns, but didn't transform them. When we learned to sense our shared field, everything changed. Instead of seeing ourselves as two separate people with conflicting needs, we began feeling the single field of Consciousness expressing through both of us. The pattern wasn't happening to us, it was happening through us and we could choose to allow something new to emerge by shifting our observation point."

Phases of Consciousness Evolution

Understanding the natural phases of the evolution of Consciousness helps us recognise and navigate shifts in relation to it.

Recognition Phase

The recognition phase marks the beginning of conscious evolution beyond a particular pattern. You will likely notice an increased awareness of limitations that previously operated outside your conscious recognition. What once seemed normal or inevitable now reveals itself as a constructed pattern rather than absolute reality.

Along with this recognition often comes a natural dissolution of old ways, things that once required effort may begin falling away spontaneously. Insights and revelations appear, sometimes in dreams, sometimes in ordinary moments, illuminating aspects of yourself or reality that were previously hidden. Through all of this runs a growing sense of new possibilities, an intuitive knowing that something fresh is emerging, even if you cannot yet articulate what that might be.

During this phase, the key is allowing awareness without forcing change. Simply noticing how patterns operate creates space for natural evolution without the interference of effort or attempts to control. Your witnessing presence itself becomes the catalyst for transformation.

Transition Phase

As evolution actively progresses, you enter the transition phase, often characterised by intense periods of reorganisation across multiple levels of your being. This is when the chaos gets unleashed. You might experience physical sensations as energy patterns shift, emotional waves as old feelings surface and transform and mental disorientation as familiar thought structures dissolve. Temporary disorientation is common during this phase, you may feel caught between worlds, no longer fully identified with old patterns but not yet stable in new ones. Rapid pattern dissolution can create both exhilaration and fear as familiar reference points disappear.

Alongside these challenges, you will notice the emergence of new capacities, new ways of perceiving, understanding and relating that were not available within your previous configuration. Rest in the In-Between Space; you are between worlds.

This phase can be challenging as familiar reference points dissolve before new ones have fully established. The key is maintaining presence through this disruption, trusting the intelligence to guide the evolutionary process, even when you do not understand.

Integration Phase

Eventually, the intensity of transition gives way to integration as new possibilities stabilise and become your natural way of being. You will experience the natural expression of expanded Consciousness without effort or maintenance; what once required conscious practice now happens spontaneously. You will notice the effortless transcendence of old limitations that previously seemed immovable despite years of effort.

Often, evolution spreads beyond the original area of focus, creating spontaneous evolution in multiple areas of your life as the field responds to your Wholeness rather than isolated parts. Perhaps most significantly, you will develop a deeper trust in natural unfolding as you witness the intelligence of evolution operating through your life in ways your limited mind could never have planned or created.

Alex describes moving through these phases, "The recognition phase felt like waking up to patterns I hadn't previously seen. It wasn't painful, just illuminating, like suddenly seeing the structure of a magic trick. The transition phase was much more intense. There were days when I didn't know who I was anymore as old identities dissolved. What carried me through was trusting the process even when I couldn't understand it. The integration phase has been beautiful, I'm discovering capacities and ways of being that feel completely natural, as if they were always there beneath the patterns."

The Revolution of Being

Remember, you are not a limited being trying to become whole. You are Consciousness itself, temporarily focussed into patterns for the purpose of evolution and expression. What we perceive as limitations are actually opportunities for Consciousness to know itself in new ways. You already are an experience of Wholeness recognising itself.

Richard, who had spent decades in conventional therapy and self-improvement, describes this shift, "I had always approached my journey as a project of fixing what was broken in me. Understanding field principles completely inverted my approach. Instead of identifying with my wounds and working to heal them, I began identifying with the Wholeness that already existed beneath the patterns. This wasn't about denying challenges but about shifting where I placed my primary attention and identity."

This revelation in perspective transforms how we approach every aspect of evolution:

- ✦ Instead of fixing problems, we allow Wholeness to emerge.
- ✦ Instead of battling limitations, we expand beyond them.
- ✦ Instead of improving ourselves, we allow our true nature to express itself.
- ✦ Instead of seeking completion, we recognise the perfection already present.

Perhaps the most liberating aspect of field-based evolution is the end of struggle as a primary path to transformation. When we recognise that Consciousness naturally evolves towards greater Wholeness unless impeded, our role shifts from forcing change to allowing natural unfolding.

Laura, who had exhausted herself through decades of spiritual striving, shares her discovery, "I had made my spiritual journey into such hard work, constantly pushing, analysing and disciplining myself towards awakening. The breakthrough came when I realised that evolution happens not through effort but by reframing my relationship with the interference. When I stopped trying so hard and simply allowed natural intelligence to operate, transformation happened effortlessly."

This does not mean we become passive or abandon commitment. Rather, our commitment shifts from forcing specific outcomes to creating conditions where natural evolution can occur unimpeded. We remain engaged but without the struggle of trying to make things happen through willpower alone.

Present Moment Power

At the heart of field-based evolution is the transformative power of pure presence, the capacity to be fully with what is without trying to change, understand or control it. This quality of awareness creates a field of possibility where patterns naturally reorganise into greater alignment with Wholeness.

The field of possibility exists in an eternal now. When we are fully present, we access its infinite creative potential rather than being bound by past patterns or future projections. This transforms our relationship with time, our access to possibility and our creative capacity.

This understanding is particularly transformative when working with the Core Wounds. The Unloved Wound keeps us fixated on painful past experiences or worried about future abandonment. The Unworthy Wound has us constantly seeking validation to feel adequate. The Unknown Wound drives us to control future outcomes out of fear. When we bring our attention fully into the present moment, we temporarily step outside these time-bound wound patterns.

Loren describes this discovery, "After years of sophisticated spiritual techniques and practices, I found that the most powerful catalyst for transformation was simple presence. By fully being with my experience without trying to fix or transcend it, I created space for natural evolution to occur. What I couldn't accomplish through years of effort often happened spontaneously through moments of complete presence."

Presence is truly the most powerful creative force available to us. When we are fully present with what is, without the distortion of resistance or the interference of forcing, we allow the natural intelligence of the field to operate unimpeded. This presence becomes both the method and the goal of evolution; we evolve through presence into greater capacity for presence.

The Ongoing Journey

This evolution does not end with some final state of enlightenment or completion. It is an ongoing exploration of Consciousness through ever-evolving forms of expression. Each Core Wound pattern that dissolves reveals new dimensions of possibility and each possibility that manifests creates new opportunities for evolution.

Dianna shared her understanding after years of field-based living, "I used to think spiritual evolution was about reaching some final state of liberation where I'd never feel Unloved, Unworthy or Unknown again. Now I recognise it as an infinite journey of Consciousness, knowing itself through ever-expanding expressions. There is no endpoint, no final achievement, just the endless adventure of being and becoming. This understanding has brought such freedom and joy to my journey.'

The path ahead is about embodying more fully what you have always been beneath the patterns of feeling Unloved, Unworthy and Unknown that seemed to define you. Having traversed the Pain Portal, moved through Dying to the Limited Self and awakened to the field of infinite possibility, you are now free to live beyond these Core Wound patterns, creating from Wholeness rather than lack. You begin dancing with infinite possibility. Moreover you participate consciously in the greatest adventure of all; the evolution of Consciousness, knowing itself through your unique expression in the world.

As we close this exploration of infinite possibility, you may find yourself standing at a threshold of profound potential. The patterns that once seemed to limit you now reveal themselves as doorways to greater freedom. The quantum field that appeared separate from you now responds to your conscious participation. You have begun to experience reality as a living extension of your own Consciousness. Yet there remains one final frontier to explore, perhaps the most revolutionary understanding of all:

- What if everything you have experienced, from your deepest wounds to your most transcendent moments, has been part of an exquisite design?
- What if the very architecture of Consciousness itself has been carefully crafted to guide you home?
- What if nothing has ever gone wrong in your journey and the path of separation was always meant to lead you back to Wholeness?

In our final chapter, we will explore the Divine architecture behind everything you have been experiencing. Here, the fragments of understanding we have gathered throughout our journey come together in a unified vision that transforms how you perceive every aspect of your experience. You will discover how your body, emotions, relationships and challenges all serve as sophisticated technologies of awakening and remembrance of truth.

Take a moment to honour how far you have come. The journey has not always been easy, but your willingness to explore these depths speaks to the courage of your soul. Now, let us step into the culmination of all we have explored, the profound recognition that Consciousness itself possesses a Divine architecture designed for your awakening.

CHAPTER FOURTEEN
The Divine Design

Everything I have shared so far is part of the gift of the development of one essential relationship...my relationship to Consciousness.

Everything that exists comes from and returns to Consciousness, so connecting and developing a deep relationship with this field of infinite possibility has become my core priority for myself and my teachings set out in *The Consciousness Method*™. I recognised that Consciousness itself possesses a Divine architecture designed for our awakening and that it orchestrates challenging and profound experiences for us to know ourselves. This final chapter invites you to understand this Divine design and sink deeper into your own relationship with it. **There is nothing more valuable than your relationship to expanded Consciousness.**

The Threshold of Transformation

When we truly understand that we are reality creation beings, something profound shifts in our relationship with existence, it is a visceral recognition reverberating through every cell of our being. The realisation dawns that every moment of separation has been orchestrated by our own Consciousness, creating elaborate patterns of disconnection that mirror our original fracture from Source. This understanding becomes the gateway to our liberation.

As Sophie describes after integrating the principles from previous chapters, "I suddenly realised that everything I had experienced, every painful relationship, every moment of feeling unworthy or unloved, wasn't evidence that something had gone wrong. It was all part of an exquisite design allowing Consciousness to know itself through me. This wasn't just a comforting idea; it was a direct recognition that changed everything about how I engaged with life."

In this profound moment of recognition, we begin to see how every experience, every relationship and every challenge has served as a curated aspect of our awakening journey. The very patterns that seemed to prove our separation reveal themselves as intricate threads in the tapestry of remembrance. Our understanding of it transforms our lives into a portal of awakening. Then we literally wake up in Consciousness.

The Mechanics of Manifestation: A Deeper Understanding

Our Consciousness operates as a sophisticated interface with the quantum field, far more intricate than previously understood. Each thought, each emotion, each perception acts as a frequency signature, attracting matching experiences from the field of infinite potential. Yet this process is not happening to us, we must understand we are the architects of this Divine design. The very mechanisms we have used to create separation can become tools for reunion when understood properly.

Consider how this plays out in daily life: when you experience anxiety about a future event, you are not merely having an emotional response, you are engaging in a complex quantum dialogue with reality itself. Your nervous system, which seems to betray you with its hypervigilance, is simply responding to the frequency patterns you are emanating into the field. This understanding transforms anxiety from an enemy to be conquered into a sophisticated feedback system showing you where you have temporarily forgotten your true nature. To be clear this is beyond the familiar adage that 'your thoughts create your reality'. Instead, it is about realising that your whole internal design (thoughts, emotions, unconscious programs, nervous system and energy) is projecting a design pattern onto reality. This awareness takes us deeper and more profoundly into our power as creators as much as it highlights our sense of being out of control and a victim to reality. Both exist; we are projecting unconsciously and simultaneously need to develop a relationship with Consciousness to project with full awareness.

Melissa shares her experience, "I spent years battling my anxiety, seeing it as a broken part of me that needed to be fixed. The breakthrough came when instead I recognised it as a powerful feedback system showing me where I was creating from separation rather than Wholeness. My anxiety wasn't my enemy, it was simply projecting a reality that was not in alignment with my greater design pattern. This shift in understanding transformed my relationship not just with anxiety but with all my emotional states."

Beyond the Pain Body: The Sacred Architecture of Wounds

With this awareness, one of the most powerful reality projectors is our unconscious pain. The pain we have carried, whether through the Unloved Wound, the Unworthy Wound or the Unknown Wound, has created specific frequencies of engagement with reality. These frequencies act like tuning forks, resonating with and attracting matching experiences. Yet these wounds are not meant to be transcended or escaped but met completely.

What emerges through deeper exploration is the recognition that these wounds do not operate in isolation. They form an intricate system of Consciousness, like a trinity of spirals through our experience that invite a remembrance of Divine intelligence. Understanding this system, rather than trying to heal individual wounds, becomes another gateway to transformation. When we understand that the three wounds co-create the design patterns, we can get closer to how they are powerfully reinforcing each other.

Consider three examples of how this cascade of wound response can begin from any wound and ultimately incorporate all the wounds.

Louise started to feel the pull of the Unloved Wound as she

prepared for a difficult conversation with her partner. As she sat across from him, her chest began to tighten, the Unloved Wound activated with its familiar message: *he's pulling away from me.* This immediately cascaded into her solar plexus clenching as the Unworthy Wound engaged: *what did I do wrong? I'm not enough to keep his attention.* Within moments, her throat constricted as the Unknown Wound completed the pattern: *he doesn't really see who I am anyway.* This shows how the Unloved spiralled to the Unworthy and into the Unknown. This can all happen in a split second and can occur in our unconscious until we become consciously aware of the wounded trilogy.

Aileen shared how the Unworthy Wound struck her first as she stepped into the boardroom for a crucial presentation. Her solar plexus tightened with the familiar grip of: *I don't belong here with these executives.* This instantly triggered her chest to collapse as the Unloved Wound joined: *they don't value my contribution, they're just tolerating me.* Finally, her throat constricted as the Unknown Wound sealed the pattern: *they can't see the real insights I have to offer. I'm invisible in this room.* From there she is projecting an energetic signature in the field that will co-create with the field to affirm this separation from her true capacity and cause others to correspond to her wound.

For Stella, attending her high school reunion, the Unknown Wound led the dance. Walking into the crowded room, her throat immediately tightened with: *no one here really knows who I've become.* This quickly pulled her heart into collapse as the Unloved Wound responded: *they probably don't even remember me or care that I'm here.* Her solar plexus then clenched as the Unworthy Wound concluded: *and why should they? I haven't accomplished anything impressive enough to matter.* This again, was the internal conflict that she was swimming in as she interacted with her former classmates and felt disconnection and judgement in a way that created a distortion of the field.

These cascades reveal how our Consciousness creates elaborate symphonies of separation. The wounds do not simply coexist, they amplify and maintain each other through intricate feedback loops, regardless of which wound initiates the pattern. Any disruption in one area immediately recruits the others to maintain the familiar experience of limitation.

At the somatic level, this system operates with remarkable precision. Louise's constricted chest (Unloved) restricts her breathing, which increases anxiety and activates her solar plexus armour (Unworthy), which then constricts her throat and voice (Unknown). Each physical pattern reinforces the others, creating a self-perpetuating cycle that maintains the experience of separation even in moments when connection is actually available.

The Systemic Intelligence: Why the Wounds Need Each Other

Lea discovered this systemic intelligence in the interactions between her wounds, giving her a life changing shift in her perception of healing. For years, she had focussed on her Unworthy Wound and the constant need to prove herself through achievement. She had made significant progress, developing a more stable sense of self-worth, but found herself hitting a wall. Her anxiety would still spike in social situations and she could not understand why.

True insight came when she recognised how her Unworthy Wound had been unconsciously supported by the other two wounds. Her drive to achieve (Unworthy) was fuelled by a deep fear of being abandoned (Unloved) if she did not perform and maintained by a perception that people could not see her true value anyway (Unknown). When she began healing the Unworthy Wound, the other two intensified their patterns to maintain the familiar experience of separation.

"I realised I was playing whack-a-mole with my wounds," Lea reflects. "I'd work on one pattern, only to have another pop up more intensely. It wasn't until I understood them as a system that real transformation became possible. They weren't three separate problems, they were three expressions of a single design for forgetting my true nature."

This systemic intelligence operates across multiple dimensions simultaneously. At the nervous system level, each wound creates specific patterns of activation and shutdown that support the others. The hypervigilance of the Unloved Wound feeds information to the performance anxiety of the Unworthy Wound, which then creates the social withdrawal that reinforces the invisibility of the Unknown Wound.

At the energetic level, the wounds create complementary frequency patterns that maintain a specific vibrational signature. For example, the seeking energy of the Unloved Wound creates a field of lack that the proving energy of the Unworthy Wound attempts to fill through achievement, while the hiding energy of the Unknown Wound ensures this achievement never feels truly satisfying.

At the micro level, the cellular intelligence of this system is equally precise. When any of the wounds activate, it shifts cellular membrane permeability, affecting how cells receive nourishment and energy. It literally creates the experience of not being fed by life. This cellular disruption then influences the nervous system, our experience of pain and fear and the way we interface with reality.

The Cascade Effect: When One Wound Begins to Heal

Sophie experienced the cascade effect firsthand when she began to truly receive love from her partner. For months, she had been working specifically with her Unloved Wound, learning to notice and receive the love that was present in her relationship. As this pattern began to shift, something unexpected happened, her Unworthy Wound intensified dramatically.

"Just as I was beginning to feel loved, I was hit with the most intense wave of unworthiness I'd ever experienced. I started obsessing over whether I deserved this love, whether I was good enough for my partner, whether I would inevitably disappoint him. It felt like my progress was going backwards, but I was actually witnessing the system reorganising itself," she shared with me.

As Sophie learned to stay present with the Unworthy Wound without trying to prove her value, the Unknown Wound emerged with startling intensity, "I became convinced that my partner didn't really know who I was, that he was loving some version of me that wasn't authentic. I wanted to tell him everything. Every flaw, every fear, every dark thought, to test whether he would still love the 'real' me."

This cascade reveals the profound intelligence of the wound system. As Consciousness begins to remember its true nature through one portal, the other aspects of forgetting intensify to maintain the familiar experience of separation. This is evidence of how perfectly designed the system is to create the experience of limitation.

The somatic expression of this cascade is equally intelligent. As Sophie's heart began to open (Unloved healing), her solar plexus initially contracted more intensely (Unworthy intensifying) before eventually beginning to soften. This then allowed her throat to open in a new way (Unknown transforming), but not without first experiencing a period of even greater constriction as the system attempted to maintain its familiar patterns.

The Transformation Portal: Understanding Dissolves the System

The breakthrough comes when we recognise the wounds as a sophisticated design for experiencing separation. Then the entire system begins to transform and the truth begins to emerge. Rachel discovered this when she stopped trying to fix her Unknown Wound and instead began to appreciate its intelligence "I spent years trying to become more visible, to speak my truth more clearly, to help people understand me. But the real shift happened when I recognised that this wound was perfectly designed to help me forget my inherent knowability. The moment I saw the intelligence in the design, the wound began to reveal its gift."

This understanding operates simultaneously across all dimensions of experience. At the cellular level, the recognition of the wound's intelligence shifts the actual frequency patterns within the cells. The cellular memory of separation begins to reveal a deep level of understanding. At the nervous system level, the recognition of the wound's sacred purpose supports us to stretch the system beyond its current limits and relax its hypervigilance, creating space for new patterns of engagement.

At the Consciousness level, this understanding reveals the wound's truest expression of love. A love so profound that it was willing to forget itself completely in order to experience the joy of remembering. Each wound becomes a testament to the creative power of Consciousness, evidence of its ability to create such convincing experiences of limitation that even it could temporarily believe them.

As Sophie shares after this recognition, "I finally understood that my wounds weren't evidence of damage or trauma. The same intelligence that could create such convincing experiences of being unloved, unworthy and unknown could just as easily create experiences of profound love, inherent worth and deep recognition. The wounds weren't obstacles to my true nature, in truth they were expressions of it."

Within this understanding, the sacred architecture of the wound system reveals itself. The Unloved Wound creates the experience of separation that motivates the journey back to Wholeness. The Unworthy Wound creates the questioning that refines discernment between true value and false identification. The Unknown Wound creates the mystery that maintains humility and wonder in the face of infinite being.

Together, they form a perfect system for Consciousness to experience the full spectrum of remembering itself. Each wound contains not only its own healing but the key to transforming the entire system. When we truly understand one wound completely, we understand them all, because they are all expressions of the same fundamental design, a sacred platform for remembering the love, worth and knowing that we inherently are.

The Divine Design: Understanding the Sacred Architecture

What emerges through this deeper exploration is a profound understanding that nothing has gone wrong. The separation Consciousness that has created such elaborate patterns of disconnection is itself a Divine design, allowing Consciousness to know itself through the experience of forgetting and remembering.

This understanding operates on multiple levels simultaneously. At the cellular level, each cell in your body carries both the frequency of separation and the potential for Wholeness. Your cellular memory contains bioelectric fields storing trauma patterns and membrane receptors tuned to specific wound and survival patterns. Perception systems influence your DNA expression, while mitochondrial responses shift in response to separation Consciousness. Yet these very patterns, when understood, become instruments of transformation. Each cell operates as a mini-brain, carrying both the wound and its healing potential.

Your nervous system serves as a bridge between dimensions, translating separation perceptions into physical patterns and creating specific somatic expressions of each wound. While it maintains familiar trauma loops, it simultaneously holds the potential for pattern transformation. Understanding this architecture reveals how your nervous system is operating exactly as designed to facilitate your awakening.

At the level of Consciousness itself, we begin to see how every pattern of separation serves awakening. Each wound contains its own healing, while all experiences point towards Wholeness. Reality itself becomes a mirror reflecting our state of Consciousness, offering continuous feedback about our relationship with truth.

As Jessica shares after integrating this understanding, "I used to see my trauma responses as evidence that my nervous system was broken. Now I recognise them as part of a Divine design. Each physical tension, each emotional trigger, each limiting perception points me towards the truth of who I am beneath these patterns. I realised at that moment the perfection of the design."

The Challenge of Self-Perception: Why We Need Mirrors

While this architecture is perfect in its design, there remains an inherent challenge in the human experience: we cannot easily see our own blind spots. This is not a flaw but a complex aspect of the design itself. If we could instantly see through all our illusions, we would not have the full experience of separation necessary for profound remembering.

The very nature of the Core Wounds creates specific perceptual blind spots. Just as the eye cannot see itself without a mirror, Consciousness cannot easily perceive its own conditioning without reflection. Our wound patterns become so deeply embedded in our identity and nervous system that they become invisible to us, not because we have limited awareness, but because this is exactly how the design works.

This is why even those with decades of dedicated inner work often cycle through the same patterns. The wound itself creates specific perceptual distortions that make it nearly impossible to see the very thing creating the distortion. This is simply confirmation of how challenging the design truly is.

As Carla describes after years of spiritual practice, "I'd done so much inner work but kept hitting the same walls. I couldn't understand why I couldn't see what was holding me back. The breakthrough came when I realised that what I was seeking to heal was the very thing creating my blind spot. My wound was designing my reality in a way that made it invisible to me, so I needed help to see that."

This is where the sacred value of mirrors becomes apparent. While books, practices and spiritual teachings can take us far, there comes a point in many journeys where having someone who can accurately read your Consciousness becomes invaluable. Not because you are incapable of awakening on your own, but because the design of Consciousness itself creates these blind spots.

Through the Mentorship space, I have observed how providing a Consciousness mirror to the unconscious aspects of self can significantly accelerate transformation by illuminating where and how your specific wound patterns operate outside your awareness. When we honour the design itself and recognise that just as wounds were created in the unconscious state, certain aspects of healing happen most efficiently in conscious reflection.

The Nervous System's Sacred Journey: A Path That Requires Support

One of the most challenging aspects of this transformation involves the nervous system itself. As we begin to shift our Consciousness, the nervous system, which has been wired for survival through our wound patterns, often experiences this shift as a threat. This creates what I have observed as the 'nervous system paradox'; the very change that will bring freedom is initially perceived as dangerous by the system designed to keep us safe.

The process of rewiring the nervous system requires specific support that many traditional modalities do not fully address. This is because nervous system transformation operates across multiple dimensions simultaneously, requiring a sophisticated understanding of both the trauma patterns and the spiritual awakening process.

Through *The Consciousness Method*™ Mentorship, I have developed specific approaches to nervous system reconfiguration that honour both the biological reality of trauma patterns and the spiritual dimensions of awakening. This methodology creates a container that supports the system through the profound destabilisation that naturally occurs during transformation, providing the specific tools needed to navigate this territory safely. Instead of regulation we create expansion and an upgraded internal safety.

As Karen shares after struggling with traditional approaches, "I'd tried everything to heal my trauma including talk therapy, somatic experiencing and mindfulness. But I kept hitting a wall where my nervous system would crash. I didn't understand why my body seemed to rebel against the very healing I sought. Through *The Consciousness Method*™, I learned how my nervous system was operating perfectly, according to its programming and how to provide it with the specific support it needed to reorganise around truth rather than protection. For the first time, I experienced a transformation that didn't lead to collapse."

Your body becomes the technology for this transformation. Every physical sensation contains information about your current relationship with reality, while each tension pattern points to where you have temporarily forgotten your true nature. All symptoms serve as sophisticated feedback mechanisms, as body wisdom guides your return to Wholeness.

Emotionally, this understanding transforms how you relate to your feelings. Emotions serve as frequency indicators, while triggered states reveal where healing is available. Emotional patterns point to core perceptions, as feeling states directly create your reality.

In conscious creation, you recognise that reality responds to your frequency rather than your wishes. Creation happens through resonance rather than force and manifestation occurs through alignment rather than effort. Transformation emerges through understanding rather than struggle, completely reversing conventional approaches to change.

Michael shared how this transformed his professional life, "I used to approach work challenges head on, trying to overcome obstacles through sheer will. But understanding the architecture of Consciousness completely transformed my approach. When I align my frequency with what I'm creating, things unfold with an ease I never thought possible. Challenges still arise, but I approach them as a mirror to my internal world and where to evolve next."

The Sacred Integration: Living this Understanding

As this Consciousness stabilises, we enter a new paradigm of creation. No longer victims to reality but conscious participants in its unfolding, we begin to create from Wholeness rather than separation. We recognise patterns as they arise and choose presence over reaction. Our alignment shifts from programming to truth, as we live from essence rather than identity.

Our engagement with life transforms completely as we begin to see challenges as awakening opportunities. Triggers become portals rather than problems, while wounds transform into wisdom gates. Reality itself becomes a mirror reflecting our state of Consciousness rather than a series of random events happening to us.

We begin to embody new possibilities, allowing patterns to reveal their wisdom rather than trying to fix or escape them. Trust in the intelligence of experience develops, as we follow body wisdom rather than mental concepts. The entire journey of remembrance becomes sacred, with each step honoured as an essential aspect of awakening.

Bella describes how this understanding transformed her daily life, "Before, I was constantly trying to avoid triggers and challenges, seeing them as obstacles to peace. Now I recognise every trigger as a portal to deeper awakening. When old patterns arise, whether feeling unloved, unworthy or unknown, I no longer try to escape them. I meet them with presence, allowing them to reveal their wisdom. This completely transforms how I engage with life, turning every challenge into an opportunity for deeper remembrance."

The Ongoing Journey: Embracing the Evolution

Remember, you will never reach a final destination where patterns never arise or triggers never activate. Instead, it is about developing a new relationship with the very nature of existence. We learn to navigate with wisdom, recognising when we have slipped into separation Consciousness and knowing how to return to Wholeness. Trust in the process of awakening deepens, as we honour each step of the journey rather than trying to skip the challenging parts.

Perhaps most importantly, we learn to embrace the human experience in its entirety. We accept all aspects of the journey, honouring both light and shadow as essential aspects of Wholeness. Transformation happens through presence rather than avoidance, allowing us to live fully while simultaneously awakening.

Josh shares his ongoing experience, "I used to think awakening meant reaching some final state where I'd never again experience limitation or challenge. Now I understand it is about developing a new relationship with the entire spectrum of human experience. Patterns still arise, triggers still activate, but I engage with them differently, they become exciting aspects of the journey to embrace.

This understanding brings such freedom to the process, allowing me to be fully human while simultaneously awakening."

The Bridge Between Modalities: When Support Becomes Essential

While many spiritual and therapeutic approaches provide valuable tools, there often comes a point where traditional modalities reach their limits. This is because certain aspects of transformation require specific support that bridges psychological and spiritual dimensions. This is particularly true when confronting the void space, that critical threshold between Wound Reality and Wholeness where identity itself undergoes dissolution. This transition often creates profound disorientation, as the nervous system processes what it perceives as a 'death' while Consciousness reorganises around truth rather than protection.

Through my work developing *The Consciousness Method*™ Mentorship, I have observed how this transition point is where many seekers either retreat back into familiar wound patterns or attempt to bypass the process altogether through spiritual concepts that have not been fully embodied. This is why I have created a specific container designed to support this exact threshold crossing and to honour the profound nature of what is occurring during this transition.

As Claire shares after years of personal development work, "I'd been doing the inner work for over a decade and I have transformed in many ways, but there was still a resistance in reality to reflect this shift. I was still looping in the same patterns and feeling fractured. *The Consciousness Method*™ Mentorship provided the missing piece. It helped me identify and transform the unconscious parts of me, limiting my capacity to be present with my whole experience. It connected all the inner work I'd done with a new amazing life."

The approach I offer is designed to amplify your inner guidance, providing specific support for the blind spots that are inherent in the human experience. This Mentorship becomes most valuable when you have reached the limits of what you can see on your own, not because of any failure on your part, but because of the very design of Consciousness itself.

The Call to Remember: Your Role in Evolution

You stand at the threshold of a profound transformation in human Consciousness. The very understanding you now hold can transform every aspect of your life, if you choose to live from it. You engage with life more consciously, more creatively, more completely.

Remember, you are not a victim of reality. You are its creator. The very Consciousness that designed these patterns of separation can now consciously create patterns of Wholeness. The journey from victim to creator is not just your personal path, it is the evolutionary edge of human Consciousness itself.

This understanding is truly an invitation to live differently. To engage with life not as something happening to you but as something happening through you and as you. Each moment becomes an opportunity to remember your true nature, to align with your essence, to create from Wholeness rather than separation.

The Sacred Container: Support for Your Journey

For those who feel called to deeper support in this remembrance process, I offer *The Consciousness Method*™ Mentorship as a container designed specifically for this transformation. It provides the support needed during the critical threshold crossings of awakening.

I developed this method after observing the specific challenges that arise when moving from Wound Reality to Wholeness, particularly the blind spots that even the most dedicated seekers encounter. Through working with hundreds of individuals, I have refined an approach that addresses both the spiritual dimensions of awakening and the nervous system reconfiguration necessary for embodied transformation.

As Jasmine shares, "When I first met Allura, I thought I had a strong sense of self-awareness, thanks to over 10 years of personal growth work. But despite all the therapy I had tried, I still felt stuck and alone, constantly hitting a ceiling I just couldn't break through. Mentorship turned out to be the missing piece in my personal growth journey, helping me finally break through that barrier! I was already aware of most of my wounds and thought I had done enough work on them, but with Allura, I could approach them from a completely new perspective." This offering comes from a genuine recognition that we are designed to heal in connection. Just as our wounds were created in relationship, certain aspects of healing occur most efficiently with skilled support that can illuminate our blind spots with love and precision.

The Mentorship I offer includes nervous system support during the often challenging transition through the void, clarity on processing pain and fear without feeling isolated and the ability to read consciousness patterns that might otherwise remain invisible to you. Most importantly, it provides a sacred container where the dissolution of old identity can occur safely, allowing your essence to emerge more fully. The support allows you to develop a new way of being and a new relationship to your internal terrain and your relationship to reality. When you have high level support everything becomes possible and you begin to understand how powerful you are.

As you embrace this understanding, you begin to see how every aspect of your life, from the most mundane to the most profound, serves your awakening journey. The very patterns that once seemed to prove your separation reveal themselves as intricate threads in the tapestry of remembrance.
This is the architecture of awakening.

As we conclude this exploration, remember that you have always been on this journey, even in your moments of deepest forgetting. The very patterns that seem to separate you from truth are also the material of your realisation. Nothing has gone wrong. Nothing has been wasted. Every experience has served your awakening.

Now, with this understanding, you are invited to live differently, not as a separate self struggling against reality but as Consciousness itself, dancing with the very patterns it created for its own evolution. This is the gift and the challenge: to live from this truth not just in moments of insight but in the ordinary moments of daily life. As you embrace this understanding, reality itself transforms from a problem to solve into a miracle to behold, the miracle of Consciousness knowing itself through you, as you, in every moment of your human journey.

I look forward to journeying with you.

In Wholeness,

Allura

Glossary

Alternate Space – The observation point where the Core Wound patterns do not exist, are untrue or do not operate in their usual way. A space that is free of wounding but one that we may have repeatedly missed or ignored.

Betrayal Wound – This wound affects our ability to trust life itself, creating a fundamental suspicion of reality that colours every experience and relationship. It instils a deep-seated vigilance that keeps us perpetually on guard, scanning for potential threats and betrayals. This hypervigilance manifests as chronic anxiety, a constant state of alert that exhausts our nervous system and depletes our capacity for joy and spontaneity.

Choice Point – What a trigger point can be transformed into when you are able to stay completely present when a triggering experience begins. It is the difference between unconsciously repeating old patterns rooted in feeling Unloved, Unworthy, Unknown and consciously creating new realities from a place of Wholeness.

Consciousness – The fundamental field of awareness from which all reality emerges and unfolds. It is not something we possess or exist within, but rather the primary fabric of existence itself, an interconnected whole expressing through individual perspectives and experiences. Rather than being separate observers navigating an external world, we are integral aspects of Consciousness participating in its continuous creation through our attention, choices, and observation. This understanding dissolves the illusion of separation, revealing that what appear as isolated events, objects, and individuals are actually interconnected expressions of a single, unified field.

Core Wound(s) – Specific energetic patterns that move in repeated, unconscious, fractalised designs. These patterns are based on our deepest sense of separation from Source and self and our desperate desire to repair this separation through external connection and completion. They create the foundations upon which all our limitations are built. Our wounds are born in the invisible realm of energy, severing us from who we truly are. We then confirm them by gathering 'evidence' from the external reality, which creates ongoing illusion and separation. This rupture becomes a relentless inner voice whispering the same devastating lies: You are Unloved. You are Unworthy. You are Unknown.

Dying to the Limited Self – The practice of surrendering to the limited, wounded identity that keeps us separate from the Divine, expanded connection to Source. An energetic, emotional and spiritual mechanism for liberation, that moves us beyond healing wounds to a complete realignment of the pattern and a release to a new level of identity and reality.

Energetic Reclamation – Actively reclaiming and calling back our energy from external investments and addictions. Withdrawing the energetic resources that would typically fuel our management strategies, hypervigilance or reactive responses and bring all those resources back into the body via the sternum point, a unique multi-dimensional point used in *The Consciousness Method* ™.

Energetic Self-Sufficiency – When you reclaim all the energy you have invested outside yourself, from all patterns of unconscious separation and bring it back within your body. The state of Wholeness.

Energetic Sovereignty – When we complete the energetic cycle within ourselves rather than continuously seeking its completion by outside experiences and relationships. This is the ultimate level of freedom as it is on the foundational level of our energetic relationship with ourselves. When we become energetically sovereign we are beyond the external pressures of coercion, domination and control.

Evidence in Absence – The natural falling away of problematic situations, relationships and issues as we experience Dying to the Limited Self and the spontaneous appearance of opportunities that seemed impossible within our old reality structure.

Field Intelligence – The natural intelligence of the quantum energy field that surrounds us, which communicates through sensations, images, emotions and direct knowing; effectively bypassing conceptual thinking.

Holographic Principle – The principle that states whatever is present within you projects a reality around you. This projection may come from the wounded part of self, the unconscious self or the whole self. This principle allows us to witness the external as a mirror for what is needing to be witnessed, processed and reconnected with internally.

Illusion of Safety – A false perception that things, relationships, behaviours are safe because they are familiar and the outcome is predictable, even though that known reality might be painful, limiting or soul crushing. The creation of the Illusion of Safety comes from feeling unsafe internally so looking to create a fabricated external safety.

In-Between Space – The experience of Consciousness between stimulus and response. A reality holding pattern, the quantum field itself, a state of nothingness where our old patterns can dissolve and new ones can form (see also Void).

Interface – The space between our inner world and our external experience, between unconscious programming and conscious choice, between the stories we have inherited and the truth we discover through direct experience of relating from a place of truth with reality.

Interface Architecture – The reconfiguration of how we interact with all the systems and programs of reality around us: healthcare systems, financial institutions, relationship dynamics, work environments and social structures, anything that contains a level of programming or expectation of our behaviour and energy.

Interface Problem – When we are trying to fit ourselves into system designs without regard for our authentic needs, intuitive knowing or individual path to fulfillment.

Internal Safety – An unshakeable connection to our essential self, the part of us that remains whole, intact and protected within regardless of external circumstances.

Pain Portal – The journey through the pain to release the stored cellular and emotional density that becomes trapped in the body from the experience of separation. It asks us to actively transverse the fear protecting the pain, to meet and experience the sensation of pain within the body without thoughts of suffering. When we transverse the Pain Portal we release ourselves into an expanded Consciousness but also release attachment to a limited painful version of reality.

Quantum Projection – The external reality we create from our internal design patterns, be it from our wound or our Wholeness. Every thought pattern, every emotional charge, every perception system we carry acts as a frequency that we broadcast into the quantum field. This field responds by organising experiences that match our internal state.

Rejection Wound – This wound relates to our fear of not being accepted or welcomed. It creates programs around social anxiety and withdrawal, excessive conformity, fear of self-expression and people-pleasing behaviours.

Source Consciousness – The unified field of the All, the Divine, God. The Source of all creation; all timelines, all potentials, all possibilities.

Stretching Your Nervous System – An active practice of consciously challenging our nervous system's resistance to change. Doing the exact thing our nervous system fears the most to expand us beyond the confines of fear.

The Consciousness Method™ – Is a unique, multidimensional method that is taught via Mentorship. It is a comprehensive pathway to live from a relationship with Consciousness which allows for a complete transformation of the Core Wounds and any level of separation from self. It moves us from being a victim to the ultimate creator of our human experience. It transforms pain, fear, limitation, loops and lack into the ultimate portals of awakening.

The Unknown – The intelligent, unknowable realm of possibilities that can be tapped into when we operate from our Wholeness. Where we rest, after Dying to the Limited Self, and allow the Source of self to begin to flow and manifest our external reality.

Trigger Point – An access point in reality where you become hooked into an unconscious mode of operating. It is where something in your external environment; whether it is seeing people act in certain ways, receiving a particular message or witnessing specific events, activates a familiar pattern stored in your nervous system. This external stimulus ignites an existing program within you, launching you into an automatic, unconscious response.

Unknown Wound – This wound originates from the absence of the Source of knowing. It manifests through behaviours that desperately seek understanding, safety and knowledge while paradoxically creating more separation and uncertainty.

Unloved Wound – This wound stems from the original abandonment of Source connection. It creates distinct patterns in how we approach, maintain and exit relationships, often unconsciously recreating the very abandonment we fear.

Unworthy Wound – This wound emerges from the contrast between our Divine Source perfection and our perceived human limitations. It manifests through behaviours that attempt to prove worth, while paradoxically reinforcing the perception that we are fundamentally flawed and do not deserve good things in life.

Unwanted Wound – A persistent sense of being an outsider, even in intimate relationships and familiar environments. This wound creates patterns of self-erasure where we habitually put ourselves last, cancel our own plans to accommodate others and struggle to assert any preferences or boundaries.

Void – The quantum field of pure potential that exists before new patterns emerge. A space of 'nothingness' that holds the potential for everything. The space that emerges when we stop feeding the addiction externally with our wounded patterns. What remains when everything we thought we were has been stripped away. Also a resting place to allow for transformation to occur.

Void Space of Truth – The state of pure infinite awareness beyond identity and form that we enter into when we no longer inhabit a body, whether through an out of body experience or death. In this space, our awareness merges with the All, revealing the true freedom and unconditional love that exists beyond our limited constructs. It is the natural state of Consciousness when it is not contracting around protection and identity.

Whole – Our natural, unseparated state of being.

Wholeness – The state of unified Consciousness that exists within us. It encompasses all aspects of ourselves, all the wounded and separated parts and offers a path to the completed self. It is a state of energetic self-sufficiency that we realise once we have fully reclaimed our energy from all patterns of unconscious separation.

Wholeness Reality – A deep inner knowing that we are complete in the now. Not that everything is perfect or that challenges disappear, but that we are no longer defined or diminished by external circumstances. Instead, we use every situation as an opportunity to explore our own evolution. When difficulties arise, we meet them with curiosity rather than reaction.

Wound Addiction – Our unconscious compulsion to move away from the pain of our Core Wounds into repetitive thoughts, feelings and behaviours that confirm a predictable level of reality and cause us to avoid the internal connection to ourselves. This addiction is often unconscious and can also be disguised within 'positive traits' and spiritual advancement. Overcoming wound addiction involves raising Consciousness, stretching the nervous system and traversing the Pain Portal.

Wound Bonds – Wound Bonds operate like emotional addictions across what could be called 'fractal patterns', the same core pain playing out with different characters throughout our lives. We form unconscious agreements with others to maintain familiar patterns of pain. We become emotionally addicted to predictable cycles of hurt because the known suffering feels safer than the unknown possibility of genuine connection.

Wound Lens – When a wound creates a form of tunnel vision that causes us to negate other experiences that are contrary to its limited perception.

Wound Pattern – The intricate systems of response that we develop in our childhood in order to manage our fear and pain. We create thought processes that attempt to make sense of our environment, emotional attachment patterns that help us navigate relationships and behavioural strategies designed to minimise perceived threat and maximise external safety. This happens at the expense of true, internal safety.

Wound Reality – A fabricated experience of reality due to the stories or illusions we make up based on past experiences and then mistake for truth. These are deeply ingrained narratives that form the foundation of our identity, the lens through which we interpret everything. Challenging the Wound Reality can feel like a threat to our very existence. It is the survival mode where we forget the truth that we are infinite, eternal, Divine beings having human experiences and that nothing external can truly impact our essential nature.

About Allura Halliwell

Allura is a pioneering Consciousness mentor, author and founder of *The Consciousness Method*™, a revolutionary framework for personal transformation. She developed it after a profound out-of-body experience created a radical shift in Consciousness that fundamentally altered her perception of reality. She came face-to-face with her own humanity and multidimensional nature. Through this experience, she gained immense clarity about the constructs of programs, illusions, nervous system responses and Core Wounds that keep humanity trapped in repetitive loops and how to transform them.

Allura's multidimensional approach rewires the energetic patterns of the Core Wounds of feeling Unloved, Unworthy and Unknown, empowering individuals to live lives of true creation, freedom and sovereignty. While she holds a postgraduate degree in Psychology and certifications as an Advanced Quantum Meditation teacher, Psych K facilitator, Non-violent Communication Specialist and Quantum Healing Hypnosis Technique (QHHT) Practitioner, her transformative modality is primarily sourced from her own exploration of Consciousness and the fundamental design of reality.

Her mission is clear: to support all beings in experiencing Wholeness by making unconscious patterns visible and completely restructuring them. Through her powerful Mentorship programs, heart-centred retreats and podcast *The Consciousness Method*™, she guides high-level spiritual seekers, coaches, mentors and aware individuals beyond intellectual understanding into embodied freedom.

Allura serves as a bridge between the human and Divine for all she meets, dedicated to the evolution of humanity and bringing advanced Consciousness work out of the shadows and into daily life she shifts people from survival mode to full-spectrum living.

'My mastery and purpose is as a conduit to your own expanded Consciousness and evolutionary path.' Allura

Connect Here

Book Resources including meditations, masterclasses and community at www.unlovedunworthyunknown.com/resources

Podcast: *The Consciousness Method*™ Podcast on all providers
Youtube: @allura_halliwell
Social media: @allurahalliwell
Email: connect@allurahalliwell.com

www.ingramcontent.com/pod-product-compliance
Lightning Source LLC
LaVergne TN
LVHW041622060526
838200LV00040B/1400